STEAM
AROUND SHEFFIELD

MIKE HITCHES

AMBERLEY

To Jenny, Gordon, and Steve

First published 2011

Amberley Publishing
The Hill, Stroud,
Gloucestershire, GL5 4ER

www.amberleybooks.com

British Library Cataloguing in Publication Data.
A catalogue record for this book is available from the British Library.

ISBN 978 1 84868 445 4

Typesetting and Origination by Amberley Publishing.
Printed in Great Britain.

CONTENTS

INTRODUCTION

Being situated at the confluence of five fast-flowing rivers and surrounded by hills that contained such raw materials as coal, iron ore and millstone grit (used in grindstones) made Sheffield an ideal setting in which water-powered industries could be developed. Indeed, as early as the fourteenth century, the town had become known for the manufacture of bladed goods as water mills originally constructed for grinding corn were converted to the production of blades. Even further back, the first cutler known to have worked in Sheffield was mentioned as long ago as the late thirteenth century.

By 1600, Sheffield had become the main town in England for production of cutlery, although other trades existed within the area, such as weavers and horners (the latter making knife handles from cow horn). The population at this time stood at around 2,207. In 1624, the Company of Cutlers was formed to oversee the trade and they had the power to mark such goods once they reached a certain quality standard. By the late seventeenth century, the population of Sheffield had grown to around 5,000 and trades were becoming more specialised. Along with cutlers, there were file smiths, scythe smiths, sickle smiths, woolshear smiths and awl blade smiths – all blade manufacturers. It is interesting to note that Britain was still very much an agricultural economy at this time, the products made in Sheffield reflecting the market.

As the seventeenth century faded and the next century developed, Sheffield became a major centre for the manufacture of iron and steel, fuelled by coal mined from collieries around Barnsley, Wakefield and Rotherham. By the 1740s, clockmaker Benjamin Huntsman had invented a process called 'Crucible Steel' (no doubt this is from where the Crucible Theatre in Sheffield, famous as the home of the World Snooker Championship, took its name). Huntsman had improved the quality of steel over that which had been available at the time.

In the same period, Thomas Bolsover had invented a way of fusing a thin sheet of silver onto copper, which produced a form of silver plating, becoming famous as 'Sheffield Plate'. Such were these developments that Sheffield was given its own silver assay office in 1773. As the century reached its end, Britannia metal was developed in the town. This pewter-based alloy had a similar appearance to silver but was, of course, cheaper.

In the same period, out of necessity, communications to other towns were improved. By 1751, the River Don became navigable right up to Sheffield and the turnpike road, from Sheffield to Chesterfield and Derby, was opened in 1756, followed two years later by a road from Sheffield to Barnsley and Leeds. These roads linked Sheffield to places like Buxton, Glossop, Intake, Penistone, Tickhill and Worksop. In 1774, a 2-mile wooden tramway was laid at Nunnery Colliery, but this was destroyed by rioters who thought that the tramway was part of a plan to raise the price of coal (such a necessity in those days, not just in industry but as a domestic fuel). This tramway was replaced by John Curr in 1776 using 'L'-shaped rails; this was one of the earliest cast-iron tramways and, perhaps, a model for the later railways, although none favoured the 'L' pattern. Large-scale transport of freight could still not be undertaken until the Sheffield Canal was opened in 1819.

With so much industry, the population of Sheffield increased rapidly and a survey of 1763 suggested that the town had as many as 10,000 souls living there, virtually double the population of half a century previously. However, Sheffield had gained an unwanted reputation of being 'exceedingly dirty and ill paved'. Daniel Defoe described the town thus:

> This town of Sheffield is very populous and large, the streets narrow, and the houses dark and black, occasioned by the continued smoke of the forges, which are always at work: Here they make all sorts of cutlery-ware, but especially that of edged-tools, knives, razors, axes, and nails; and here the only mill of the sort, which was a use in England for some time was set up, for turning their grindstones, though now 'tis grown more common.

By the time of the first national census in 1801, Sheffield had a population of over 31,000 (a large town in its day), growing to some 135,000 fifty years later. The town still had a reputation as a grimy and dirty place, which should not be too much of a surprise given the nature of the industries situated in Sheffield.

Throughout the nineteenth century, the iron and steel industries continued to thrive, aided by the invention of the Bessemer process in 1856. The Bessemer converter made a better quality steel than the Crucible method, and at a lower price. Henry Bessemer's invention was not well received by local steelmakers, so he built his own steelworks using his new process in Sheffield. As production increased and competition became effective, the Bessemer process was undercutting the competition by as much as £20 a ton, establishing the Bessemer converter as the most economical way of producing steel.

In 1840, silver plate was being produced using an electroplate process, which replaced the famous 'Sheffield Plate'. However, cutlery was still the main industry in Sheffield. Perhaps the most famous cutlery to emanate from Sheffield was made from stainless steel. It was discovered by accident in 1913 when one Harry Brearley was developing improved alloys for gun barrels. One such alloy with a high chrome content failed a trial and was left out in all weathers for several weeks. In that time, this alloy refused to rust, so Brearley gave samples to be made into cutlery blades, thus founding a booming market not just for cutlery but other metal household products.

Production of steel and its products in the nineteenth century involved long working hours in unpleasant conditions, with little or no consideration given to safety. An example of conditions for working people in the town was described by Friedrich Engels, friend of Karl Marx, in 1844:

> In Sheffield wages are better, and the external state of the workers also. On the other hand, certain branches of work are to be noticed here, because of their

extraordinarily injurious influence upon health. Certain operations require the constant pressure of tools against the chest, and engender consumption in many cases; others, file-cutting among them, retard the general development of the body and produce digestive disorders; bone cutting for knife handles brings with it headache, biliousness, and among girls, of whom many are employed, anaemia. By far the most unwholesome work is the grinding of knife-blades and forks, which, especially when done with a dry stone, entails certain early death. The unwholesomeness of this work lies in part in the bent posture, in which chest and stomach are cramped; but especially in the quantity of sharp-edged metal dust particles freed in the cutting, which fill the atmosphere, and are necessarily inhaled. The dry-grinders' average life is hardly thirty-five years, the wet grinders' rarely exceeds forty-five.

Given such working conditions, it is no surprise that Sheffield became a centre of trade union militancy, leading to such outrages as explosions and murders. Things were put on a more political footing with the formation of the United Kingdom Alliance of Organised Trades, forerunner of the Trades Union Congress, following a Trades Council meeting in Sheffield in 1866.

Since Sheffield was a centre of steel production in the nineteenth century, there were demands for bulk transport to export its finished products to other areas of Great Britain and abroad. Such transport was also required to bring in raw materials from the South Yorkshire coalfields around the Rotherham and Barnsley areas. These coalfields also needed outlets themselves to send their coal to other parts of the United Kingdom. While the Sheffield Canal could take much bulk cargo, it was slow and subject to weather conditions (water freezing in winter or evaporating in summer), all of which could delay transit of goods. What was required was a more rapid and reliable form of bulk transport and the fledgling railway companies would have taken interest in building railways around Sheffield and the South Yorkshire coalfields in order to make substantial profits from more rapid transit of massive amounts of freight, along with potential passenger traffic.

The first railway to reach Sheffield was the Sheffield & Rotherham Railway, arriving at the passenger terminus of Wicker in 1838. The next railway into the town was the one which bore its name as part of its title: the Sheffield, Ashton-under-Lyne & Manchester Railway. Its line into Sheffield arrived in 1845 to a single-platform station with a wooden shed at Bridgehouses. This little station was to remain in existence until the Manchester, Sheffield & Lincolnshire Railway (as the SA&MR had become from 1847) opened its new Victoria station in 1851 on the through line to Gainsborough and Lincoln. The MS&LR was to have grandiose ideas, becoming the Great Central Railway in 1893, the same year that Sheffield obtained its city status. The last of the 'big' companies to arrive in Sheffield was the Midland Railway, gaining access to the town via a 3½-mile branch from the Derby–Leeds main line between Treeton and Brightside on the Sheffield & Rotherham Railway. The MR Sheffield Midland station was opened on 1 February 1870, replacing the station at Wicker.

Although only connected to Sheffield via the MS&LR, Doncaster was to achieve importance as the centre of locomotive construction for the Great Northern Railway, whose line bypassed Sheffield at Retford to reach Doncaster, and the London & North Eastern Railway. The GNR was involved in lines throughout South Yorkshire coalfield areas, one such being the South Yorkshire Joint Railway in which it shared ownership with the GCR, MR, North Eastern Railway and Lancashire & Yorkshire Railway.

The L&YR also had an influence in South Yorkshire, having a freight line for coal traffic from Barnsley to Goole, and having its own station at Barnsley Exchange. Also operated by the L&YR was the Dearne Valley Railway which ran from Brierley Junction, on the Hull & Barnsley Railway, to Edlington, south of Doncaster, where it made connections with the GCR, GER, GNR, MR and NER. It also made a useful connection with the South Yorkshire Railway. Like the SYR, the DVR was primarily a freight line which served the many local collieries, but also operated limited passenger trains, these being operated by steam railmotor trains. The SYR operated passenger services, these being run by the GCR. The MR also operated passenger trains into Barnsley, these terminating at Barnsley Court House station. Services were connected to the main Leeds–Derby line via a shuttle service from Court House to Cudworth.

Cudworth Midland station was also shared by the unique Hull & Barnsley Railway, being the last of the Victorian independent railway companies. As its title suggests, the H&B connected the coalfields at Barnsley with its own Victoria Dock at the Port of Hull, which allowed onward shipment of coal to foreign customers and to the shipping companies that needed the coal to power their ships. The line obtained most of its revenue from such coal traffic, but the railway operated passenger services without much success. The line did, however, have branches to Denaby, where it made a connection with the DVR, and to Wath (for the GCR), this latter being the more successful passenger branch of the H&B due to its link to the GCR Manchester and Sheffield main line.

Just prior to the 1923 'grouping', the Hull & Barnsley Railway merged with the North Eastern Railway in 1922. Thus, along with the GCR and GNR, it became part of the London & North Eastern Railway as a constituent of the NER. The MR and L&YR became constituents of the London, Midland & Scottish Railway. The DVR became part of the LMS, while the SYR was jointly owned by the LMS and LNER. These colliery branches and lines continued to operate a myriad of coal trains but passenger trains were few and far between.

By nationalisation in 1948 such passenger services were dwindling or had ceased to exist. DVR passenger services ceased in 1951, while SYR regular passenger trains ceased in 1929 (although there were efforts to reintroduce a passenger service in 1935 without success). Outward excursions ran until 1966, after which a few rail tours operated over the branch. As steam traction headed towards its demise, much freight and coal traffic was lost to the railway as road competition began to bite, much having disappeared by 1966, forcing closure of the many branches.

As a last hurrah, an all-Pullman service, *The Master Cutler*, was operated by Eastern Region and was usually headed by a Thompson B1 4-6-0 running between Sheffield Victoria and London Marylebone. Steam gave way to diesel traction on this train from 1958, and the service was transferred to Sheffield Midland and London St Pancras in 1968. Another named train operating at Sheffield was *The South Yorkshireman*. This train operated between Bradford (Exchange), Huddersfield, Sheffield Victoria, and

London Marylebone. The train was usually hauled between Bradford and Sheffield by an ex-LMS 'Black 5' or 'Jubilee' 4-6-0 and then taken on to Marylebone by an ex-LNER locomotive.

Although the new British Railways had remained committed to steam traction, new forms of motive power were starting to appear by the mid-1950s. At Sheffield, a new electric passenger service was inaugurated on 14 September 1954 between Manchester and Sheffield, via Woodhead, using 1,500-volt DC electric locomotives with power supplied by overhead wires. Journey times from Sheffield to Manchester were reduced to an hour and, for the first time, the Woodhead Tunnel became smoke-free.

Ironically, only six years later, the whole of the GCR main line between Sheffield and Marylebone was to close, all services to be concentrated on the Sheffield Midland station. The old MR line also lost services between Sheffield and Leeds by 1967 due to subsidence over old mine workings between Barnsley and Leeds. Victoria station survived until 1970 because electric services to Manchester continued to operate, but its days were also numbered. Although Dr Beeching had not recommended closure, the West Coast Main Line, which included Manchester, was to be electrified on the 25kV AC system, leaving the Woodhead line as an anachronism, although an argument could have been made to have the Woodhead line so treated; but, as the old GCR line had gone, it would have been isolated at Sheffield. Thus, the last passenger train ran on 4 January 1970, while freight lasted until 1981, when all goods traffic was transferred to the ex-MR Hope Valley line. The whole of the Woodhead line closed at the same time and the remaining electric locomotives were sold to the Dutch railways, the last one retiring from service in 2010.

With all passenger services now concentrated on Sheffield Midland station from 1970, Victoria station was completely demolished in 1989. The local populace remember Victoria with great affection, as it was 'the station to be seen in', along with its upmarket hotel which still exists.

With so many railway companies operating trains in the Sheffield and South Yorkshire areas, there was much diversity in locomotive design in steam days, along with the locosheds that maintained and serviced them. Also, at Doncaster, there was a works which built many famous engines that operated in the locality. Stations were numerous and always staffed, something rarely seen today. Both freight and passenger traffic were plentiful, creating such a variety to enjoy. It was all of these things that made the steam railway such a place of fascination for young and old alike. I hope that I have managed to capture some of the fascination and sheer diversity which applied to the railway in the days of steam, much of which has been lost in these days of modernisation and so-called efficiency.

ONE

THE MANCHESTER, SHEFFIELD & LINCOLNSHIRE RAILWAY

The Manchester, Sheffield & Lincolnshire Railway (MS&LR) had its origins in the Sheffield, Ashton-under-Lyne & Manchester Railway (SA&MR), whose 2-mile line from Guide Bridge to Stalybridge, via Ashton, was opened on 23 December 1845, the SA&MR becoming the MS&LR from 1 January 1847. The SA&MR had promoted a scheme for a railway between Sheffield and Manchester, receiving its Act in 1837. Its 42-mile line used the Don Valley to the east, with Longdendale and Etherow Valleys in the west. To bring the railway through the Pennines, the 3-mile-long Woodhead Tunnel had to be constructed at a thousand feet above sea level. Construction began from both ends, with the eastern section from Sheffield to Woodhead being completed in July 1845 and the single track finally being finished five months later. The first trains between Sheffield and Manchester began operating from 22 December 1845. It took 1,500 navvies to build the tunnel and 26 lives were lost, construction conditions being very bad. The first stations were opened at Dunford Bridge and Penistone, with Hazelhead added in 1846 (renamed Hazelhead Bridge from 1850). Following the formation of the MS&LR in 1847, a second single-bore tunnel was approved and completed in 1852, the death toll reaching 28 – due this time to an outbreak of cholera.

The section from Penistone to Sheffield was opened in 1845 as part of the SA&MR line from Manchester, via Woodhead, also following the course of the River Don. From Deepcar the valley was wide enough for the railway to follow it; for the first five miles it included the four-arch Rumtickle Viaduct (there's a name to conjure with) and the 350-yard Thurgoland Tunnel. From Penistone, stations were opened at Oxspring, Thurgoland, Wortley, Deepcar, Oughty Bridge and Wadsley Bridge. A further station was opened, between Wadsley Bridge and Sheffield, at Neepsend in 1888, which lasted until 1940. The first Sheffield terminus was a single platform, with a wooden shed, at Bridgehouses; this was replaced in 1851 when the MS&LR opened a new station, Sheffield Victoria, on the through line to Gainsborough and Lincoln, via Retford, which followed the title of the railway company, running as it did from Manchester, through Sheffield, to Lincolnshire.

Destinations south and east of Sheffield Victoria were reached by construction of lines out to Rotherham (between 1864 and 1868), Annesley (for access to Nottingham, between 1890 and 1892) and the London extension south from Annesley (begun in 1899).

Although the MS&LR had become a reasonably large organisation, it was not a particularly prosperous one. Indeed, the railway had gained the unfortunate epithet 'Money Sunk and Lost' as a reflection of the poor return on investment in the MS&LR. The company, however, harboured ambitions of reaching London and beyond following the appointment of Sir Edward Watkin as general manager in 1853. Having been under the influence of the mighty London & North Western Railway, the MS&LR decided to strike out on its own and sought an alliance with the Great Northern Railway instead of harassing the King's Cross company, as it had done in the past. A joint Manchester–King's Cross service was inaugurated in 1857.

Watkin had, however, resigned from the MS&LR and gone to Canada, but returned to the Sheffield company as general manager in 1863. He was finally elected to the MS&LR board as chairman in 1867. Watkin continued trying to take the MS&LR to London, seeking various partners, but all were suspicious of him. Thus, he became chairman of the South Eastern Railway in 1866 and of the Metropolitan Railway in 1872. At the same time, he took an interest in a new company that wished to build a tunnel under the English Channel. By these means, Watkin could bring the MS&LR down from Annesley to join up with the Metropolitan Railway (allowing access to London) and then emerge on to the South Eastern Railway, via the East London Railway, and thence to the Channel coast. If the Channel Tunnel were built, then the MS&LR would be able to operate its trains all the way through to Paris from Manchester and Sheffield, which may well have done wonders for the economies of these two great cities; it would have provided direct access to the European mainland for the export of cotton products from Manchester and the products of the 'Steel City' of Sheffield. As it transpired, however, there would be no Channel Tunnel until the late twentieth century, despite all the nineteenth-century efforts to construct one. Direct Manchester/Sheffield–Paris expresses and freight traffic to mainland Europe would remain a pipe dream. Indeed, the north of England still awaits a direct rail service to Paris.

Despite such thwarted ambitions, Watkin did manage to see through a Parliamentary Bill for the extension of the MS&LR, which received Royal Assent in 1893. As if to highlight the future ambitions of the MS&LR, the railway company was renamed the Great Central Railway in the same year. Access to the GCR terminus at London Marylebone was via the Metropolitan Railway, and is now the only evidence, along with Marylebone station itself, that the MS&LR once existed. Had access to mainland Europe come to fruition, Marylebone could well have remained the London railway gateway to Europe instead of the old Midland Railway terminus at St Pancras. Indeed, it could be argued that the GCR itself may well have survived at the expense of another main line into London. One can only speculate as to which of these lines would have been sacrificed.

The new line to Marylebone was completed in 1907 and gave the once-provincial MS&LR/GCR access to the great metropolis and gave Sheffield an alternative route to London, setting up competition with the rival Midland Railway.

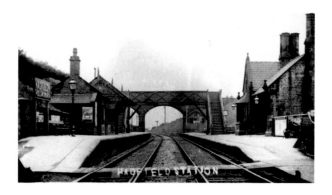

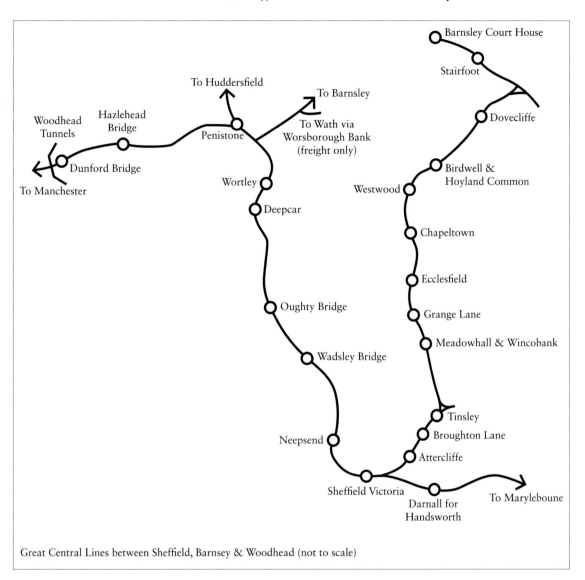

Great Central Lines between Sheffield, Barnsey & Woodhead (not to scale)

The GCR routes from Woodhead Tunnel to Sheffield Victoria and thence to Dovecliffe, Stairfoot and Barnsley. On the Woodhead line, there was a junction with the Lancashire & Yorkshire Railway at Penistone for trains to Huddersfield, followed by a junction for Barnsley, where Exchange station in the town was shared with the L&YR. There was also a freight branch to Wath, via Worsborough Bank, which had a colliery junction and small locoshed at Wentworth. Near Deepcar, the private Stocksbridge railway left the main line, serving Fox's steelworks. (Author)

Opposite: Approaching Woodhead from Manchester lay the station at Hadfield (for Hollingworth), seen here in the early twentieth century, followed by Crowden station, thence to Woodhead. (LOSA)

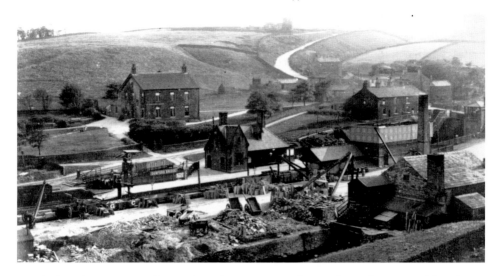

Dunford Bridge station with a coal yard in view, complete with small crane and handcarts, along with goods yard, water tower, station buildings and tunnel to the extreme right. The setting appears rural, belying the fact that the major steel city of Sheffield is not far away. By the time this picture was taken, the GCR line here was becoming overloaded with passenger trains trying to gain access between the myriad of coal trains from South Yorkshire pits. Trains operating between Manchester and Sheffield were now augmented by expresses running through to London Marylebone via the new extension which had been opened by the GCR in 1907. The station here was closed in 1970 when the electric railway was closed. The next station of Hazelhead Bridge was not so lucky, as it closed in 1950. (LOSA)

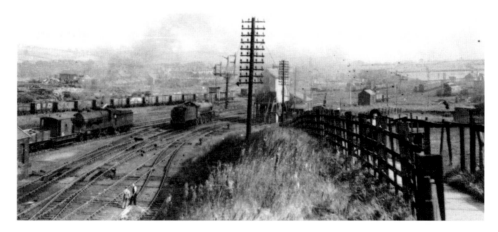

Penistone, looking towards the Huddersfield junction in 1947, with an ex-GCR 4-6-0 on shunting duties and an unidentified Thompson B1 4-6-0 waiting its turn of duty. The siding here appears to be full of coal wagons awaiting transit to Huddersfield and on to Lancashire, via the L&YR, or to Manchester via the GCR. The section between Penistone and Sheffield was opened in 1845 as part of the SA&MR line from Manchester to Bridgehouses until the MS&LR opened its new station at Sheffield Victoria. At Penistone, the GCR was joined by the Huddersfield & Sheffield Junction Railway in 1850, bringing in trains from Halifax and Bradford. By 1905, the Penistone–Sheffield section was dealing with GCR expresses from Liverpool and Manchester to Marylebone, and Great Northern Railway trains to King's Cross. There were also trains to Grimsby, Cleethorpes and the Norfolk coast, along with excursions to Plymouth and boat trains to Hull and Harwich. There were also stopping trains from Manchester and Penistone (five and six respectively on weekdays in 1922). These services were the first to go, ceasing in 1959. (R. Carpenter)

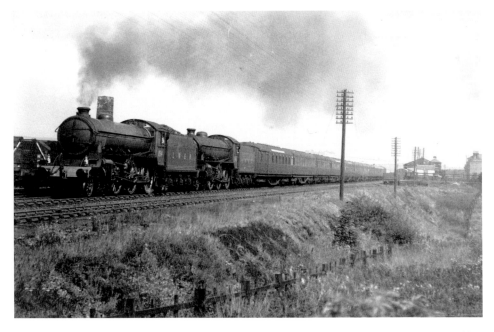

A pair of Thompson B1 4-6-0s, the leading engine numbered 1154 (BR No. 61154), still in LNER apple-green livery, head an express of Gresley teak stock past Penistone goods siding in 1947. Close to this spot, there was once the steelworks belonging to Cammell Laird, which was closed during the Depression years in an effort to rationalise steel production at a time when demand was poor. (R. Carpenter)

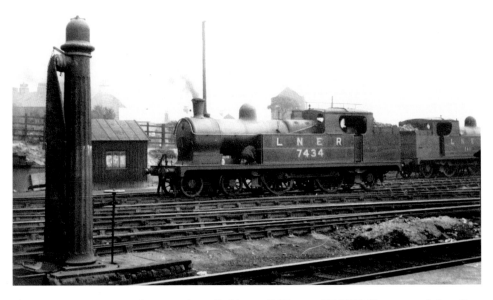

Shunting at Penistone in the 1930s is ex-Robinson GCR 4-4-2T LNER No. 7434 of class C13, built between 1903 and 1905. The whole class were still in service in 1952, but scrappage started in 1955, the last going in 1960. (H. Boulter)

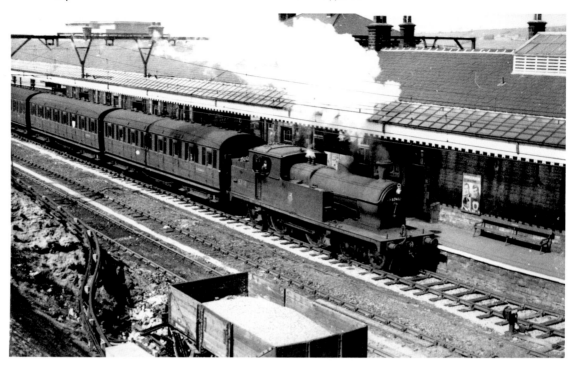

Another of the ex-GCR 4-4-2Ts, No. 67411, at the head of a local train at Penistone station on 19 April 1954. As a major junction, Penistone was the scene of several railway accidents. Indeed, only a short while after the station opened, the first accident occurred on 6 October 1845 when a train hit a cow. The 1880s saw several accidents at Penistone; there were two persons injured during a shunting accident on 8 December 1882. A more serious accident occurred on 16 July 1884 when a passenger train broke an axle, derailing the train, which fell down the embankment, killing four and injuring sixty passengers. A year later, on 1 January 1885, an excursion train collided with a coal train; four people were killed. On 1 September 1886, a locomotive hit carriages too hard when coupling up, injuring twenty passengers. In the same month, a year later, another locomotive hit carriages hard when coupling up but there were no injuries. It would seem that practices involved in coupling up here left a lot to be desired and, hopefully, the Board of Trade accident investigators made recommendations to prevent such things happening again. Another broken axle caused the death of one passenger and several injuries at Penistone on 30 March 1889. On 10 October 1897, a train collided with a carriage, killing one and injuring a further two persons. There were no further accidents at Penistone until 2 February 1916, when an embankment and end arch collapsed at the Penistone end of the viaduct, north of the station. A train went down with the collapse, although no injuries were recorded. The cause was subsidence after heavy rain. The final accident at Penistone occurred on 27 February 1927, when the signalman allowed LMS 2-4-2T No. 10760 to enter the main line after accepting a Manchester to Marylebone express. Having been turned, the little tank engine was returning to couple up to its train to Huddersfield just as the signalman had cleared the line for the express that was hauled by ex-GCR 4-4-0 No. 5437 *Prince George*. The driver of the tank engine thought the signals were for him and proceeded towards Sheffield to clear a set of points which, after reversing, would send the tank engine back to its train. The fireman of 10670 saw the express heading towards them and warned the driver before jumping out. The driver opened up his regulator to increase speed and reduced the impact, which almost certainly saved lives. (E. Morton)

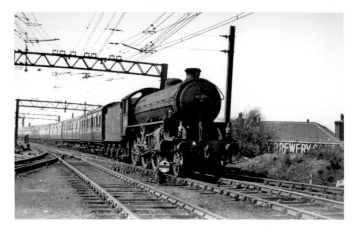

Ex-LNER Thompson B1 4-6-0 No. 61288 heads an 'up' Manchester express through Penistone on 19 April 1954, under the wires of the newly electrified Woodhead route that opened to electric train services in the same year. The B1 here was built by the North British Locomotive Company (build No. 26189), entered service on 16 February 1948 as a BR engine and was given the running number of E1288, being renumbered 61288 on 24 June 1950. The locomotive started working life at Darlington before being transferred to York on 26 September 1948, where she spent the fleeting fourteen years of her life before being condemned on 6 January 1964. She was cut up at her first home, Darlington, on 27 January 1964. (E. Morton)

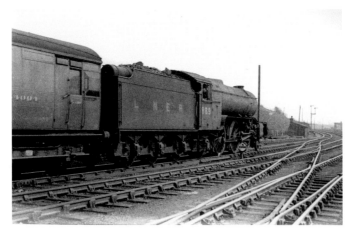

An empty stock train, hauled by LNER V2 2-6-2 No. 889, passes Wentworth Junction on the Worsborough branch on 18 April 1947. This was something of a rarity as empty stock workings usually went via Barnsley. The branch was usually used for heavy coal trains from Wath and local mines. Coal had been worked around Worsborough from the 1830s, although only in a small way and it was not until the development of railways in the area that real exploitation was possible. The South Yorkshire Railway had opened in 1850 with single-track lines to the various collieries in the area, the Worsborough line also being single until doubled in 1876. By 1886, there were five collieries at Swaithe, Worsborough, Strafford, Wentworth and Sovereign, with only three (at Swaithe, Strafford and Wentworth) at the turn of the century. By the 1930s, Strafford had been purchased by the Denaby Colliery Company and closed. Most output from the Worsborough collieries went via the SYR to Doncaster, for onward shipment to Hull and Grimsby, while the remainder went by the GNR to London and East Anglia. There was also a market for coal from South Yorkshire in places like Manchester, Cheshire and south Lancashire; thus the decision was made to build the Worsborough line to connect Penistone with Barnsley, which avoided the town and opened up a major route for traffic to the north-west of England. (H. Casserley)

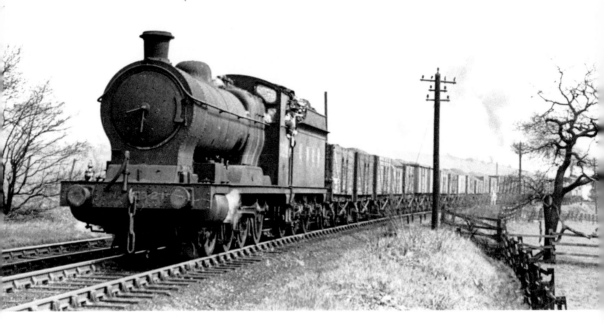

Ex-GCR Robinson Q4 0-8-0 No. 3219 is working a full load from Wentworth Colliery to the Barnsley Junction yard at Penistone on 18 April 1947. Wentworth had its own depot, with nine sets of men for the three locos involved in banking work here, which included the Beyer-Garratt and two 04 2-8-0s. If the Garratt was out of use, two further 04s were sent from Mexborough, which supplied all the locos here. Wentworth depot was merely a small cabin for signing on and for storage of lubricating oil. Men could also wait here if traffic was light – a rare event. Coal was available at nearby Wentworth colliery and water was provided in both directions. Along with local men, Wentworth could have men from places like Neasden, Ipswich, March, Retford, Northwich and Frodingham stationed there. (H. Casserley)

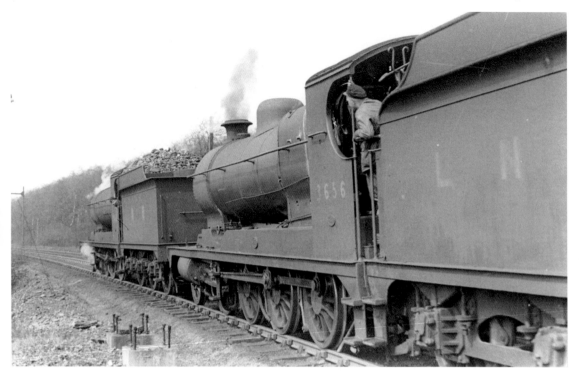

A pair of ex-GCR class 04 2-8-0s, Nos 3710 and 3656, at the head of a heavy train drawing up to the Wentworth starting signal, prior to the banker buffering up at the rear. (H. Casserley)

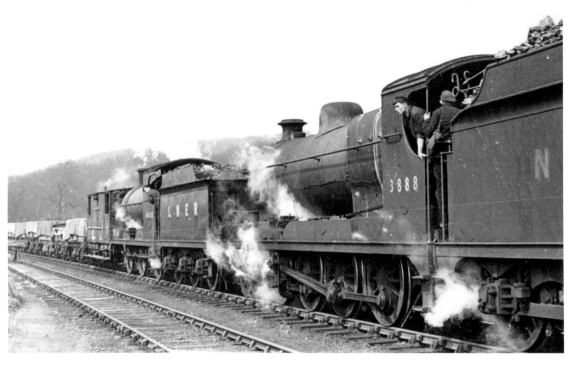

Banking a heavy coal train at Wentworth Junction on 18 April 1947 are ex-GCR Robinson J11 class 0-6-0 No. 4400 with class 04 2-8-0 No. 3888. The 0-6-0 was an unusual sight banking on such trains, as they were usually banked by the Garratt or a pair of 2-8-0s. (H. Casserley)

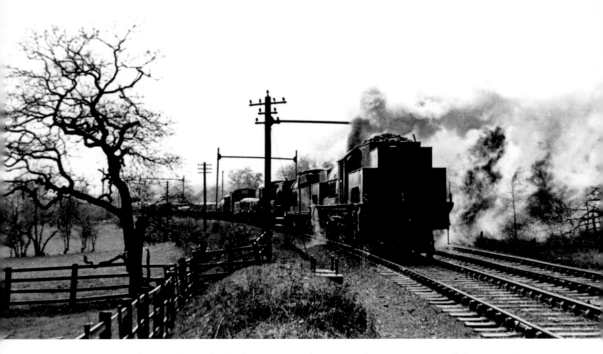

A heavy coal train is being banked at Wentworth Junction by an 04 2-8-0 and the Beyer-Garratt 2-8-0 0-8-2 No. 9999 on 23 April 1947. The Garratt was based on a design by Nigel Gresley from his three-cylinder class 02 2-8-0s, giving six cylinders and a tractive effort of 72,940 lb. The engine was delivered by Beyer-Peacock from its Gorton works to Darlington for display in the Darlington Centenary Exhibition of 1925. From there it went to Wentworth for use as a banking engine. The locomotive was not popular with enginemen from Mexborough, Barnsley or Wentworth. Firemen certainly did not like it because they were doing the work of two men. So much so that it was forbidden to fire the Garratt on consecutive days, so it was an 'every other day' roster. The Garratt was taken out from Mexborough on a Monday morning and was regarded as a job to avoid. The crew signed on at 2.15 a.m. and an allowance of two hours was made to prepare the engine. The 56.5 square feet of grate meant that shovelling coal for twenty minutes had no real effect. Leaving at 4.15 a.m., the loco had to be at Wentworth for 5 a.m., when the Mexborough men were relieved by Wentworth men. The Worsborough branch was electrified in 1951/52, with the whole of the Sheffield–Manchester line energised in 1954, which meant that other work had to be found for the Garratt and it went to the Lickey Bank, near Birmingham, causing a few accidents at Bromsgrove when coupling up to passenger trains and damaging rear coaches. It also suffered from water starvation when climbing the bank, causing it to be withdrawn in 1955. (H. Casserley)

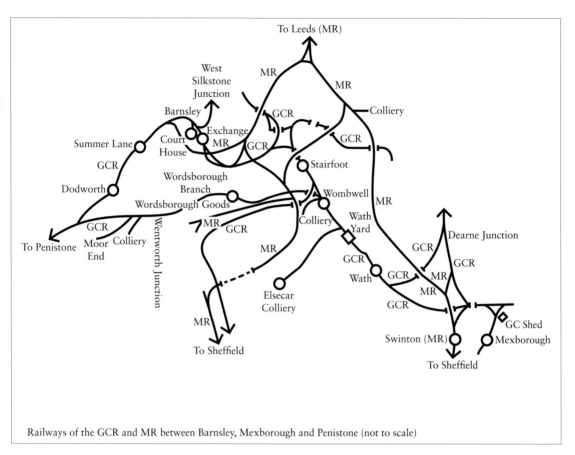

Railways of the GCR and MR between Barnsley, Mexborough and Penistone (not to scale)

A map showing the Worsborough branch and its connections. The branch was built to relieve congestion in Barnsley, where the line from Stairfoot to Summer Lane and Dodworth had gradients starting at 1 in 76, steepening from Barnsley Exchange to 1 in 50 through Summer Lane to Pogmoor, necessitating the use of banking engines for heavy coal trains. A busy level crossing at Jumble Lane, right in the centre of Barnsley, also dealt with passenger trains of the MS&LR and the L&YR, creating a great deal of congestion. In 1876, MS&LR management decided to extend the 1850 Worsborough branch from Moor End to join the Barnsley–Penistone line at West Silkstone Junction, 2½ miles away. This extension was difficult to build and involved driving two tunnels – Silkstone No. 1 of 75 yards and Silkstone No. 2 of 290 yards – taking four years to complete. The line was laid to a gradient of 1 in 40, steeper than the Barnsley line but preferable to the delays and costs of running through Barnsley, thus the need for banking. (Author)

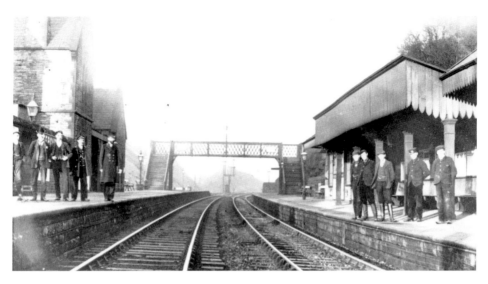

Deepcar station with staff at the beginning of the twentieth century. By an Act of 1874, a line was built from the MS&LR at Deepcar station to run into the steelworks at Stocksbridge, opening in April 1877. As well as industrial use, the Stocksbridge railway also carried passengers in its early days, although the service was infrequent and often did not run at all. A small siding, just at the side of Deepcar station, was provided for these trains, which would arrive and depart with both clerical and manual staff and run into the station at Low Yard of Fox's. Schoolchildren who attended Penistone Grammar school were taken to Deepcar railway station for the Sheffield to Penistone train and were met at Deepcar on the return journey. Passenger carriage ceased in 1931 when local bus services in the area became more regular. From the closure of the Woodhead line, the only traffic operating over the line was from Nunnery to Deepcar in connection with traffic from Stocksbridge, and that ceased in 1983. The railway cutting just north of Deepcar station was filled in to carry the Stocksbridge bypass. (LOSA)

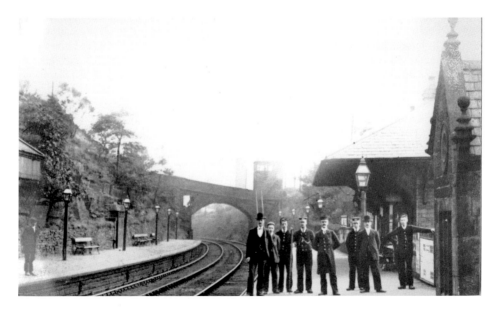

Oughty Bridge station of the GCR with stationmaster and staff posed for the photograph. Discontinuation of local services in 1959 meant the end for Oughty Bridge and it closed in the same year. (LOSA)

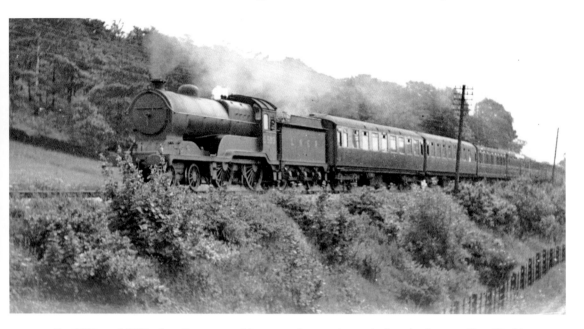

Ex-GCR, as LNER class D11, 4-4-0 No. 5503 *Somme* (named after the famous First World War battle which cost many thousands of lives) is seen passing through Beeley woods, between Oughty Bridge and Wadsley Bridge, at the head of a train for Sheffield in 1933, when the line was busy. (R. Carpenter)

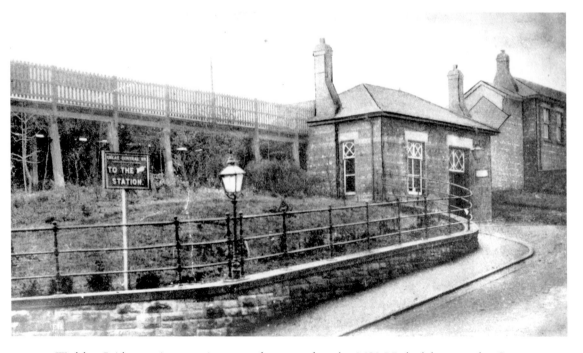

Wadsley Bridge station exterior around 1910, after the MS&LR had become the Great Central Railway. Although the station lost its local services in 1959, it did remain open to deal with football specials because it was close to the Hillsborough ground of Sheffield Wednesday Football Club, famously known as 'The Owls'. (LOSA)

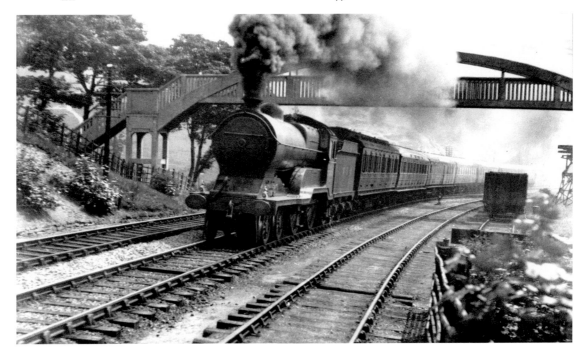

At Neepsend is ex-GCR Robinson 'Director' class, 011, 4-4-0 No. 5509 *Prince Albert* with a Manchester-bound express in 1933. (R. Carpenter)

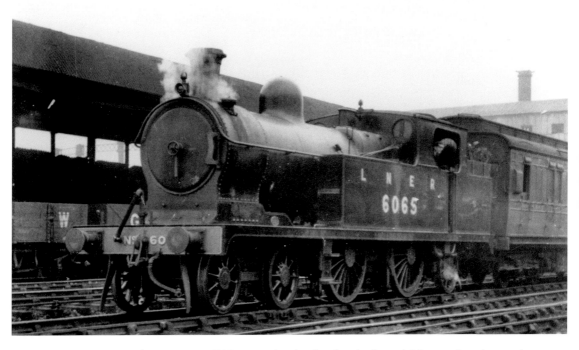

Ex-GCR LNER class C13 4-4-2T No. 6065 heads a local train through Neepsend station on 6 June 1936. Interestingly, Great Western coal wagons are in the goods siding here, a long way from home. (H. Casserley)

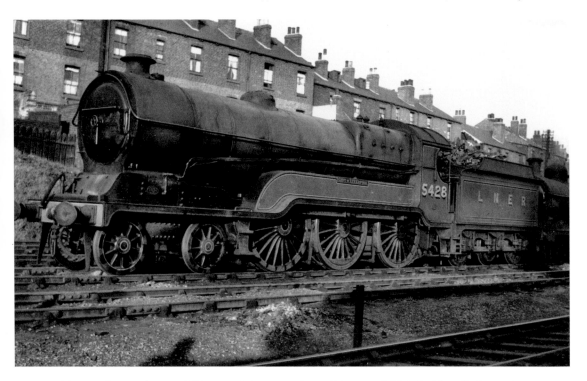

Also at Neepsend is ex-GCR 4-6-0 No. 5428 *City of Liverpool*. This inside-cylinder engine was of LNER class B2 and is seen here on 10 May 1936. None of this class survived into British Railways ownership. (N. Glover)

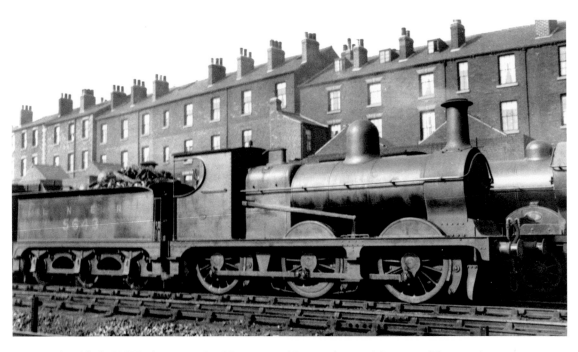

An elderly LNER class 0-6-0 J10 No. 5643 at Neepsend on 19 May 1929. These engines were built by Parker for the MS&LR at Gorton works from 1892 to 1902 and many were long-lived, the last having been scrapped as late as 1962. (N. Glover)

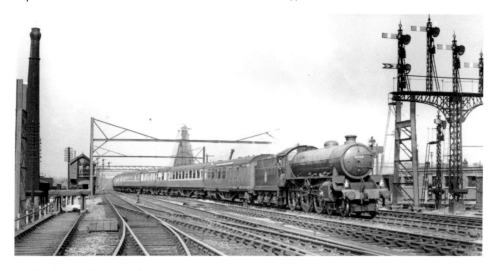

At the head of a Manchester to Marylebone train is ex-LNER Thompson B1 4-6-0 No. 61157 at Priory Junction on 17 August 1952. The locomotive was built by Vulcan Foundry (No. 5515) and entered traffic on 9 May 1947, being renumbered 61157 on 30 October 1948. She was first allocated to Gorton and then moved to Stratford on 5 October 1952, only a few months after this picture was taken. She then went to Doncaster on 19 October, where she remained until condemned on 1 August 1965. She was sold for scrap to T. W. Ward of Brighton in September 1965. (B. Green)

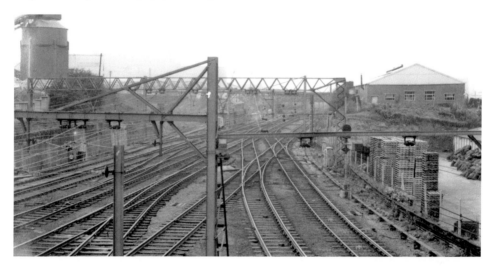

Woodburn Junction, Sheffield, as it appeared on 4 October 1969, shortly before the line closed. All of the overhead lines for the electric service are still intact. Electrification of the Woodhead line had first been mentioned as early as 1913 following a visit by the GCR locomotive superintendent to the USA, where he saw a 1,500-volt DC system operating. The plan was to use such a system on the difficult Worsborough Bank section of the Barnsley–Penistone line. The plan was, however, abandoned due to cost, but the idea was later considered by the LNER for electrification of lines from Sheffield, Wath and Barnsley to Penistone and through Woodhead to Manchester, at an estimated cost of £2.5 million, to include eighty-eight locomotives, only one of which was built by the outbreak of the Second World War. Work resumed in 1946, but the deteriorating condition of Woodhead Tunnel forced the LNER to plan for a replacement at a cost of a further £2.8 million. The escalating cost of the whole scheme, £12 million by 1950, led BR to cut the project back drastically, especially the number of locos. Despite this, the cost of a new double-track Woodhead Tunnel alone cost £4.6 million. (R. Carpenter)

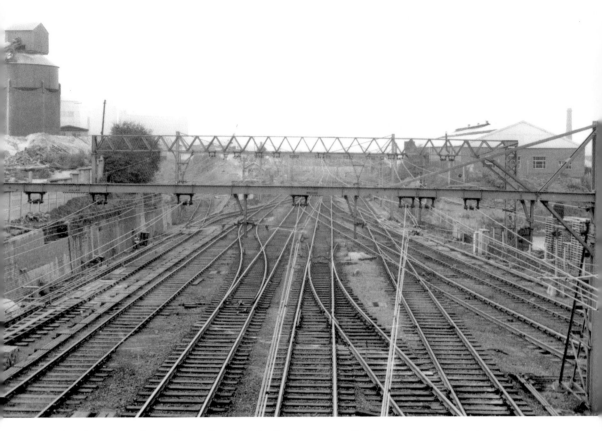

Another view of Woodburn Junction in October 1969. By January 1955, electric services between Sheffield and Manchester were fully operational, but in 1960 through services from Manchester, Sheffield and London Marylebone ended. Oddly enough, although the Woodhead line was not proposed for closure by Dr Beeching, BR proposed giving priority to freight by switching Sheffield–Manchester services to the longer ex-MR Hope Valley line. After a two-year inquiry, consent was given to withdraw Woodhead passenger services in 1969. On 4 January 1970, the last timetabled electric passenger train left Sheffield and resulted in the closure of Dunford Bridge station and the ex-GCR platforms at Penistone. Much of the reason for closure was the 1,500-volt DC system in use on the Woodhead line, while the 25kV AC system was being developed on the West Coast Main Line which served Manchester. Decline of coal traffic and the policy of using other routes had seriously reduced freight traffic over the Woodhead line and BR exercised its right to close the line. The last freight train was the Harwich–Liverpool 'Speedlink' service, on 18 July 1981, after which the line was completely closed and even the single line through the tunnel was removed in 1986 and the portals sealed off. Many of the locos were sold to the Dutch railways, the last one being withdrawn in Holland in the last few years. (R. Carpenter)

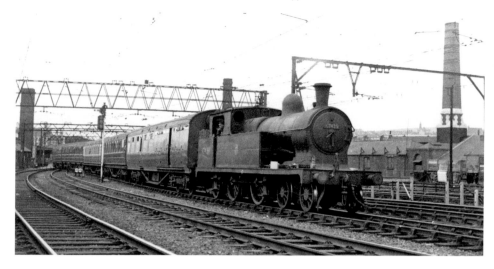

Ex-GCR/LNER C13 class 4-4-2T No. 67434 at Sheffield Victoria station on pilot duties on 14 June 1958. The train is on the Wicker Viaduct, known as Wicker Arches, designed by John Fowler, who went on to design the famous Forth Bridge in Scotland. The construction of Wicker Arches was begun by contractors Blackie & Shortbridge in the mid-1830s to bring trains from the original Bridgehouses terminus of the SA&MR to a new MS&LR station at Victoria, which was under construction at the same time. The construction cost of the arches was £80,000 and the edifice was seen as a new modern wonder, bringing a great deal of interest from locals. Some thought that the arches would not be strong enough to carry any trains when opened, a criticism of many major structures built at that time which appeared to be borne out when, in 1848, machinery and other equipment collapsed, killing four workmen. Very shortly afterwards, a whole arch collapsed with no injuries, but this gave the doom mongers further ammunition. However, only shortly afterwards, the first steam train crossed the viaduct on 16 December 1848 and no further mishaps occurred for the remainder of its working life. The entire viaduct spanned 650 yards on a 72-feet-wide arch that commenced at Bridgehouse station and continued into Victoria station. (R. Carpenter)

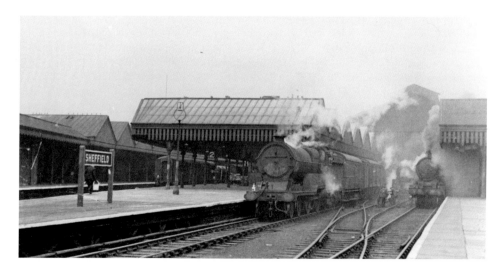

Sheffield Victoria station on 23 April 1947 when still in LNER ownership, and a little over a year before nationalisation. Ex-GCR 'Director' class 4-4-0 No. 2654 *Walter Burgh Gair* stands at the head of a fitted freight train on the left and ex NER B16 4-6-0 No. 1405 is about to depart with a London bound train on the right. (H. Casserley)

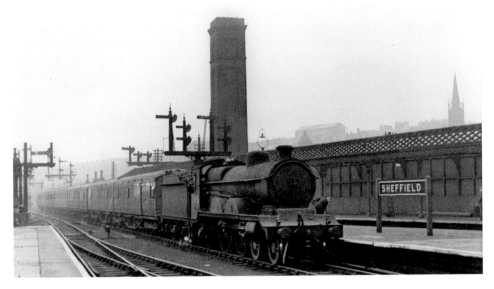

Ex-GCR Robinson C4 class Atlantic No. 2915 heads a train of Gresley teak rolling stock into Sheffield Victoria station on 23 April 1947. (H. Casserley)

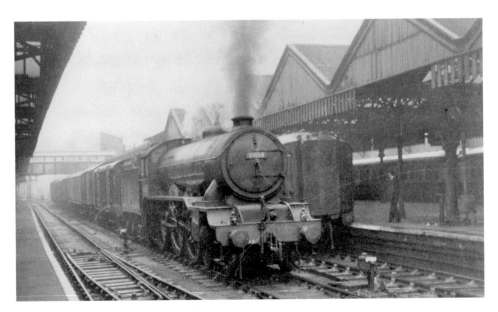

LNER class B17 4-6-0 No. 61658 – at this time a March engine – *The Essex Regiment* arrives at Sheffield Victoria with a fitted freight train. The loco was built at Darlington in 1936 as No. 2858 for the ex-Great Eastern Railway where axle loadings were restricted due to the strength of bridges on the line. The whole class had an axle loading of only 18 tons. This engine entered traffic on 28 May 1936 at Neasden, went to Stratford on 19 June 1936, Parkeston on 21 August 1938, before returning to Stratford on 7 July 1940. From there, she went to March on 11 April 1942, back to Parkeston on 7 October 1946, and then back to March on 10 June 1951. After her sojourn at March the loco then went to Colchester on 7 May 1955, back to Stratford on 14 December 1958, and then returned to Colchester on 8 February 1959. Her final allocation was Stratford from 1 November 1959. Less than a month later, on 3 December 1959, she was condemned and cut up at Doncaster. The engine was renumbered 1658 from 21 December 1946, becoming 61658 on 5 June 1948. (H. Casserley)

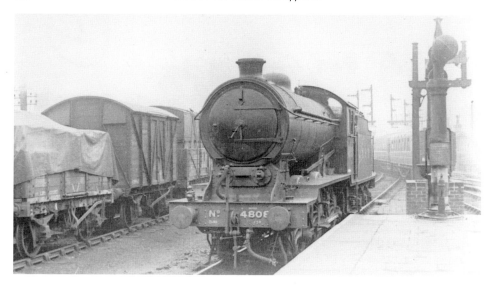

Ex-GNR Gresley 03 class 2-8-0 No. 4808, one of a class of twenty built at nearby Doncaster between 1913 and 1919, waits outside Sheffield Victoria station on 23 April 1947. The whole class was withdrawn between 1947 and 1952, so this photograph captures the last period of its life. (H. Casserley)

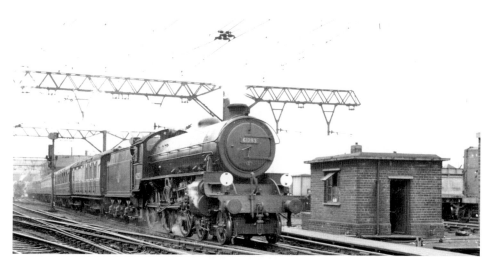

Leaving Sheffield Victoria under the wires for the new electric railway is ex-LNER B1 class 4-6-0 No. 61283 at the head of a Manchester-bound train in the early 1950s. The B1 here was built by the North British Locomotive Company (works No. 26184) and entered traffic from Colwick shed on 2 February 1948 with the running number 1283, becoming 61283 on 27 November 1948. From Colwick, the engine was transferred to Leicester on 6 November 1949 and returned to Colwick only a month later, on 18 December, and went back to Leicester on 5 February 1950, returning to Colwick on 12 March. From Colwick she was transferred to Woodford on 7 November 1954, then went back to Colwick on 20 February 1955, to Leicester on 15 November 1956, back to Colwick on 9 December (was there something wrong with this loco?), thence to King's Cross on 5 May 1957, to Cambridge on 20 October 1957, then to Norwich on 20 November 1960, and finally to Stratford on 10 September 1961 – much-travelled indeed. The engine was condemned on 16 September 1962 and transferred to Doncaster for cutting up on 26 November 1962 after a hectic life of some fourteen years. (B. Collins)

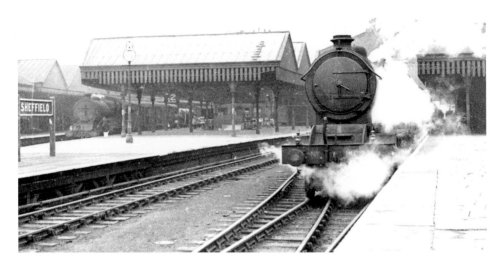

Sheffield Victoria station on 23 April 1947, with ex-LNER B16 4-6-0 No. 1405 at the head of an LNER train for Marylebone. An ex-GCR loco is on the left at the head of what appears to be a parcels train. Sheffield Victoria station was opened to fanfare in 1851, occupying a high position. Access was via a flight of steps from the Wicker or up the hill on Victoria Station Road to access the ticket office. Although not easy to access, the station was popular and was *the* place to be seen. Its Royal Victoria Hotel, adjoining the station, was well known for its civic functions and grand balls, being popular with the wealthy of Sheffield. The hotel remains today as part of the Holiday Inn chain. (H. Casserley)

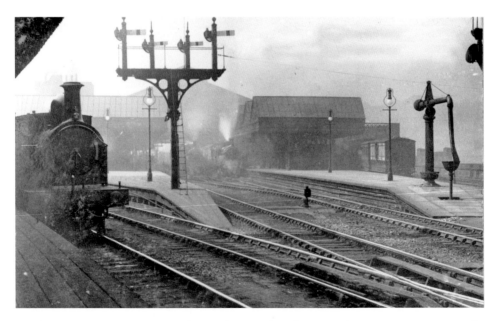

Sheffield Victoria station in GCR days with examples of trains and motive power in use at the time. In the near foreground appears to be a GCR 0-6-0 while a couple of expresses, headed by GCR 4-4-0s, are in the distant centre of the picture. The station looks rather grubby when compared to the previous photograph dating from immediately after the Second World War. (LOSA)

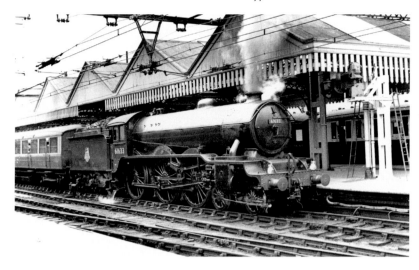

Ex-LNER B17 class 4-6-0 No. 61633 *Kimbolton Castle* is at the head of a Harwich boat train on 29 May 1954. The B17s were often found on this service until they disappeared in the late 1950s. This particular example was built at Darlington and entered traffic as No. 2833 from Doncaster shed on 28 May 1931. The engine was renumbered 1633 from 15 September 1946, becoming 61633 on 14 August 1948. After leaving Doncaster after running in, the engine spent much of her life in East Anglia, being based at Cambridge from 30 October 1938. After twelve years, she was transferred to March on 4 June 1950, returning to Cambridge on 18 March 1956, then going back to March from 25 November 1956. For just under three years, she remained at March before being condemned on 30 September 1959 and was cut up at Doncaster. (B. Green)

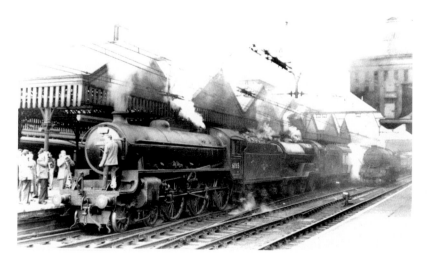

A busy scene at Sheffield Victoria on 21 September 1958, with ex-LNER B1 4-6-0 double-heading ex-GCR 'Director' class 4-4-0 on an RCTS excursion with photographers taking their pictures. In the background, what appears to be a Gresley 2-6-0 is waiting on the centre road. The B1 is No. 61165 and was built by Vulcan Foundry (works No. 5523) and entered traffic from Gorten on 28 May 1947. From there, she was allocated to Mexborough from 14 June 1947 as No. 1165. The loco was still based there when this excursion was operated and, it could be assumed, the trip started from here. The ex-GCR loco may also have been allocated to Mexborough at this time. Becoming 61165 from 5 August 1949, she was transferred to Canklow from 11 March 1962 and condemned there on 1 November 1962 and sold for scrap to Draper's of Hull in January 1965. (H. Boulter)

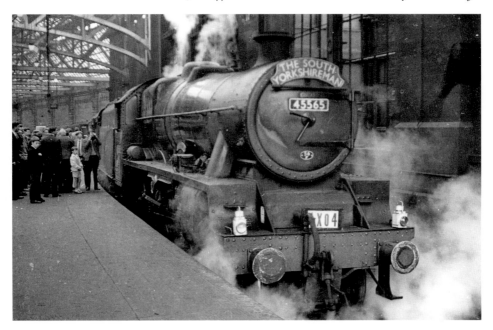

Among the named trains which ran through Sheffield Victoria was *The South Yorkshireman*, which ran from Bradford Exchange to Marylebone, via Huddersfield. This train was only given its name from 1948, even though it had been operating since GCR days. By the 1950s, the train was operated from Bradford to Sheffield Victoria by ex-LMS 4-6-0s. Here, at Bradford, is ex-LMS Jubilee class 4-6-0 No. 45565 *Victoria* about to depart with the train. (LOSA)

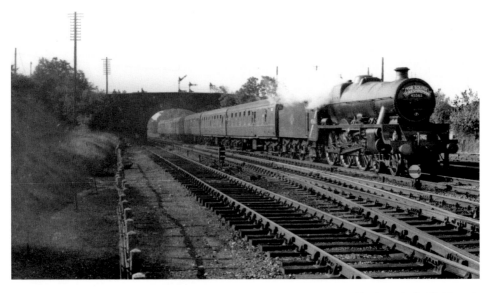

Another view of *The South Yorkshireman* running between Bradford and Sheffield with another Jubilee 4-6-0, No. 45562 *Alberta*, at the head. (LOSA)

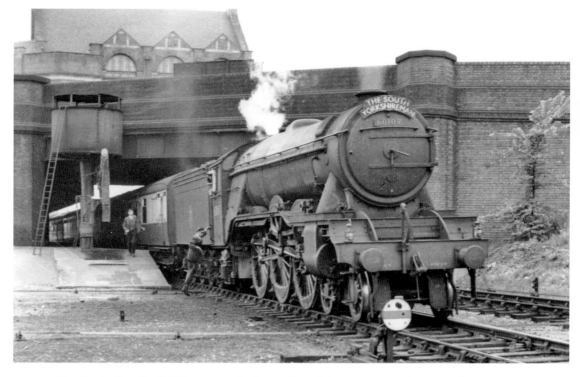

Heading back to Sheffield Victoria with *The South Yorkshireman*, ex-LNER A3 Pacific No. 60107 *Royal Lancer* makes ready to depart from Rugby Central in the early 1950s. (R. Carpenter)

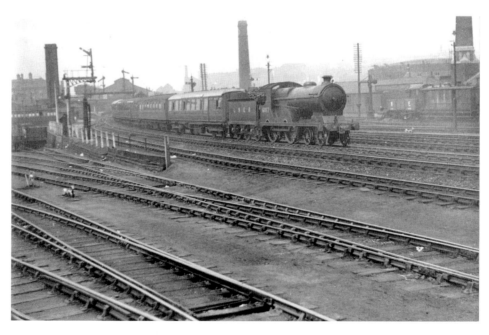

Heading an 'up' local train past Sheffield Victoria is ex-GCR D9 class 4-4-0 No. 6017 in the early 1930s. Just under forty years later, Victoria station was closed, in 1970, when the final electric services had gone and the GCR main line had closed. The station had a brief reprieve in 1972, when the Midland station was being modernised, but was finally demolished in 1989. (R. Carpenter)

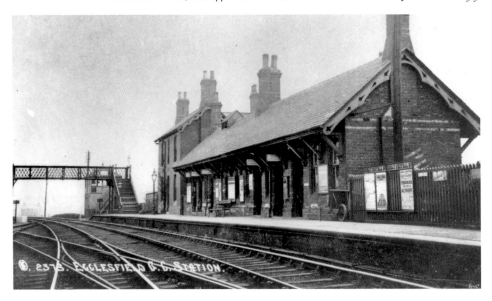

Ecclesfield station on the GCR Sheffield–Dovecliffe–Barnsley line. Construction of the line from Barnsley to Sheffield was started by the Sheffield, Rotherham, Barnsley, Wakefield, Huddersfield & Goole Railway with the building of a 2,278-yard tunnel at Birdwell in 1847. However, work stopped the following year after 6,000 cubic yards had been excavated from six shafts. When the South Yorkshire Railway resumed work on the line in 1851, local coal owners wanted a surface route further east and the tunnel was abandoned. The new route climbed at 1 in 63 to Birdwell and then descended on a similar gradient. It ran from an east-facing junction at Adlam (on the Barnsley–Mexborough line), with stations at Smithley (later Dovecliffe) and High Royd (which only lasted a year), to Birdwell. Further stations were built at Westwood, Chapeltown, Ecclesfield (shown here), Grange Lane and Meadowhall and Wincobank before the line joined the MR into the original Sheffield terminus at Wicker. (LOSA)

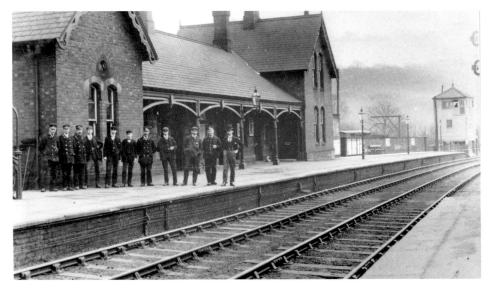

Chapeltown station on the Barnsley line. In 1860, the SYR began construction of a Sheffield extension, but its line into Victoria did not open until after MS&LR takeover in 1864. There was an intermediate station at Broughton Lane, with Tinsley added in 1869. Attercliffe was added two years later. (LOSA)

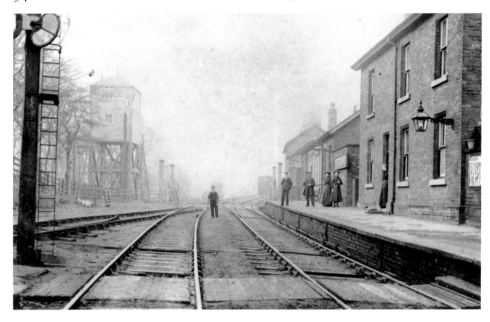

Westwood station on the line to Barnsley, with the line doubled after the MS&LR had done this in 1876. The stations here and at Ecclesfield were replaced in the same year. The following year, the MS&LR opened a new connection at Adlarn which gave direct access to Barnsley Court House station. Court House had been adapted by the MR in 1871–2 and was seen as a great improvement on the L&YR Exchange station, which was viewed as 'an awful place'. Westwood station was closed in 1940; given that a sparse passenger service was being run at this time, little protest was raised. (LOSA)

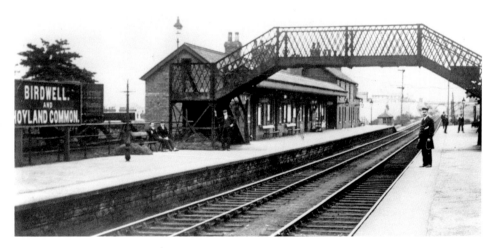

Birdwell and Hoyland Common station at the end of the nineteenth century. In 1897, the MR extended its freight-only Chapeltown branch, which ran parallel to the MS&LR through to Barnsley and began a competing passenger service. The two lines survived into BR days and it was the MS&LR line which closed in 1953. Excursion trains continued for a further six years and its Sheffield extension carried passenger trains from Rotherham until 1966. Goods traffic on the Chapeltown section was cut back progressively as collieries closed, finally ceasing in 1986. (LOSA)

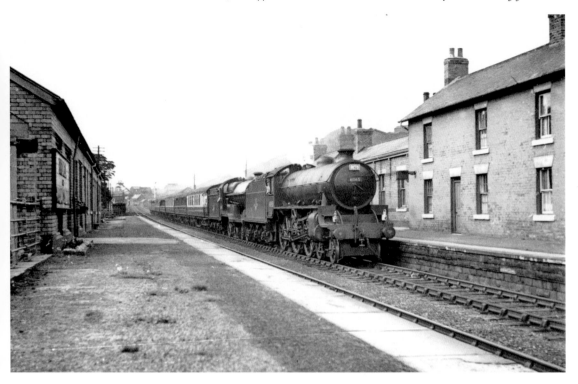

The RCTS excursion, headed by B1 4-6-0 No. 61165 and ex-GCR 4-4-0, last seen at Sheffield Victoria, passes through Birdwell on 21 September 1958. (H. Boulter)

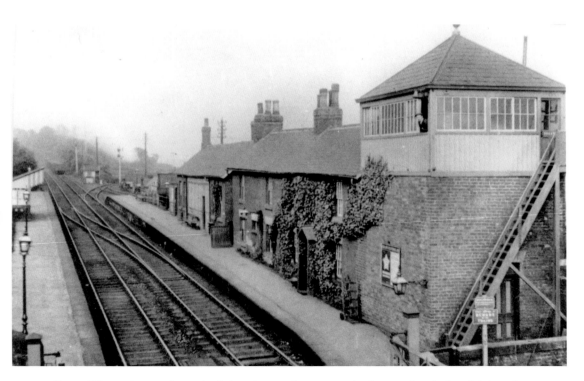

Dovecliffe station at the end of the nineteenth century, the last station before joining the Barnsley line at Adlam Junction. (LOSA)

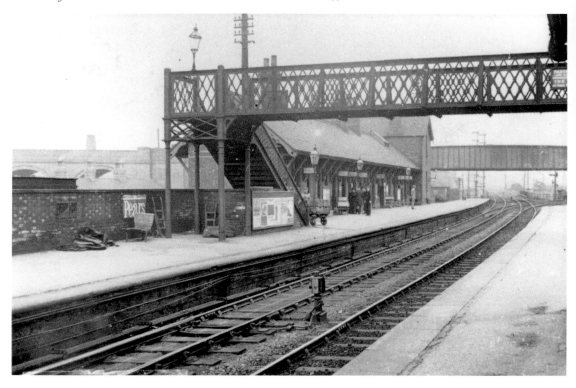

Stairfoot station on the line from Barnsley to Adlam Junction, giving access to Sheffield via the MS&LR line. (WSA)

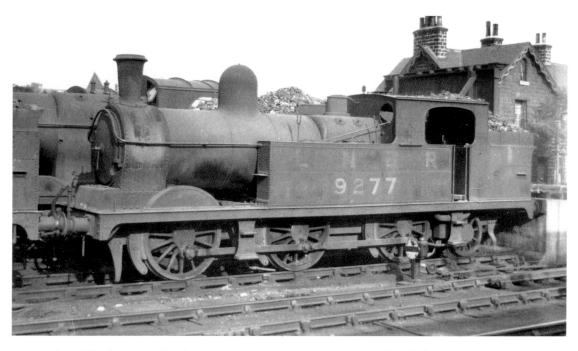

In LNER days, ex-GCR class N5/2 0-6-2T No. 9277 sits at Barnsley shed in 1947. The shed was built by the GCR to replace a single-road shed north of the L&YR Barnsley Exchange station. (R. Carpenter)

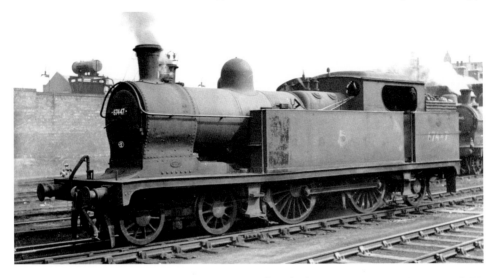

Ex-GCR C14 class 4-4-2T No. 67447 at Barnsley shed on 1 May 1958. As an ex-GCR locoshed, although next to the L&YR Exchange station, locos allocated at the two-road shed were mostly of GCR origin, although there was a presence of LMS types in later years. Coded 41G in BR days, the shed closed in 1960, allowing Exchange to add a second platform to its station. (H. Boulter) The allocation for 1950 was as follows:

GCR Q4 0-8-0	63220, 63229, 63235
GCR o1/o4 2-8-0	63697, 63727, 63883, 63904, 63913
GCR J11 0-6-0	64290, 64366, 64391, 64398, 64399, 64425, 64436, 64448, 64452
MS&LR N5 0-6-2T	69268, 69278, 69285, 69291, 69303, 69320, 69325, 69334, 69345, 69348, 69355, 69357, 69365, 69367, 69368
	Total: 33

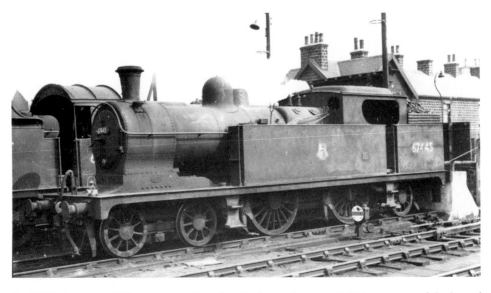

Ex-GCR C14 4-4-2T No. 67445 at Barnsley shed on 1 May 1958. This was one of the last of its class, the majority having been withdrawn a year earlier. Indeed, this loco may well have been awaiting its fate here and would be gone very soon. (H. Boulter)

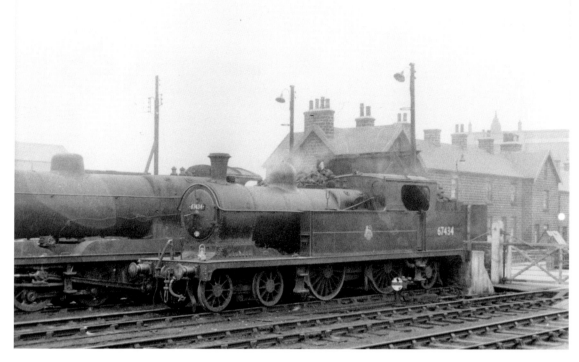

Ex-GCR class 4-4-2 No. 67434 on shed next to Jumble Lane level crossing, Barnsley. The level crossing divided the town and the sheer volume of traffic caused a lot of congestion until the freight-only Worsborough branch opened. (H. Casserley)

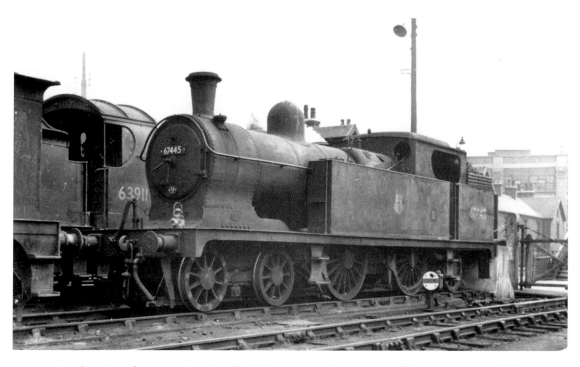

Another view of 67445 at Barnsley shed. She is seen in the company of No. 63911, an ex-GCR 2-8-0 of the 04 class (H. Boulter)

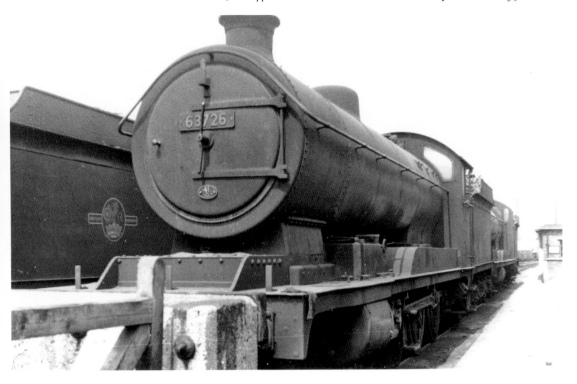

Ex-GCR 04 2-8-0 No. 63726 at Barnsley shed on 25 July 1959. The engines allocated here were usually to work on heavy coal trains from the collieries in the area or for local passenger traffic, hence an allocation of 4-4-2 and 0-6-2 tank engines. (D. Green)

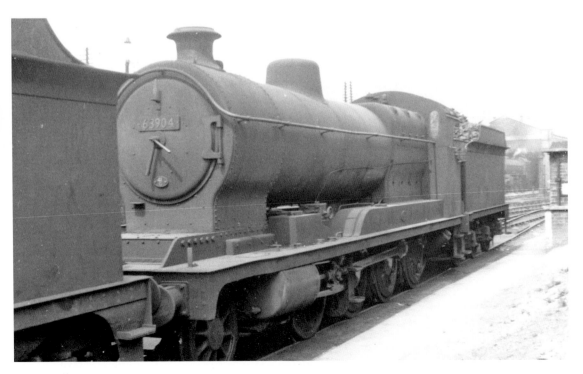

Another 04 2-8-0, No. 63904, at Barnsley shed on 25 July 1959. (D. Green)

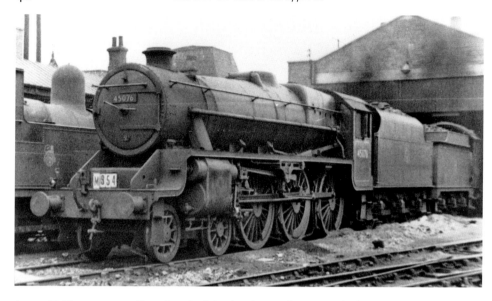

An ex-LMS presence at Barnsley shed, in the shape of Stanier Black 5 4-6-0 No. 45076 on 30 June 1957. (R. Carpenter)

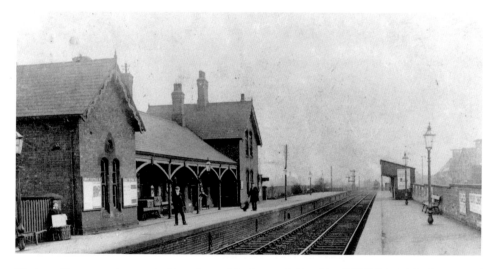

Wath-on-Dearne station on the Barnsley to Mexborough line. The SRBWH&GR had proposed a link between Mexborough, in the Don Valley, and Barnsley. In 1847, the SYR reached agreement with the SRBWH&GR to purchase the latter's routes south of Barnsley and obtained an Act for a Mexborough–Barnsley line. The following year, the SYR wanted a link from Barnsley to Penistone, but this went to the MS&LR, who completed the line in 1859. The SYR line from Mexborough to the SRBWH&GR Barnsley station (later named Exchange by the L&YR) opened in 1851 with basic stations at Wath, Wombwell and Ardsley to provide a Doncaster–Barnsley passenger service, originally operated by the GNR, the SYR more interested in coal traffic from local pits. The two companies did discuss amalgamation, but in 1853 the GNR cut passenger services to once a day, leaving the SYR having to use motive power and coaches borrowed from the MR. In the end, the SYR was leased by the MS&LR, who had absorbed the SRBWH&GR in 1864, taking complete control a decade later. The MS&LR made improvements, including moving to Barnsley's Court House station, rebuilding stations at Wath and Wombwell, and re-siting Ardsley station and changing its name to Stairfoot. (LOSA)

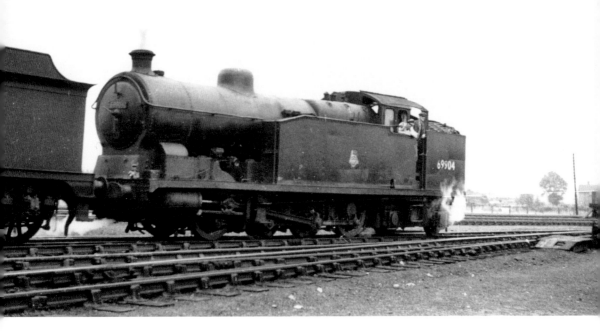

In 1907, the GCR made major changes to the way it handled freight traffic with the development of a huge marshalling yard at Wath. It was the largest goods yard in the country at the time and it was designed to concentrate all coal traffic from the South Yorkshire coalfields. Wath was a hump shunting yard, using gravity instead of locos to marshal wagons into trains. The GCR built four 0-8-4Ts to work in the yard. Known as 'Wath Daisies', these locomotives were designed by CME John Robinson and built between December 1908 and January 1909. They had a length of 45 feet and weighed 99 tons. With a tractive effort of 34,000 lb, they were the most powerful tank engines in the country. Designated class S1/1 by the LNER, No. 6171 (BR No. 69901) had a booster unit fitted in 1932 to improve its tractive effort. Here No. 69904 is seen at Wath yard on 7 August 1958 awaiting its duties, one of Gresley's 1932 developments of the S1/1 class being designated class S/3. Closure of the Woodhead line greatly reduced freight traffic, but Wath yard survived until 1986, when the whole of the Barnsley–Mexborough line disappeared. (H. Boulter)

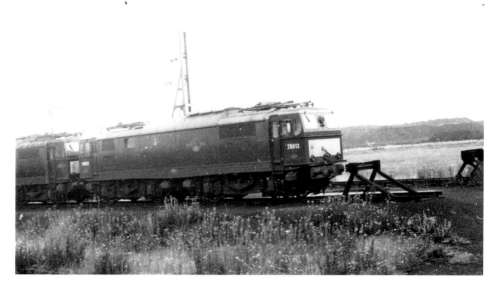

A pair of the 1,500-volt DC Bo-Bo electric locos on 13 August 1966 at Wath, where they were shedded. The shed containing these electric engines was built of asbestos in 1951 and of a lightweight construction due to the nature of the site, with large collieries close by and the possibility of subsidence. The shed contained two roads, and it found several uses after the electric services were discontinued, but was finally demolished in 1994. (H. Casserley)

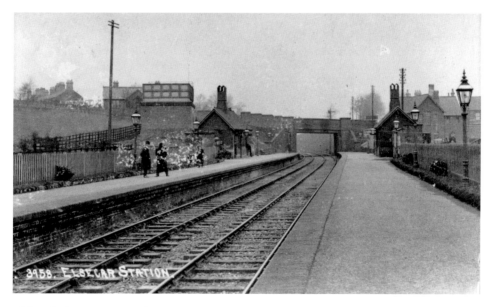

Although there appears to be no mention of the station, this view of Elsecar station is seen at the end of the nineteenth century, possibly serving the nearby colliery. Passenger services on the Barnsley–Mexborough line were usually Penistone–Barnsley–Doncaster trains, introduced by the MS&LR in 1859. By 1922 these comprised ten weekday trains, with two on Sundays. Little changed right through to withdrawal in 1959 despite many objections because of the popularity of the service. A much-reduced passenger service did operate until 1970. Passenger services returned to the Penistone–Barnsley line in 1983, but not on the Barnsley–Mexborough line. (LOSA)

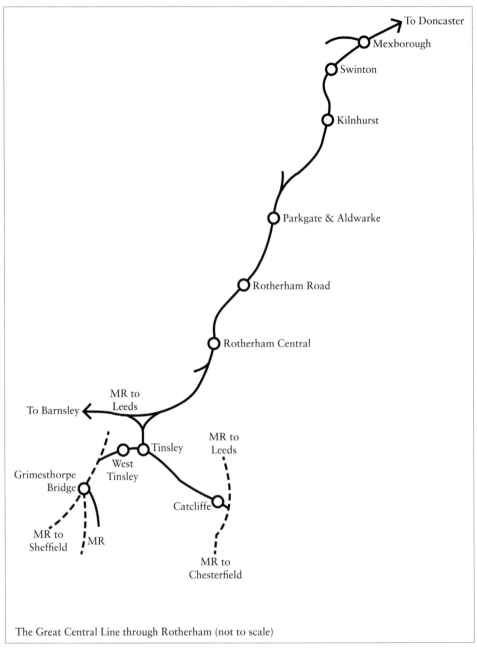

The Great Central Line through Rotherham (not to scale)

A map of the GCR line through Rotherham. This was a line planned by the SYR, but no construction was undertaken until after takeover by the MS&LR. At Tinsley, a major marshalling yard was opened by Dr Beeching on 29 October 1965. This large yard was to have only a short life of twenty years. It seems that BR was very wasteful with its assets, what with the closure of such a major project after only two decades, not to mention the indecent haste to rid itself of steam traction, having only decided to continue with it after nationalisation and building new locos right up until 1960, while being rid of such motive power within the next eight years. Indeed, some engines of the B1 class had a life of only fourteen years. Along with this, the Woodhead line closed after millions of pounds had been spent on a new Woodhead Tunnel and on the development of electric traction which, perhaps, could have been converted to 25kV AC to provide a fast service between Sheffield, Manchester and the West Coast Main Line instead of complete closure. (Author)

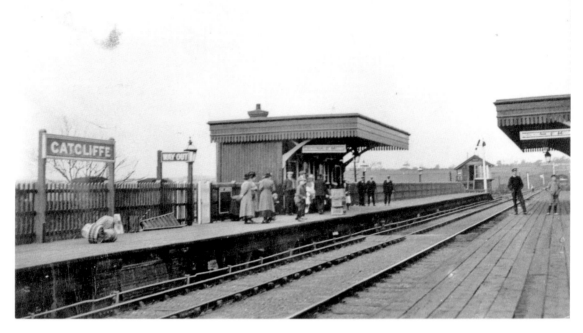

Catcliffe station, first on the line to Rotherham with Tinsley coming next before the line made a junction with the line to Barnsley. From there, the line then ran up through Rotherham Central and Rotherham Road and passed Parkgate and Aldwarke before entering Kilnhurst. (LOSA)

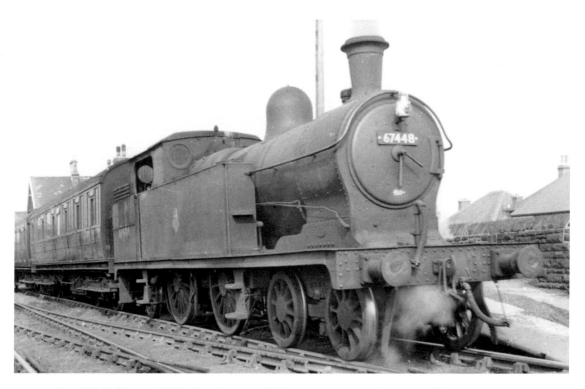

Ex-GCR Robinson LNER class C14 4-4-2T No. 67448 on a local train at Silkstone on 1 May 1948. (H. Boulter)

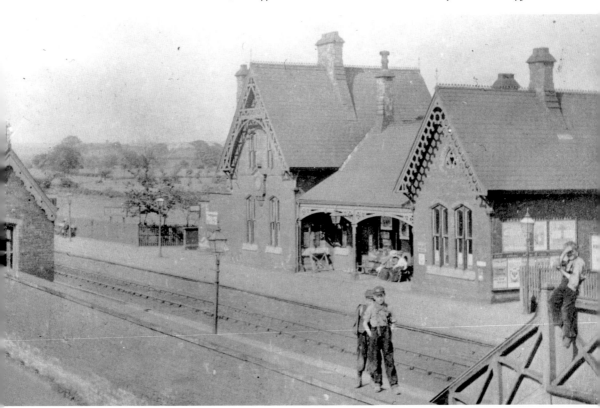

The important station at Kilnhurst in GCR days. The SYR had absorbed the Don Navigation alongside which the railway through Rotherham would run and no Act of Parliament was obtained. This led to problems where the line ran under the 1838 Sheffield and Rotherham line, as the only possible route meant using the canal. Thus, the MS&LR was forced to divert the canal for half a mile, then fill in the canal bed and lay track on its former course. This was one reason why the cost of the project had more than trebled by 1867, when work was suspended. Work began again the following year when the line reached a temporary terminus in Rotherham, and it was not until 1871 that the line was completed to join the original SYR line at Mexborough; this was only possible by using the 1863 Mexborough–Kilnhurst potteries branch. The 7-mile double-track line to Mexborough from the SYR Sheffield extension at Tinsley was never more than half a mile from the MR route, which had been completed in 1840. Even the stations at Rotherham Central – which had replaced the temporary station in 1874 and was known as Rotherham & Masborough from 1889 to 1950 – Aldwarke (Parkgate and Aldwarke from 1895), Kilnhurst and Swinton duplicated those on the MR line. Only the little-used Rotherham Road station was an addition to the system. The Midland line always had more traffic, especially on the Sheffield to Rotherham section. In 1922, the MR had forty-five weekday trains compared to eighteen on the GCR line. The GCR route was busier at holiday times, especially the 'Sheffield Works' fortnight in July and August during the late 1940s and 1950s, with departures from Victoria to the Yorkshire coast. By the 1960s, it was decided to concentrate all Sheffield services at the Midland station and ex-GCR services were withdrawn from 5 September 1966. The former GCR line was retained for freight serving factories along the Don Valley and, in the 1980s, there was a return to passenger use at Rotherham. The MR station at Masborough was over a mile away from the town centre, while the GCR station had been more centrally placed. Thus, BR decided to build a new 'Central' station on the site of the old one, which had been demolished, together with 2.5 miles of line north to Rawmarsh. The old MR station was abandoned in 1988. (LOSA)

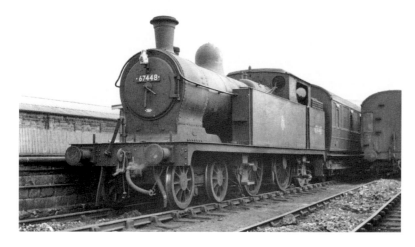

Another view of C14 4-4-2T No. 67448 at Silkstone station on 1 May 1948. At this time, the loco was shedded at Frodingham (36C). (H. Boulter)

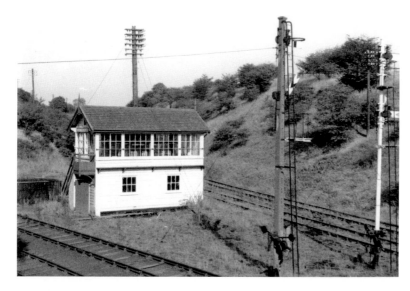

The ex-GCR/MR joint line between Shireoaks and Kilnhurst at Braithwell Junction with GCR pattern signal box in view. On the left is the line to Kilnhurst, while the H&B line to Warmsworth is on the right. (R. Carpenter)

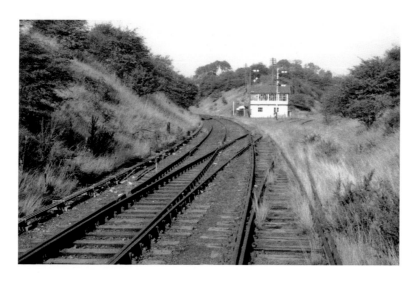

Another view of the Shireoaks–Kilnhurst line at Braithwell Junction around 1970. (R. Carpenter)

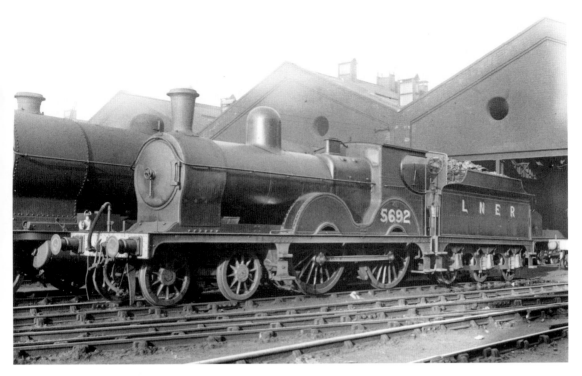

Mexborough locoshed on 23 September 1934 with ex-GCR Robinson D9 class 4-4-0 No. 5692 in view at the shed entrance. Mexborough locoshed had fifteen roads and provided motive power for the heavy coal trains operating over the Worsborough branch and local collieries. Coded 36B at nationalisation, the shed was recoded 41F in 1958 and was closed in 1964. (H. Wheeler) The allocation for 1950 was as follows:

Ex-LNER B1 4-6-0	61165, 61166, 61167, 61194
Ex-GCR O1/O4 2-8-0	63608, 63611, 63612, 63627, 63668, 63672, 63682, 63774, 63775, 63779, 63791, 63792, 63813, 63898
Ex-GCR O2 2-8-0	63924, 63927, 63969, 63970, 63971, 63972, 63975, 63976, 63977, 63978, 63979, 63980, 63981, 63982, 63983, 63984, 63985, 64288, 64296, 64319, 64334, 64352, 64356, 64374, 64377, 64400, 64403, 64404, 64432, 64442
Ex-GCR J11 0-6-0	64283, 64319
Ex-GNR J50 0-6-0T	68890, 68946, 68960, 68974
Ex-MS&LR N5 0-6-2T	69264, 69314, 69316
Ex-GCR S1 0-8-4T	69900, 69901, 69904, 69905
Ex-WD 2-8-0	90104, 90108, 90120, 90144, 90146, 90150, 90153, 90154, 90101, 90166, 90189, 90190, 90195, 90196, 90209, 90220, 90223, 90229, 90246, 90250, 90255, 90270, 90280, 90285, 90286, 90290, 90296, 90301, 90311, 90421, 90521, 90537, 90538, 90550, 90587, 90590, 90596, 90597, 90598, 90612, 90618, 90696, 90700, 90709
	Total: 107

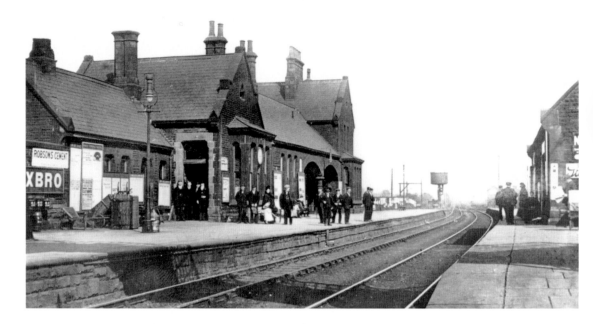

The GCR station at Mexborough (spelt Mexbro) not long after opening, showing station staff and passengers, the gentlemen in flat caps, women in long skirts, and a little girl in white with a straw hat. This was the junction of the line to Doncaster and Barnsley, via Wombwell and Stairfoot. (LOSA)

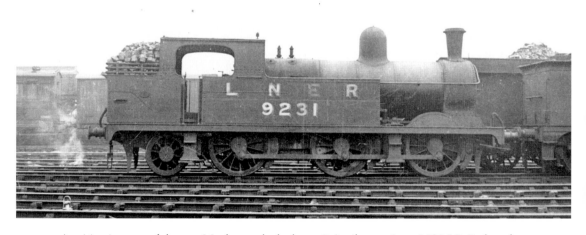

Awaiting its turn of duty at Mexborough shed on 18 April 1947 is ex-MS&LR Parker class N4 0-6-2T No. 9231, one of 55 locos built between 1889 and 1892 with round-topped fireboxes. The last of the class had gone by 1954. (H. Casserley)

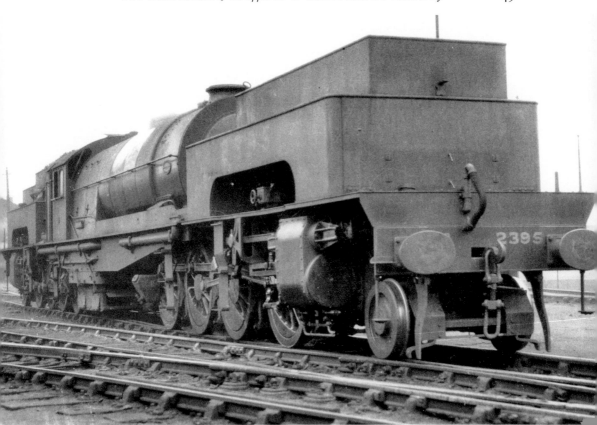

The LNER Beyer-Garratt 2-8-0 0-8-2 as class U1 No. 2395 at Mexborough shed in the 1930s. The loco had a total length of 87 feet 3 inches and would come into Mexborough shed from Wentworth Junction on a late Saturday morning, where the fire was dropped through the large drop portion of the grate and the ashes were drawn through four ash doors (two on each side). The loco was then put into the shed for its boiler washout and then placed in a convenient spot ready for the firelighters on Sunday morning and for preparation on a Monday morning. During the week, cleaning, ash raking, etc. was done at Wentworth Junction, the loco being out of service for around 90 minutes. In July 1925, less than a year after entering service, the engine found itself at Doncaster works for retubing after the water at Worsborough had quickly corroded the tubes and stays. Although the water was not pure, it turned out to be too soft, with hardly any build-up of protective limescale on the inside of the boiler. Three years afterwards, the loco was back at Doncaster for heavy repairs after it was discovered that the firebox roof stays were badly corroded. (R. Carpenter)

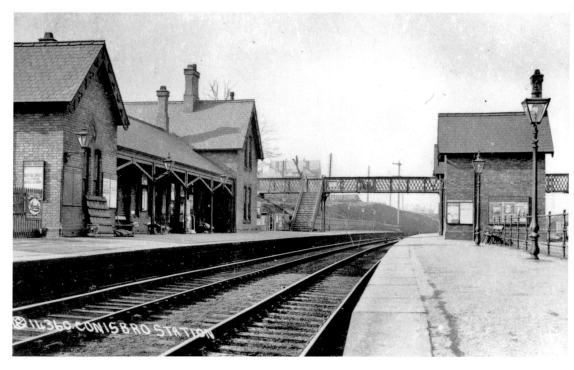

Heading towards Doncaster, the GCR station at Conisborough is seen in the late nineteenth century when part of the MS&LR, which had taken control of the SYR in 1849. (IDSA)

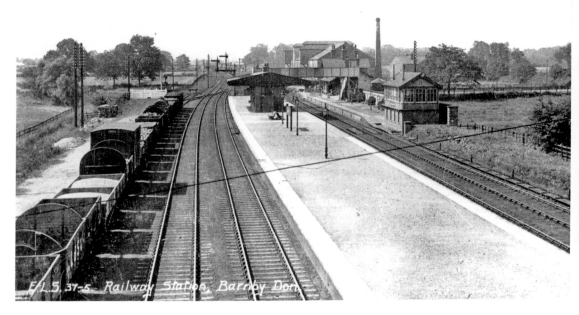

On the Doncaster–Barnetby line is the station at Barnby Dun as it appeared just before the First World War. A rake of mineral wagons is in the siding on the left; the nearest seems to belong to the London, Brighton & South Coast Railway and, if so, it is a very long way from home. (R. Carpenter)

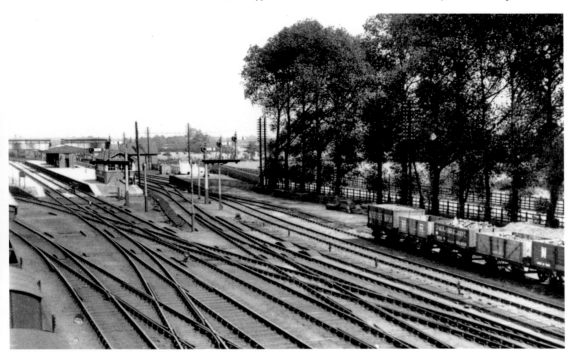

Also on the Doncaster–Barnetby line was the important station of Stainforth & Hatfield; it is shown as it appeared in 1910. (R. Carpenter)

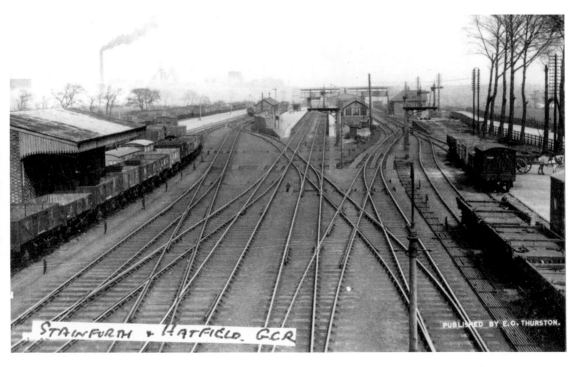

Ex-GCR station at Stainforth & Hatfield in LNER days, around 1930, with mineral wagons at the goods shed. In the distance, the chimney and pit head of Hatfield Colliery is just visible in the left distance. The colliery sidings, with plenty of coal wagons, can be seen beyond the goods shed. (R. Carpenter)

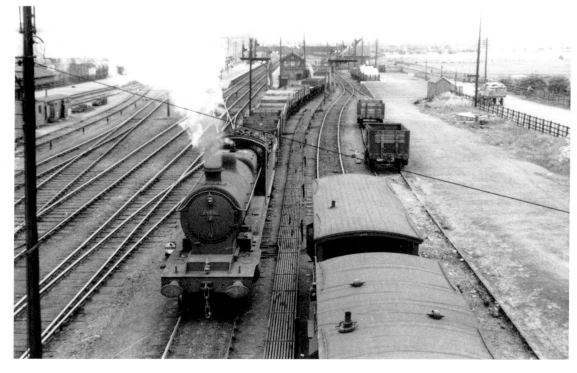

Ex-GCR Robinson class 04 2-8-0 No. 63850 is seen passing through Stainforth & Hatfield station with a rake of empty mineral wagons on 20 May 1952. (H. Casserley)

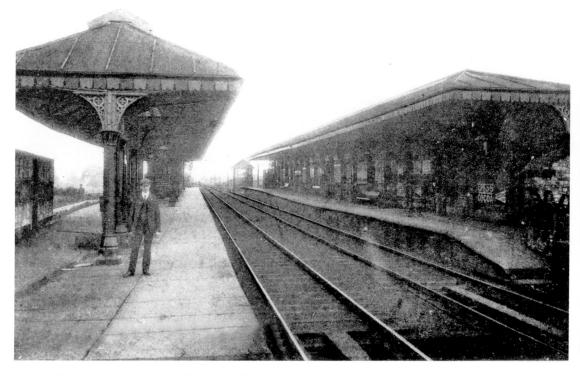

The impressive station at Thorne in GCR days on the line to Barnetby. (LOSA)

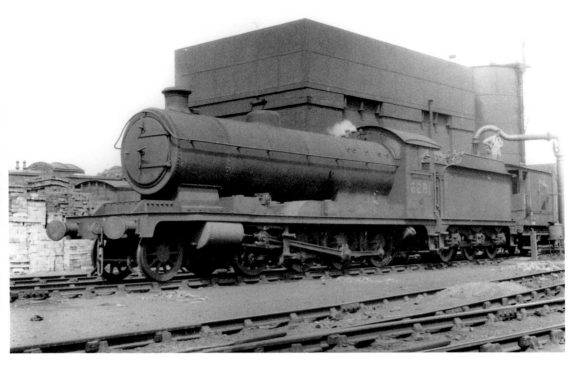

Outside Frodingham engine shed on 4 July 1946 is ex-GCR Robinson ROD 2-8-0 as LNER No. 6281 (class o4/8). (L. Perkins)

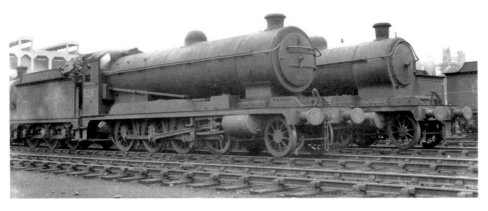

Also at Frodingham locoshed on 23 May 1937 are ex-GCR o4/4 class 2-8-0 LNER No. 6287 with another ex-GCR loco, No. 5353, a member of the o4/1 class 2-8-0. The shed here mainly provided freight engines. Virtually all locos at this time were ex-GCR types. In BR days, ex-WD 2-8-os were allocated here and, in later years, famous BR 9F2-10-os could be found on the shed. (N. Glover)

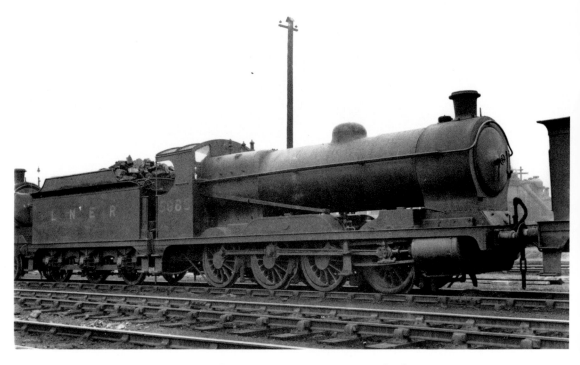

Ex-GCR 8A class LNER Q4 class 0-8-0 No. 5085 is at Frodingham on 23 May 1937. Following nationalisation, the shed was coded 36C and remained so until closure in 1966. (N. Glover) The allocation for 1950 is given as follows (virtually all freight engines):

Ex-GCR 01/04 2-8-0	63572, 63576, 63584, 63587, 63595, 63601, 63602, 63606, 63617, 63623, 63626, 63640, 63642, 63643, 63645, 63649, 63653, 63659, 63660, 63669, 63726, 63728, 63731, 63744, 63745, 63747, 63778, 63788, 63793, 63818, 63824, 63832, 63847, 63906, 63911, 63917, 63920
Ex-LNER 02 2-8-0	63922, 63934, 63937, 63939, 63944, 63963
Ex-GCR J11 0-6-0	64308, 64309, 64339, 64395, 64407, 64429
Ex-GNR J50 0-6-0T	68964, 68968, 68970, 68971, 68973, 68979
Ex-GCR S1 0-8-4T	69902, 69903
Ex-GCR Q1 0-8-0T	69930, 69932, 69934, 69935, 69936, 69937. When 69936 was withdrawn in September 1959, it was the last of the class to be scrapped.
	Total: 63

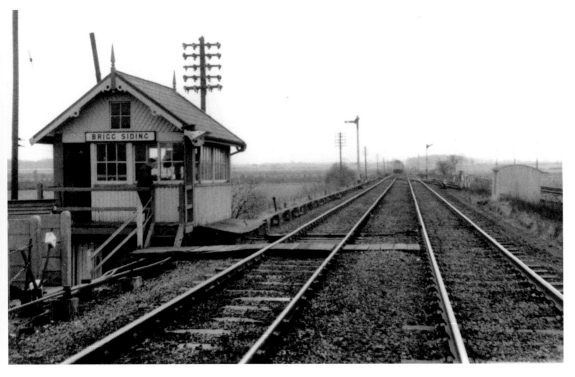

On the Barnetby–Gainsborough line lay the GCR signal box at Brigg sidings as it appeared on 2 May 1970. Diesel-electric loco No. D5697 is approaching 'wrong line' from the Gainsborough area. (R. Carpenter)

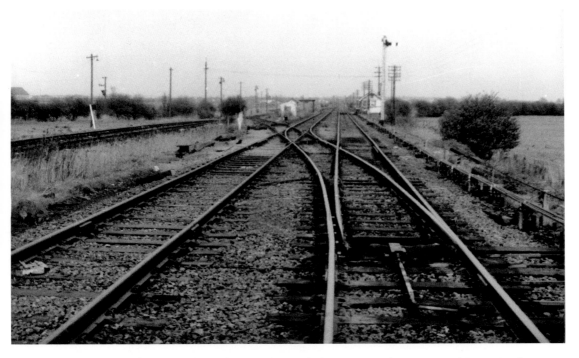

Looking towards Barnetby from the Gainsborough direction is a distant view of Brigg signal box in 1970. (R. Carpenter)

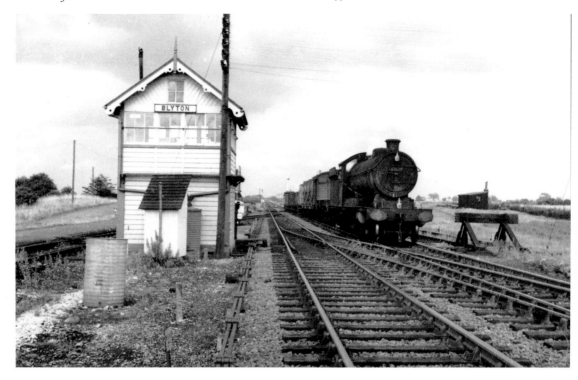

Also on the Barnetby–Gainsborough line was the signal box at Blyton, seen here on 7 August 1964 with ex-GCR 04 2-8-0 No. 63651 passing with an 'up' freight. (R. Carpenter)

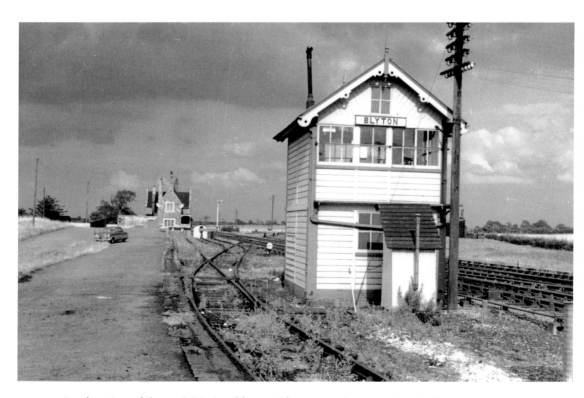

Another view of the ex-GCR signal box at Blyton on 7 August 1964. (R. Carpenter)

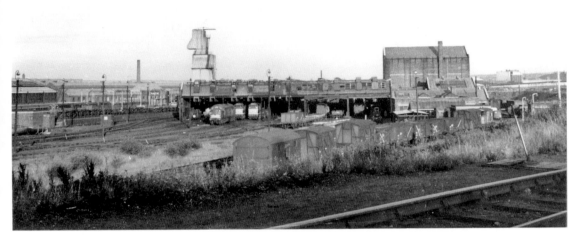

A general view of Sheffield Darnall locoshed as it appeared on 20 September 1964, with several diesel-electric locos in view, along with a single steam engine on the right. Built by the GCR, the locoshed had ten roads and could accommodate some seventy engines. The shed also had a 70-foot turntable. It was planned to be used for electric locos by the LNER but the intervention of the Second World War meant that construction of the four-road electric shed had to be abandoned in 1940. From 1943, Darnall serviced steam engines instead. The electric shed was completed in 1952, but was only used for the electric Manchester–Sheffield services for eight years, after which it was taken over by diesels, as can be seen in this view. When coming under BR control in 1948, the shed was coded 39B, becoming 41A in 1955. By 1959, the shed had an allocation of ninety-seven locos and included the ten 'Director' class 4-4-0s, the last of which was withdrawn in 1960. Only three years later, the shed itself was closed. (R. Carpenter) In 1950 Darnall's allocation was as follows:

Ex-LNER B1 4-6-0	61150, 61151, 61152, 61153, 61154, 61169, 61179, 61181, 61311, 61312, 61313, 61314, 61315, 61316, 61317, 61327
Ex-GCR O1/O4 2-8-0	63574, 63581, 63583, 63604, 63605, 63609, 63622, 63629, 63661, 63675, 63680, 63685, 63710, 63714, 63733, 63734, 63737, 63766, 63771, 63783, 63790, 63797, 63821, 63822, 63846, 63850, 63860
Ex-GCR J11 0-6-9	64291, 64360, 64373, 64387, 64412, 64419, 64441, 64447, 64449
Ex-LNER J39 0-6-0	64746, 64753, 64808, 64809, 64973
Ex-GCR C13 4-4-2T	67404, 67406
Ex-LNER Y3 shunter	68176, 68184
Ex-GNR J50 0-6-0T	68983, 68990
Ex-NER J72 0-6-0T	69015
Ex-MS&LR N4 0-6-2T	69225, 69227, 69228, 69229, 69230, 69231, 69232, 69233, 69234, 69235, 69236, 69239, 69240, 69242, 69244, 69245, 69246
	Total: 81

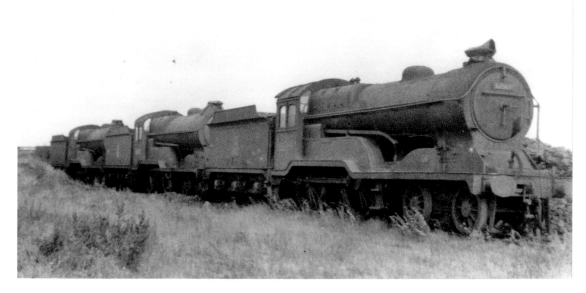

Awaiting her fate, with other members of her class, ex-GCR D11 'Director' class 4-4-0 No. 62669 *Ypres* (another of the class named after battles of the First World War) is seen on the scrap line at Darnall locoshed in late 1960. Loco No. 62666 *Zeebrugge* was the last of the 'Director' class to be withdrawn in December 1960. The preserved D11 *Butler Henderson* was withdrawn in October 1960. (LOSA)

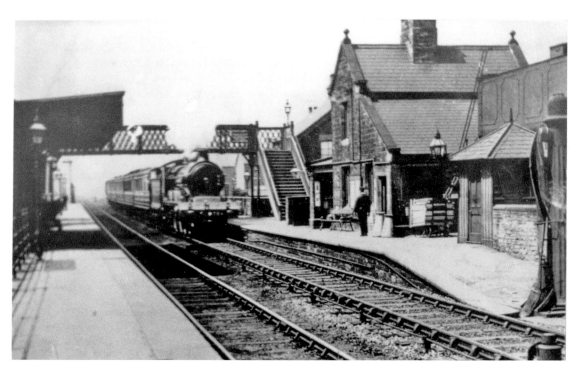

An unidentified GCR express loco runs through Darnall station at the head of a Manchester express in around 1900. (LOSA)

CLEETHORPES, LINCOLN, DONCASTER, BARNSLEY, SHEFFIELD, and MANCHESTER.—Great Central.

Down.	Week Days—*Continued.*		Sundays.	

(Dense tabular railway timetable with station lists including Cleethorpes, New Clee, Grimsby Docks, Grimsby Town, Great Coates, Healing, Stallingboro', Habrough, Hull (Cor. Pier), Brocklesby, Doncaster, Thorne, Frodingham, Barnetby, Brigg, Scawby and Hibaldstow, Kirton Lindsey, Northorpe, Blyton for Corringham, Gainsborough, Sturton, Retford, London (King's Cross), Harwich, Yarmouth (Vaux.), Lowestoft (Cen.), Cromer (Gt. East.), Norwich (Thorpe), Lincoln, Saxilby, Torksey, Cottam, Leverton, Retford, London (K.C.), Peterborough, Retford, Checker House, Worksop, Shireoaks, Kiveton Park, Waleswood, Woodhouse, Darnall for Handsworth, Sheffield (Victoria), Nottingham (Vic.), Leicester (Central), London (Marylebone), Barnetby, Elsham, Appleby, Frodingham & Scunthorpe, Gunness and Burringham, Althorpe, Crowle, Medge Hall, Thorne; and second part with Hull (Paragon), Goole, Stainforth and Hatfield, Barnby Dun, Doncaster, Conisboro', Mexboro', Wath-on-Dearne, Wombwell, Stairfoot for Ardsley, Barnsley (C.H.), Summer Lane, Dodworth, Silkstone, Swinton, Kilnhurst, Fargate and Aldwarke, Rotherham Road, Rotherham & Masboro', Tinsley, Broughton Lane, Attercliffe, Sheffield (Victoria), Neepsend, Wadsley Bridge, Oughty Bridge, Deepcar for Stocksbridge, Wortley, Penistone, Hazlehead Bridge, Dunford Bridge, Woodhead, Crowden, Hadfield for Hollingworth, Glossop, Dinting, Mottram and Broadbottom, Godley Junction, Newton for Hyde, Guide Bridge, Ashton (Park Pde.), Stalybridge, Oldham (Clegg St.), Manchester (Lon. Rd., Central), Stockport (Tiv. Dle), Warrington (Cen.), Southport (Lord St.), Liverpool (Cen.))

Notes:
c Arrives at 8 aft.
d Via Selby.
g Sets down from London on informing Guard at the preceding *stopping* Station.
i Stops to set down from Sheffield on notice being given to the Guard at Sheffield.
j Stops to set down from Penistone or beyond on informing Guard at the preceding *stopping* Station.
p Beach Station.
t Connection at Darnall.
v Stops to set down on informing Guard at the preceding *stopping* Station.
r City Station.
z Victoria Station.
* Station for Epworth and Belton.
† Parkeston Quay.
1 mile to Midland Station.
§ Frodingham & Scunthorpe.

☞ For **LOCAL TRAINS** between Cleethorpes and Brocklesby, see page 662; between Rotherham and Masboro' and Sheffield, see page 643; between Hull (Paragon) and Doncaster, see page 721.
•.• For **LOCAL TRAINS** and **intermediate Stations** between Guide Bridge and Manchester (London Road), see page 666; between Woodhouse and Sheffield, see page 673. ¶ For **intermediate Stations** between Doncaster and Barnetby, see page 648.

A 1910 timetable for GCR trains operating around Sheffield, Doncaster and Barnsley through to Manchester, Grimsby and Cleethorpes. (Author)

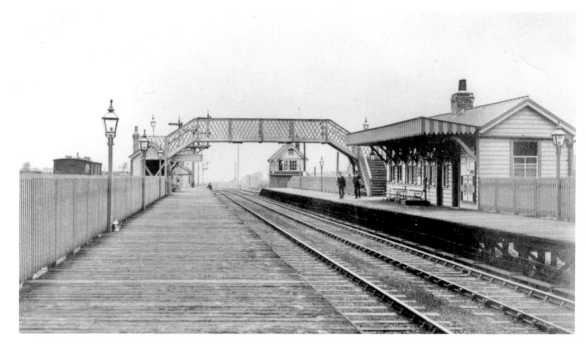

On the GCR line from Sheffield to Retford lay the station at Waleswood. Its wooden structure, seen in this early twentieth-century view, looks very neat and tidy. Those were the days when people took pride in their surroundings and this was reflected in the railway stations at the time when staff competed with one another to have the best on the line. (LOSA)

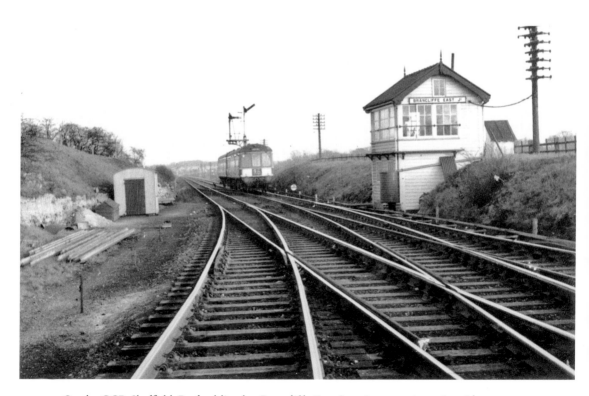

On the GCR Sheffield–Retford line lay Brancliffe East Junction, seen in 1965 with a two-car DMU approaching with a Lincoln–Sheffield Victoria train. (R. Carpenter)

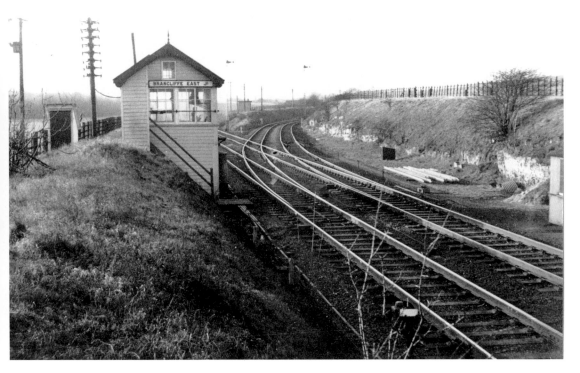

Another view of Brancliffe East Junction, on the Sheffield–Retford line. On the right-hand side is the line to Mexborough. (R. Carpenter)

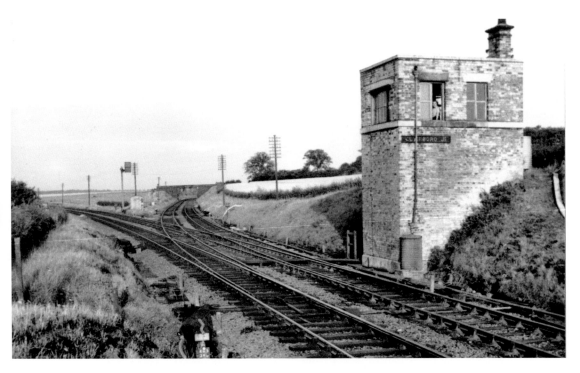

Clarborough Junction on the line to Retford, as seen in August 1964. Looking in the Lincoln direction, the line to Gainsborough veers off to the left, while the line to Retford and Lincoln veers off to the right. (R. Carpenter)

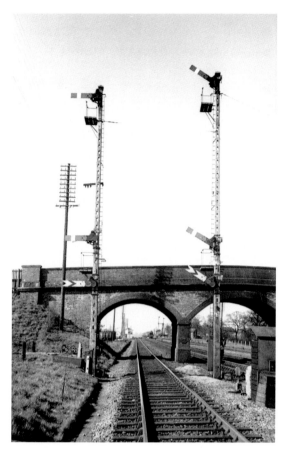

Left: Ex-LNER concrete post signal at Marshmoor in 1950, showing the down main and relief signals. (R. Carpenter)

Below: The GCR station at Hemsworth on the Sheffield–Rotherham–Wakefield (Westgate) line as it appeared in the early twentieth century. (LOSA)

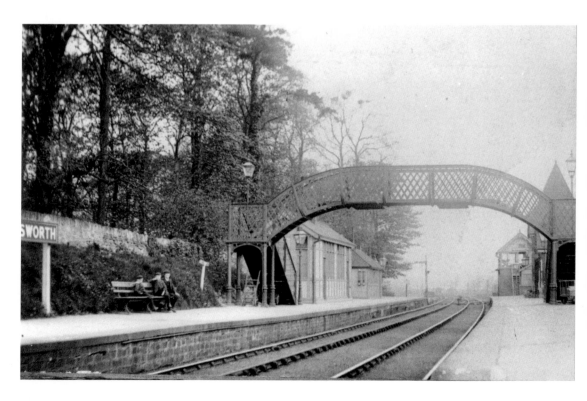

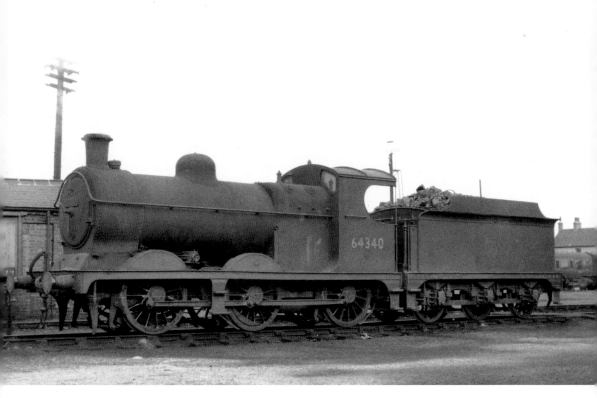

Ex-GCR Robinson J11 0-6-0 No. 64340 at Retford shed on 29 June 1958. Retford had two locosheds: one was GNR, seen here, and the other was built by the GCR. The GCR shed was closed in 1965 to make way for a flyover which removed the flat crossing of the East Coast Main Line by the GCR route. (N. Glover) Coded 36E, the allocation for 1950 was as follows:

Ex-LNER B1 4-6-0	61208, 61211, 61212, 61213, 61231
Ex-GCR O1/O4 2-8-0	63637, 63654, 63688, 63736, 63763, 63782, 63785, 63877, 63905, 63907, 63908, 63914
Ex-GNR J3/J4 0-6-0	64141, 64148, 64150
Ex-GNR J6 0-6-0	64241
Ex-GCR J11 0-6-0	64280, 64282, 64287, 64306, 64335, 64340, 64341, 64347, 64348, 64385, 64393, 64402, 64413, 64416, 64421, 64422, 64451
Ex-LNER J39 0-6-0	64759, 64906, 64908, 64956, 64961, 64970, 64987
Ex-NER J21 0-6-0	65070
Ex MS&LR N5 0-6-2T	69273, 69277, 69282, 69294, 69313, 69321, 69354
	Total: 53

SHEFFIELD, ROTHERHAM, WAKEFIELD, and LEEDS.—Great Central.

Miles	Down. Victoria Station,	Week Days.												Miles	Up. Central Station,	Week Days.										
		mrn	mrn	mrn	mrn	mrn	aft	aft	aft	aft						h	mrn	mrn	aft	k	Aft	aft		
	Sheffield............dep.	6 22	7 22	8 0	8 33	10 7	1 58	5 18	6 30	9 40				Leeds............dep.	8 8	9 48	11 33	2 41	4 48	7 5	9 40		
1¾	Attercliffe............	6 27	7 27	c	8 38		5 23						½	Holbeck............	8 11	9 51	11 36	2 44	4 51	7 8	9 43		
2¾	Broughton Lane............	6 30	7 30	c	8 41		5 26						10	Wakefield (Westgate).......	8 25	10 9	11 51	3 0	5 7	7 24	10 1		
3¾	Tinsley............	6 33	7 33	c	8 44		5 29						18	Hemsworth............	8 39	f	f		5 19	f			
5¼	Rotherham and Masboro'....	6 42	7 40	8 12	8 52	10 22	2 11	5 37	6 42	9 51			28¼	Swinton............		10 36		d	5 38		g		
10¾	Swinton......................		7 51		9 5	c		5 47	c				33½	Rotherham and Masboro'....	9 6	10 46	12 28	3 34	5 48	8 2	10 43		
21¼	Hemsworth..................	7 11			9 25		2 40	6 9	b	b			36	Tinsley		10 52		d	5 54	8			
29¼	Wakefield (Westgate).......	7 20	8 30	8 50	9 34	11 3	2 51	6 21	7 15	10 28			37	Broughton Lane.			12 35	d					
38¼	Holbeck 610, 616, 703, 718..	7 36		•	9 18•		9 51	11 22	13 10	6 38	7 33	10 45		37½	Attercliffe									
39¾	Leeds (Central)............arr.	7 41		j	9 22		9 54	11 26	13 13	6 42	7 37	10 49		39½	Sheffield (Victoria) ......arr.	9 16	11 0	12 40	3 45	6 28	8 15	10 53		

b Stop to set down on informing the Guard at Rotherham and Masboro'.
c Stop to take up for Wakefield or beyond on notice being given at the Station.
d Stops on Wednesdays to set down from Wakefield on informing the Guard at Wakefield.
f Stop to take up for Rotherham and Masboro or beyond on giving notice at the Station.
g Stops to set down from Wakefield or beyond on informing the Guard at Wakefield.
h Calls at **Ardsley** to take up for Rotherham and Masboro' or beyond on giving notice at the Station.
k Calls at **Nostell** at 5 14 aft.

A 1910 timetable for GCR passenger services between Sheffield and Wakefield, which included Hemsworth station. (Author)

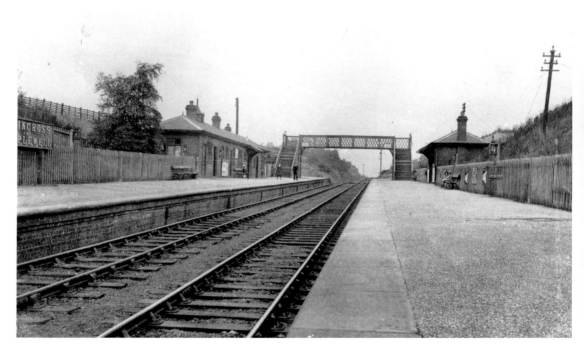

Staincross station on the Barnsley (Court House)–Stairfoot–Wakefield (Westgate) line as it appeared in the 1930s. (LOSA)

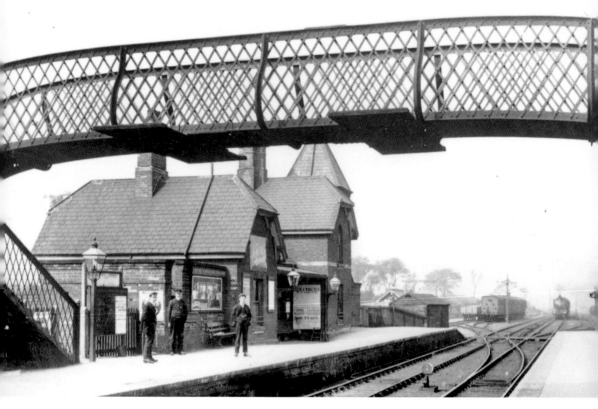

The station at Nostell, on the line to Stairfoot (for Ardsley). The line on which Nostell stood was originally started as the Barnsley Coal Railway and was promoted by local colliery owners to serve pits in the north-east of the town; the intention was to reach Wakefield. Authorisation for the line was given in 1861 and it was then taken over by the SYR in 1863. Local landowners opposed the line, which forced work to stop in 1870 at Applehaigh, five miles from Ardsley (Stairfoot), on the SYR Mexborough–Barnsley line. The MS&LR acquired the line in 1864 and obtained an Act in 1874 to extend it a further five miles to Nostell on the Wakefield–Doncaster line. Links were also made to Barnsley and the Midland main line. The MR connection was short-lived, but the extension to Nostell and the link to Barnsley allowed the MS&LR to run passenger services to Wakefield and Leeds, starting in 1882. A station was built at Staincross on the original line to Applehaigh, in addition to stations at Notton & Royston and Ryhill (becoming Wintersett & Ryhill from 1927) on the Nostell extension. By 1922, the GCR was running five weekday Barnsley–Leeds trains, with a couple of extras on Saturdays, but the GCR was unable to compete with the more direct MR services from Cudworth. Indeed, the LNER had withdrawn passenger services on 22 September 1930. The line remained in use for freight and a lot of summer passenger traffic, when it was used for excursions to relieve pressure on the MR main line. This arrangement continued until 1961 when the line north of Staincross was closed. Colliery closures meant that the remainder of the line closed in 1967. (LOSA)

BARNSLEY, RYHILL, WAKEFIELD, and LEEDS.—Great Central.

Miles	London Road Station,	Week Days.													Sundays.		
		mrn	mrn	mrn	aft	aft		aft	aft		aft					mrn	aft
	648 MANCHESTER......dep.	6 20	10 0	11 29	2 50	5 0		....	6c55		....					6 50	4 55
	Barnsley (Court House)dep.	8 16	1125	1 56	4 35	6 55		8 5	9 40		1135					1225	7 10
2	Stairfoot, for Ardsley......															1235	7 20
5	Staincross, for Mapplewell	8 25	1135	2 7	4 45	6 46	Saturdays only.	8 16	9 50	Saturdays only.	1146					1244	7 29
7	Notton and Royston	8 29	1139	2 13	4 51	6 52		8 22	9 54		1152					1250	7 35
8¼	Ryhill...............	8 34	1144	2 19	4 56	6 57		8 27	9 59		1157					1254	7 39
11¼	Hare Park and Crofton	8 39	1148	2 25	5 2	7 2		8 33	10 4		12 3					1 1	7 43
13½	Sandal................[378	8 43	1152	2 30	5 6	7 7		8 38	10 9		12 8					1 5	7 52
15½	Wakefield (Westgate)..arr.	8 46	1156	2 35	5 10	7 11		8 42	1012		1211					1 9	7 56
24¾	Holbeck (H.L.) 382, 708 "	9 18	1231	3 10	5e53	7 33		9 33	1045							1 43	8 37
25¾	Leeds (Central)........ "	9 22	1234	3 13	5e57	7 37		9 35	1049							1 47	8 41

Miles	Central Station,	Week Days.													Sundays.	
		mrn	mrn	aft	aft	aft	aft	aft		aft		aft			aft	aft
	Leeds ....dep.	7 10	9 0	1217	2 55	Saturdays only.	5 5	7 30	Saturdays only.	8 12		9 40			1 10	8 7
¾	Holbeck (High Level) .. "	7 13	9 4	1220	2 59		5 8	7 33		8 15		9 43			1 14	8 10
9½	Wakefield (Westgate).. "	7 37	9 34	1258	3 23		5 35	8 5		9 12		1023			1 40	9 20
11½	Sandal	7 41	9 38	1 3	3 27		5 40	8 9		9 17		1027			1 44	9 24
12¾	Hare Park and Crofton......	7 45	9 43	1 8	3 31		5 46	8 14		9 22		1033			1 49	9 29
16½	Ryhill...............	7 52	9 49	1 14	3 38		5 51	8 21		9 28		1041			1 55	9 35
18½	Notton and Royston	7 56	9 53	1 18	3 42		5 55	8 25		9 32		1047			1 59	9 39
20½	Staincross, for Mapplewell..	8 1	10 0	1 24	3 48		6 0	8 30		9 37		1053			2 4	9 44
23½	Stairfoot, for Ardsley..[655						6 6	10 8							2 18	9 58
25½	Barnsley (Court House)	8 10	1012	1 34	3 58		6 10	8 40		9 47		11 5			2 24	10 4
60½	655 MANCHESTER (L.R.) arr.	1015	1213	4 32	6 31		....	8 28	11 3						9 40	

b Leaves Central Station at 11 25 mrn.   *c* Leaves Central Station at 7 20 aft.
e Except Saturdays.

A 1910 timetable for trains operating between Barnsley (Court House) and Wakefield (Westgate), which included Staincross (for Mapplewell), to give it its full title. (Author)

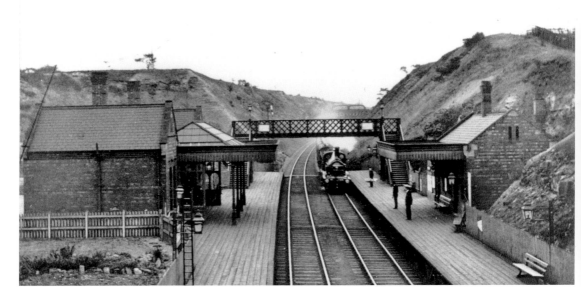

Hare Park station, close to Wakefield (Westgate), with a GCR local train arriving at the neat little station. (LOSA)

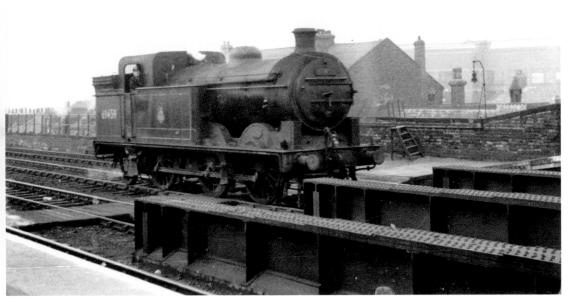

Ex-GNR Ivatt N1 class 0-6-2T No. 69459 is seen on shunting duties at Wakefield (Westgate) on 24 April 1953. In GCR days, passenger trains would call here on their way to Leeds or on the return journey to Barnsley. (H. Casserley)

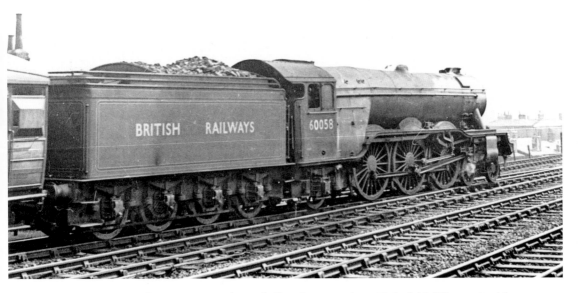

Ex-LNER A3 Pacific No. 60058 *Blair Atholl* is departing from Wakefield (Westgate) with a King's Cross–Leeds express on 30 April 1949. The loco is in early British Railways livery and may well be in the experimental blue livery used on top-link express engines. (H. Casserley)

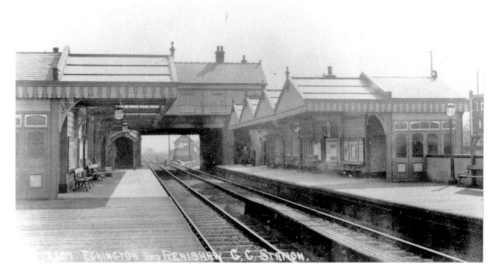

On the GCR line to Chesterfield was the station of Eckington and Renishaw, seen here in the early years of the twentieth century. Like a lot of GCR stations, the station was approached from above with ticket offices at the roadside. The platforms here have quite substantial waiting rooms and facilities, all of timber construction. (LOSA)

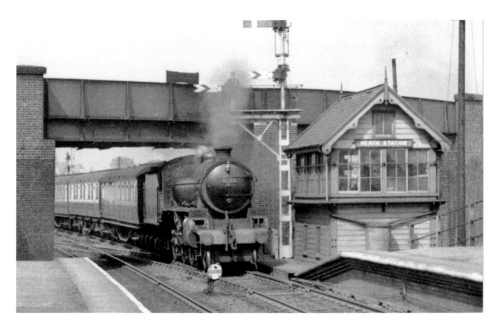

The signal box and platform end at Heath station on 12 May 1956. The 2.20 p.m. Sheffield Victoria–Nottingham Victoria local service is entering the station, hauled by ex-LNER Thompson B1 4-6-0 No. 61152. The loco was built by Vulcan Foundry (works No. 5510) and entered traffic from Gorton on 2 May 1947. It was numbered 1152, becoming 61152 on 15 January 1949. From Gorton, the engine was transferred to Sheffield on 4 June 1947, going to Doncaster ten years later, on 29 September 1957, and returning to Sheffield on 17 November. She then went to the old MR shed at Millhouses on 8 November 1959 and returned to Sheffield on 23 April 1961. Her final allocation was to Immingham on 3 March 1963, from where she was condemned on 19 April 1964 and sold for scrap to the Central Wagon Company, Ince, in June 1964. (R. Carpenter)

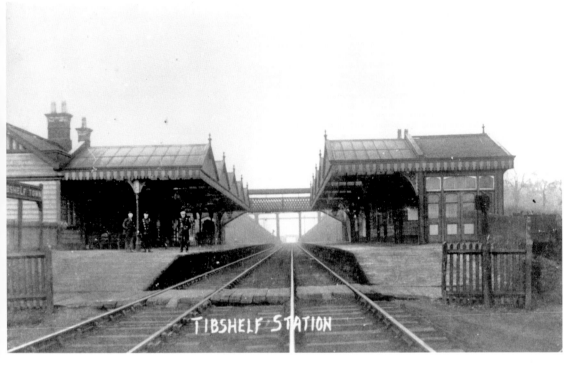

The GCR station at Tibshelf in the late nineteenth century. Today, Tibshelf is best known as a service area on the M1 motorway. (LOSA)

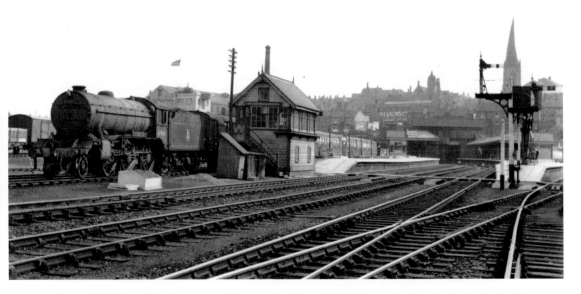

Chesterfield Central station on 12 May 1956 with ex-LNER K3 2-6-0 No. 61980 at the head of the 4.30 p.m. passenger service to Sheffield Victoria. In the right background is the church with the twisted spire which has made the town famous. Chesterfield is also the home of Chesterfield Football Club, a team that has always been difficult to beat. (R. Carpenter)

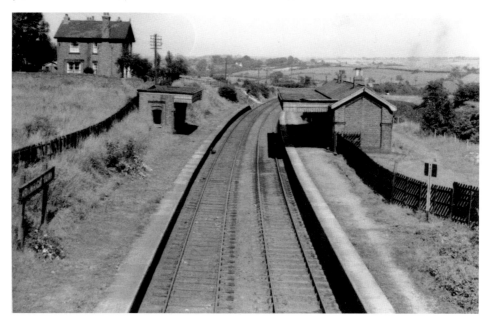

Arkwright Town station, now derelict, as it appeared on 19 July 1959. This ex-GCR line was actually built by the Lancashire, Derbyshire & East Coast Railway, which had a plan to build a line, at an estimated cost of £5 million, from Warrington to the North Sea at Sutton-on-Sea. However, the only section that was built was from Chesterfield to Lincoln, with a branch to Beighton on the GCR line to Sheffield. By 1900, a service of six LD&ECR trains ran daily between Sheffield Midland station and Langwith Junction on the LD&ECR main line. Despite having MR connections, the LD&ECR became part of the LNER in the 1923 grouping and all passenger services were gone by 1930. (H. Priestley)

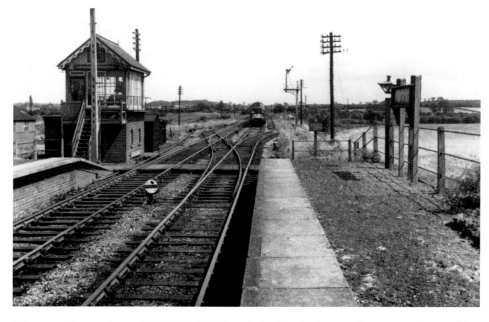

Warsop station on the ex-GCR/LD&ECR line, facing Tuxford, on 23 June 1963. Approaching is the 12.44 p.m. Skegness–Manchester Central train hauled by diesel-electric loco D6805. (H. Priestley)

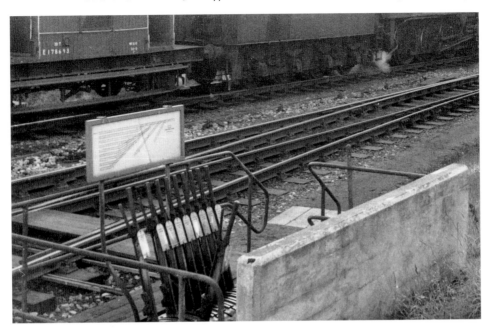

On the ex-GCR/LD&ECR line was the High Mawham sidings frame, as seen on 10 October 1964. (H. Priestley)

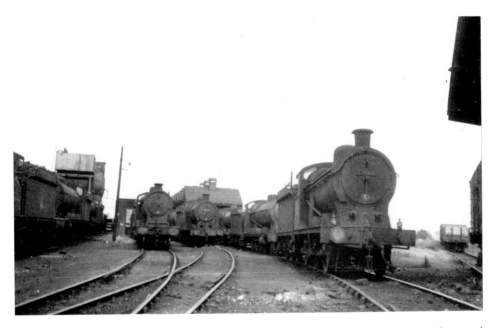

The ex-GCR (LD&ECR) locoshed at Tuxford, as it appeared on 17 August 1958 with several of its allocation of locos in view. Given the code 40D at nationalisation, it became 41K in 1958. (R. Carpenter) Virtually all of the shed's allocation of engines were freight types, as this 1950 list shows:

Ex-GCR O1/O4 2-8-0	63570, 63588, 63634, 63691, 63852, 63861, 63885
Ex-GCR J11 0-6-0	64286, 64293, 64299, 64337, 64344, 64353, 64392, 64424
	Total: 15

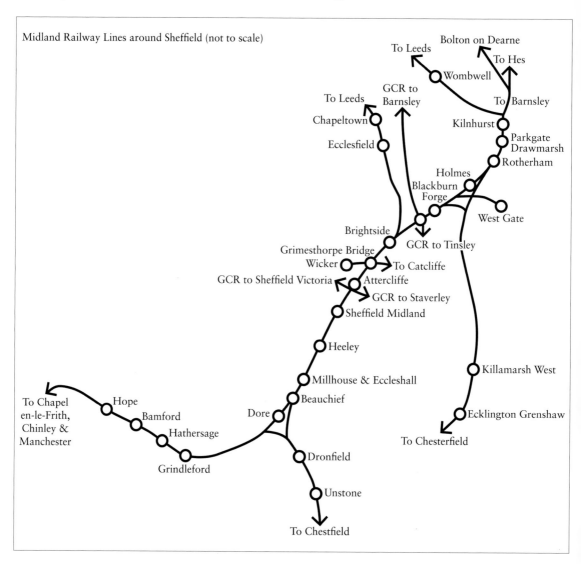

Midland Railway Lines around Sheffield (not to scale)

The Midland Railway around Sheffield. The lines to Leeds, Rotherham and Barnsley ran parallel to those of the GCR, and stations on both lines often had similar names. The line to Chesterfield and on to St Pancras can be seen on the right, and the Hope Valley line to Chapel-en-le-Frith, Chinley and Manchester can be seen on the left. It was this Hope Valley line which was to change the face of the railways around Sheffield. (Author)

TWO

THE MIDLAND RAILWAY

When the North Midland Railway opened its line from Derby to Leeds in 1840, it missed centres of population because George Stephenson had engineered the route to run along the Dearne Valley north from Rotherham, avoiding high ground. A 3-mile branch of the main MR line between Treeton and Brightside, on the Sheffield & Rotherham Railway, was built by the Lancashire, Derbyshire & East Coast Railway (LD&ECR) which proposed a £5 million scheme to connect Warrington to the North Sea, at Sutton-on-Sea. In the event, the only section to be completed was from Chesterfield to Lincoln, with a branch to Beighton (on the MS&LR line to Sheffield). The Treeton–Brightside branch had originally been promoted by the Midland Railway, but to gain access to Sheffield, the LD&ECR, with the backing of the Great Eastern Railway, agreed to build the line and operate it, running powers being granted to the MR and GER. This line opened in 1900, with stations at Catcliffe and Tinsley Road (West Tinsley from 1907) and a service of six LD&ECR trains daily between Sheffield Midland and Langwith Junction on the LD&ECR main line. The MR added a Sheffield–Mansfield service of four trains a day in 1903. Despite its MR connections, the line actually became part of the LNER in 1923.

Sheffield Midland station itself opened on 1 February 1870, replacing the old Sheffield & Rotherham Railway station at Wicker. As late as the early 1860s, Sheffield had no direct railway route south from Chesterfield, although the MR had some rough plans to construct such a line, and these plans included construction of a new, large station off Pond Street, Sheffield. Once Parliamentary approval had been granted for construction of the new line and station, 1,000 houses were compulsorily purchased and demolished on the southern approaches to the city. When opened, the new station had a canopied entrance from the drive off Pond Street, and the main building contained separate booking offices for the different classes (typical of the Victorian obsession with the class system within British society), first- and second-class ladies' and gentlemen's waiting rooms, and two classes of refreshment rooms. On the day Sheffield New Midland station opened, without ceremony, Wicker station was closed and all services transferred to the new station. In the early years of the twentieth century, the MR went on to spend in excess of £215,000 as the company continued to upgrade the station to meet increasing need.

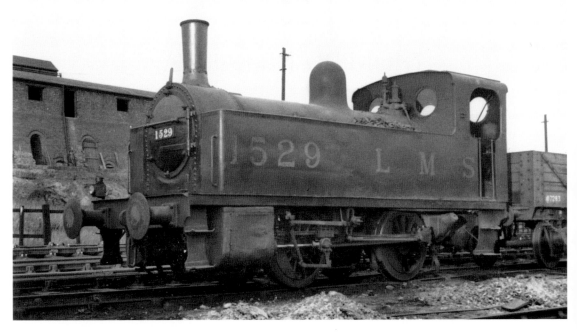

Lying between Chesterfield and Sheffield, there was an ironworks at Staveley, the MR having signed an agreement with the works to purchase the internal railway system, while being obliged to supply motive power for the next century. To maintain and service its locos there, the MR built the Barrow Hill roundhouse, coded 41E in BR days and M24 in MR days, becoming 18D in 1935 under LMS auspices. In February 1958, the depot was taken over by the Eastern Region (when it was coded 41E). The shed closed to steam on 4 October 1965, BR having fulfilled the contract to supply motive power for the works. Here, ex-MR 0-4-0T No. 1529, later BR No. 41529, is seen at the steelworks on 27 August 1939. These little engines were built by the MR between 1907 and 1922 specifically to work on yards, docks and other places where tight curves existed. All were scrapped between 1957 and 1966. The allocation at Barrow Hill shed in 1949 was as follows:

MR OF 0-4-0T	41528, 41529, 41533, 41534
MR 1F 0-6-0T	41708, 41710, 41711, 41749, 41752, 41753, 41763, 41803, 41804
MR 3F 0-6-0	43224, 43234, 43252, 43292, 43294, 43297, 43298, 43299, 43309, 43310, 43386, 43515, 43524, 43546, 43575, 43751
MR 4F 0-6-0	43857, 43862, 43863, 43886, 43914, 43920, 43993, 44006
LMS 4F 0-6-0	44066, 44070, 44104, 44122, 44129, 44147, 44154, 44182, 44299, 44590
LMS 3F 0-6-0T	47424, 47455, 47502, 47625, 47626
LMS 8F 2-8-0	48002, 48053, 48111, 48195, 48210, 48213, 48332, 48341, 48346, 48441, 48460, 48493, 48538, 48539, 48545, 48546, 48604, 48663
	Total: 70

The GCR also had a locoshed at Staveley. Coded 41H, it was a five-road shed with an allocation of thirty-four engines in 1950 and thirty-seven in 1959. Locos here were mostly ex-GCR types and included a 'Director' class 4-4-0 No. 62663 *Prince Albert*. At nationalisation, the shed was coded 38D, becoming 41H in 1958 following regional reorganisation that had brought the ex-MR roundhouse under Eastern Region control. The GCR shed was closed in 1965. (L. Perkins)

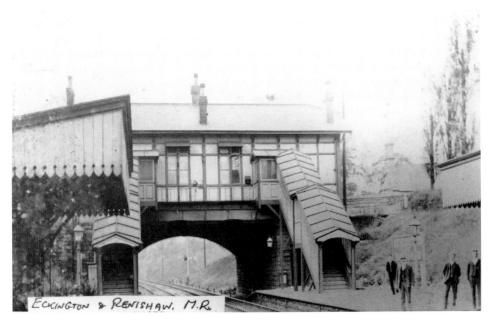

On the line from Chesterfield to Rotherham, via Staveley, was the MR station of Eckington and Renishaw. Its main building was at the roadside, with a covered footbridge down to the platforms. It appears to be of all-timber construction. Station staff are visible on the right of the picture. (WSA)

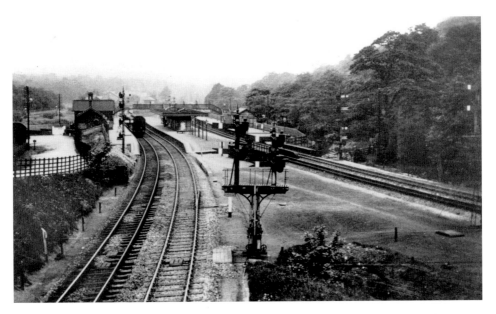

Situated at the junction of the line from Chesterfield and the Hope Valley line is the station at Dore and Totley. The station was opened on 1 February 1872 and cost £1,517 to build on two acres of land that had cost the MR £450. The line from Chesterfield to Sheffield had only been open for two years at this time, and the station catered for local services of six or seven weekday trains, with three on Sundays. In 1894, the station was at the junction of the new Dore and Chinley line, which was to become the Hope Valley line. The original northbound platform became an island and a fourth platform was built to the west. Here, a northbound train for Sheffield waits at the platform in the early years of the twentieth century. (LOSA)

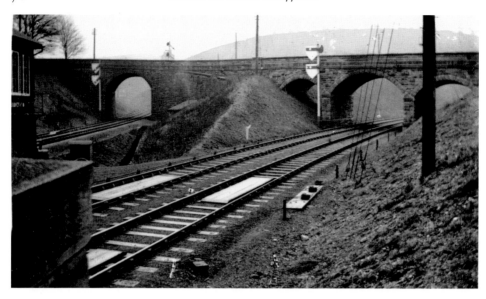

The junction at Dore and Totley with the line to Chesterfield and Derby going off to the left and the Chinley/Manchester line off to the right. Dore and Totley station was closed to main line traffic and became an unstaffed halt in 1969 (a fate which befell a good many stations at this time). By the 1980s, the station was rationalised with the island and eastern platforms demolished. Therefore, southbound trains can no longer stop at Dore and Totley. The Hope Valley line was singled in the 1980s and trains now stop at the only platform here. (R. Carpenter)

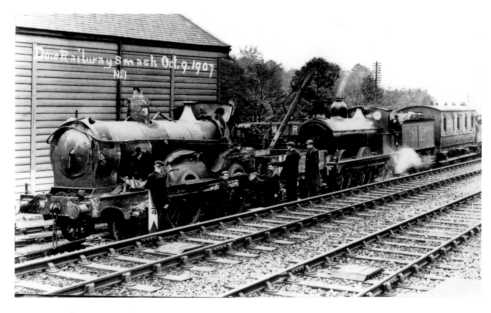

On 9 October 1907, the station at Dore and Totley saw an accident when a Sheffield to Birmingham and Bristol train jumped the points here. The train was double-headed – common MR practice on expresses at this time – and the first loco hit the platform and overturned, throwing the driver and fireman clear. The coaches, however, remained upright and there were no injuries to any of the passengers. Here, the results of the accident can be seen with Johnson 2-4-0 being prepared for removal. It would appear that this was the engine which overturned, given the damage to the cab, boiler, dome and missing chimney. A Johnson 0-6-0 appears to be assisting with recovery work. (LOSA)

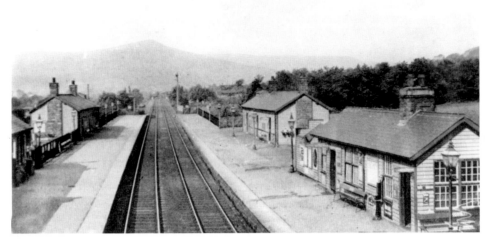

The little station at Hope, on the line to Chinley and Chapel-en-le-Frith. This was to become the Hope Valley line. In 1867, the MR extended its Ambergate–Buxton branch through the Peak Forest Hills, via the 1¾-mile Dove Holes Tunnel, to reach Manchester and compete with the LNWR for London traffic. At first, the MR used the Manchester (London Road) terminus, thanks to the MS&LR. In 1894, the Dore and Chinley line (the Hope Valley line) opened and the MR then had its own Manchester station at Central, via Cheadle Heath and the 2¼-mile Disley Tunnel. Transfer of passengers to Manchester from Sheffield Victoria to Sheffield Midland over the Hope Valley line allowed eventual closure of the Woodhead route. (LOSA)

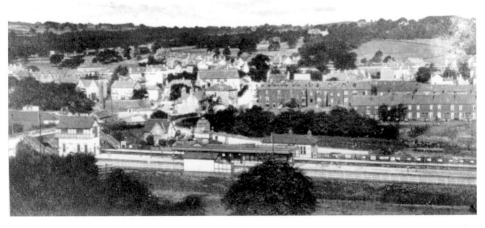

A long-distance view of the station at Millhouses, between Dore and Totley and Sheffield Midland station, showing an extensive village here at the beginning of the twentieth century. (LOSA)

MANCHESTER, BUXTON, CHINLEY, HOPE, SHEFFIELD, and THE NORTH.—Midland.

Up.	Week Days—*Continued.*								Sundays.				
Central Station,	aft	aft	aft	aft	aft	aft	aft		mrn	non	mrn	aft	aft
680 LIVERPOOL .... dep.	3 30	3 30	....	4 30	5 30	6 30	7 30		...	1115		6 10	....
680 SOUTHPORT (L. St.) "	1 15	2 45			3 55		5 25		9 0		2 0		
680 WARRINGTON (Cen.) "	3 0	3 45	....	4 55	5 56	6 55	7 55			1118		6 37	
761 BLACKPOOL { Cen...dep	12¾d	12¾d	d2 5	....	3 3				8 15		1 15		
T.Road "	1 37	1 37	2 25		3 23				7 30		1 37		
767 BLACKBURN "	2 44	2 44			5 20				11 0		2 5		
775 BOLTON (Trin. St.) "	3 25	3 25	3 53		6 3				1131		3 45		
564 MANCHESTER (V.)§ "	4 2	4 2	4 40		7 13				12 5		5 25		
Manchester (Cen.)¶ ...dep.	4 20	4 50		5 30	6 35	7 25	8 25		8 15	12 0		6 55	
Cheadle Heath "		5 4		5 20	6 48		8 42						
Stockport "	3 29			5 30		7 45	8s25		8 42	12 4		7 13	
Marple "	4 29	4 29		5 42		7 55	8s36		8 56	1231		7 3	
New Mills "	4 38	4 39		5 51		7 10	8s45		9 5	1240		7 13	
Chinley¶ .... arr	4 53	5 26	5 31	6 0	7 14	8 9	9 4		9 17	1233	1249	7 37	
Buxton ...|Dale dep	4 d4	4 52	5d12	5d35	7 30		8d22					7s10	
Peak Forest, for Peak "		5 5		6 16	7 43		9 3						
Chapel-en-le-Frith † "		5 12		6 18	7 50		9 10						
Chinley ... arr	4 45	5 15	5 43	6 23	7 53		9 15					7 46	
Chinley ....dep.	4 59	5 29	6 4	7 16	8 13	9 6			9 21	1 0		7 50	
Edale "		5 42	6 17		8 26	9 20			9 34			8 3	
Hope †† "		5 50	6 25		8 34	9 29			9 42	1 18	1 35	8 11	
Bamford "		5 54	6 29		8 38	9 32			9 46		1 39	8 15	
Hathersage "		5 59	6 34		8 43	9 37			9 51		1 44	8 20	
Grindleford "		6 3	6 38		8 47	9 41			9 55		1 48	8 24	
Dore and Totley 548.. arr	5 30	6 11	6 46		8 55	9 49			10 3		1 56	8 32	
548 CHESTERFIELD ..... arr	5 58	7 c1	7 24	8s38	9 39	1023			1112c		2 20	9 28	
548 DERBY "			8 25		1025h	1225			1145c		6 5	1218	
549 BIRMINGHAM (N. St.) "			9c42			2 7			1248c		8 32	2 7	
549 NOTTINGHAM "		8c10	8c52		1115	1158			1235c		7 27	1140	
549 LEICESTER (L. Rd.) "		8c23	9 c5		1157	1 42			2c20		7 38	1 42	
549 LONDON (St. Pan.) "			1025c			4 20			4c30		9 50	4 20	
Dore and Totley ......dep	5 32	6 12	6 48		8 56	9 50			10 5		1 58	8 33	
Beauchief and Abbey Dale.. "					8 59				10 8		2 1	8 36	
Mill Houses and Ecclesall "					9 2				1011		2 4	8 39	
Heeley "	5 39	6 18	6 55	7 51	9 6	9 56			1014	1 38	2 7	8 42	
Sheffield ** 539, 608 arr	5 43	6 22	7 0	7 55	9 10	10 0			1018	1 42	2 12	8 46	
Rotherham (Masboro') "	6 3	7 10	7 26	8 37	9 39				1 18		2 46		
" (Westgte) "						1021			2 8			9 21	
793 HULL (Cannon St.).. arr		9 18	1020	1020		6 30					6 14		
726 HULL (Paragon) "		1012	1133	1133		4 42					9 13	4 42	
539 YORK "		7 45	10 5	10 5	1133	3 31					5 22	3 31	
684 NEWCASTLE (Central) "		1016	1231	1231	1416	5 58					9 7	5 58	

a Sets down from Manchester and the Cheshire Lines.
b Takes up at 10 28 mrn. for Chinley and beyond.
c Via Sheffield.
d Stops to set down from beyond Chinley.
d Via Miller's Dale.
g Arrives at 5 10 aft. on Wednesdays.
h Arrives at 10 37 aft. on Saturdays.
i Arrives at 2 56 mrn. on Sundays.
k Via Heeley.
n Via Sheffield; arrives Chesterfield at 9 30, Derby 10 3, and Birmingham 11 17 mrn. on Mondays.
o Via Leeds.

p Leaves at 7 45 aft. on Saturdays.
q Arrives Chesterfield at 5 24; Derby at 6 10, and Birmingham at 7 20 aft. on Thursdays.
s Saturdays only.
t Arrives at 10 1 aft. on Thursdays and Saturdays.
u Leaves at 1 30 aft. on Wednesdays and Saturdays.
v Arrives at 9 55 aft. on Saturdays.
x Leaves at 9 1 mrn. on Saturdays.
† Over 1 mile to L. & N. W. Station.
§ Via Marple.
** ¼ mile to Victoria Station, G.C.
†† Station for Castleton (2 miles) and Bradwell (2 miles).

¶ For Local Trains and intermediate Stations
BETWEEN — PAGE
Manchester and Chinley....569, 570
Buxton and Chinley......558 to 560

, For other Trains
BETWEEN — PAGE
Dore and Totley and Sheffield 539 to 547

A 1910 timetable for MR trains running between Rotherham, Sheffield, Chinley and Manchester Central. (Author)

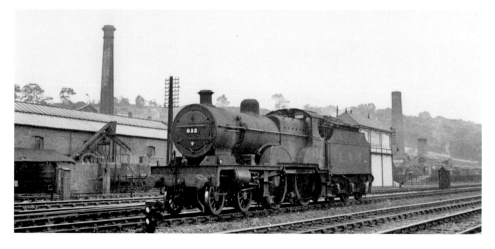

The locoshed at Millhouses, Sheffield, as seen on 2 July 1948 with LMS Compound 4-4-0 No. 932 in view. This is an example of an LMS development of MR Deeley 'Compounds', built between 1924 and 1932. Millhouses locoshed was situated between Millhouses and

Eccleshall and Heeley stations, opened by the MR in 1901. It was the MR's main shed for passenger services in Sheffield. The shed was coded 19B, becoming 41C in 1958. It was closed to traffic in 1962. (H. Casserley) Its allocation for 1950 was as follows:

LMS 3MT 2-6-2T	40082, 40139
MR 2P 4-4-0	40487, 40493, 40502, 40518, 40549
MR 3P 4-4-0	41014, 41021, 41037, 41062, 41072, 41079
MR 3F 0-6-0	43341
LMS 5MT 4-6-0	44664, 44665, 44859, 44962, 44963, 44986, 45260, 45264
LMS 5XP 4-6-0 ('Jubilee' class)	45590 *Travancore* 45594 *Bhopal* 45607 *Fiji* 45621 *Northern Rhodesia* 45664 *Nelson* 45679 *Armada* 45683 *Hogue* 45724 *Repulse*
MR 1P 0-4-4T	58067, 58068, 58071, 58076
	Total: 35

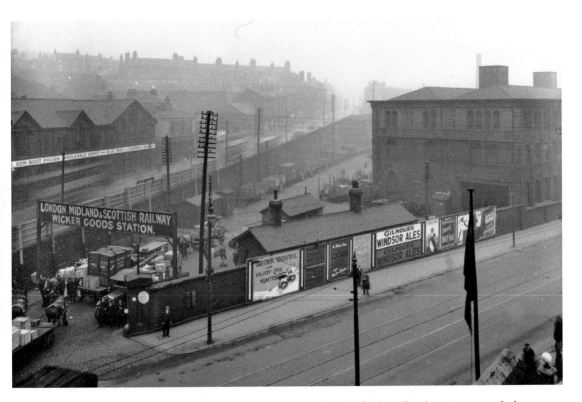

Wicker station as a goods yard in the early 1930s. After Sheffield Midland station opened, the Wicker passenger station closed and became a goods yard. The passenger station at Wicker was not missed by locals and had once been described as 'a miserable little station, dirty, dilapidated and unattractive.' No doubt the MR spent little on Wicker station due to the prospect of opening the new Sheffield station. In the 1890s, the MR spent £100,000 developing Wicker as a goods station. In July 1965 Wicker goods station was closed due to rationalisation in the Sheffield area and was burned down a year later. (R. Carpenter collection)

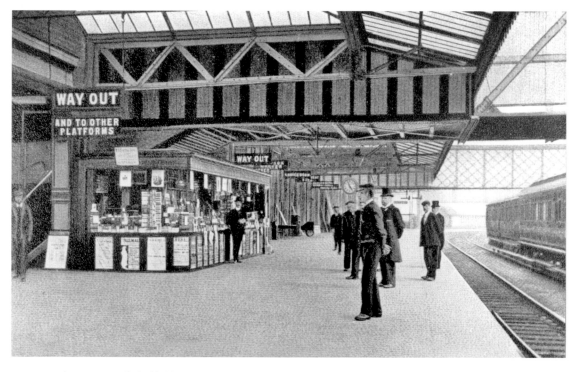

The interior of Sheffield Midland station as it appeared shortly after opening. (LOSA)

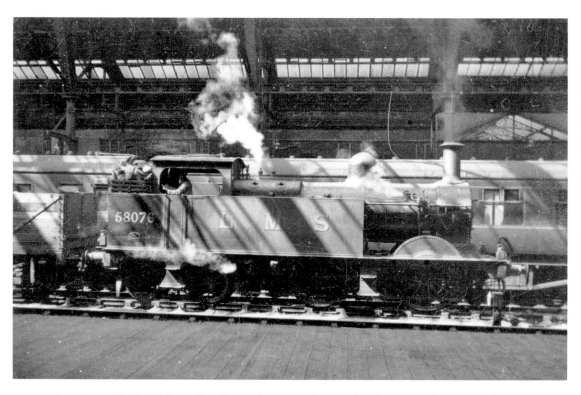

Interior of Sheffield Midland station as it appeared on 20 April 1951, with ex-MR Johnson 0-4-4T No. 58076 in LMS style and still with its pre-nationalisation ownership on the tank side. The loco appears to be passing through with a local goods train. (R. Casserley)

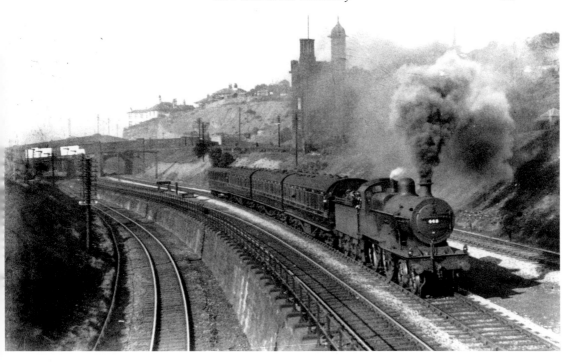

LMS 2P 4-4-0 No. 443 is seen departing from Sheffield Midland station with a southbound train in 1933. In MR days, such short, frequent trains with small locos providing motive power were common practice. (R. Carpenter)

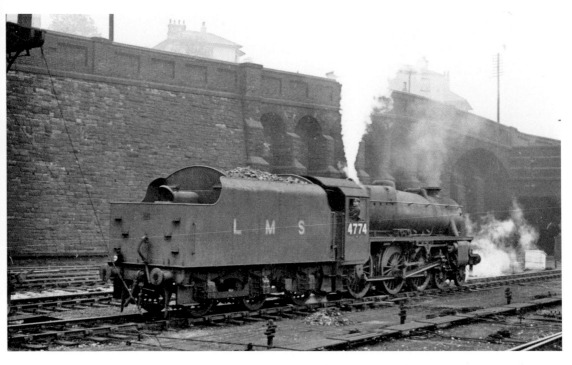

Awaiting its turn of duty on 9 July 1948, only a few months before nationalisation, is Stanier 'Black Five' 4-6-0 No. 4774 in postwar LMS livery outside Sheffield Midland station. (H. Casserley)

LONDON, LEICESTER, NOTTINGHAM, DERBY, MANCHESTER, LIVERPOOL, SHEFFIELD, LEEDS, SCOTLAND, &c.—Midland.

Offices—Derby. Gen. Man., W. Guy Granet. Sec., Alexis L. Charles, F.C.I.S.

Down. — **Week Days.**

¶ **For Local Trains and intermediate Stations**

BETWEEN	PAGE
St. Pancras and Luton	584, 585
Northampton and Wellingboro'	614, 615
Nottingham, Trent, and Derby	594, 595
Nottingham, Trent, and Chester field	596, 597
Sheffield and Rotherham	662
Sandal and Walton and Wake field	597

☞ **For other Trains**

BETWEEN	PAGE
Kettering and Nottingham, via Melton Mowbray	591
Leicester and Syston	592
Derby and Ambergate	558
Derby and Duffield	587
Dore and Totley and Sheffield	566
Sheffield and Swinton	595, 608
Methley and Leeds	785

A 1910 timetable for MR passenger services operating between St Pancras and Leeds, which included Sheffield and Rotherham. (Author)

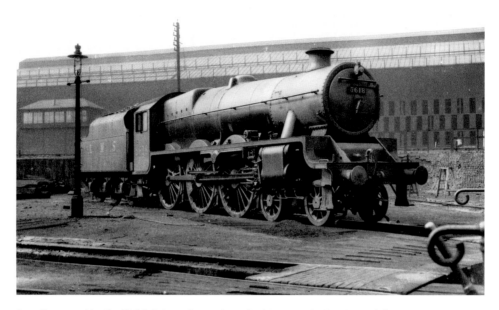

Standing outside Sheffield Grimesthorpe locoshed in 1935 is Stanier 'Jubilee' 4-6-0 No. 5618, as yet without nameplates. The engine would soon be named *New Hebrides*. The shed was opened by the MR in the 1860s as a typical Midland roundhouse. When the Sheffield–Chesterfield line opened, it soon became apparent that a larger shed would be required to improve engine servicing facilities. A new shed, with a 46-foot turntable, was built slightly north of the existing one. The shed was further expanded in the 1890s when an eight-road fitting shop was added and a traverser was fitted at the same time to avoid building extra trackwork. In 1901, a new 60-foot turntable was installed which allowed the 1860s shed to finally be taken out of use. In 1939, another new 60-foot turntable was installed at a cost of £4,397. At nationalisation, the shed was coded 19A, becoming 41B in 1958 when control was transferred to the Eastern Region. (LOSA)

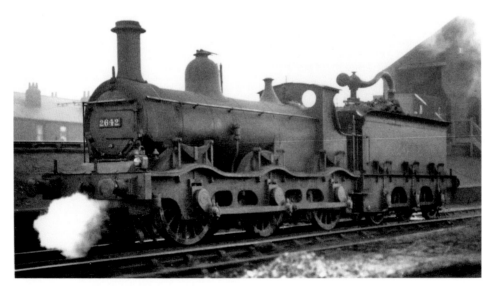

One of Matthew Kirtley's picturesque 0-6-0 goods engines, built by the MR between 1863 and 1874, at Grimesthorpe on 23 June 1926. Still in MR livery, it was numbered 2642. All of the class had gone by 1951. (H. Casserley)

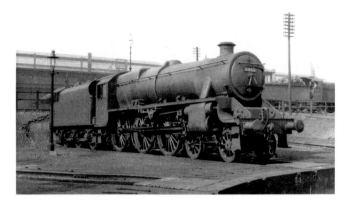

Standing outside Grimesthorpe locoshed is LMS Stanier 'Black Five' 4-6-0 No. 5048 as it appeared in the late 1930s. In 1950, the allocation at Grimesthorpe was as follows:

Ex-MR 3P 4-4-0	40728, 40729* *At this time, these were some of the last survivors of an original class of 80 Johnson 4-4-0s built by the MR between 1900 and 1905.
Ex-MR 1F 0-6-0T	41660, 41781
Ex-LMS 5MT 2-6-0	42797
Ex-LMS 4MT 2-6-0	43032, 43037, 43038, 43041, 43042
Ex-MR 3F 0-6-0	43334, 43335, 43463, 43604, 43605, 43607, 43636, 43661, 43662, 43715, 43731, 43755, 43775
Ex-LMS 4F 0-6-0	44211, 44212, 44284, 44285, 44234, 44284, 44285, 44426, 44437, 44557, 44568, 44573
Ex-LMS 5MT 4-6-0	44802, 44827, 44845, 44858, 44944, 45056, 45074, 45225, 45262, 45407
Ex-LMS 2MT 2-6-0	46450, 46451
Ex-LMS 3F 0-6-0T	47235, 47236, 47452, 47548, 47563, 47611, 47624
Ex-LMS 8F 2-8-0	48116, 48179, 48284, 48642
Ex-MR 2F 0-6-0	58139, 58140, 58151, 58165, 58175, 58190, 58225, 58232, 58276
	Total: 67

The shed was finally closed in 1961. (LOSA)

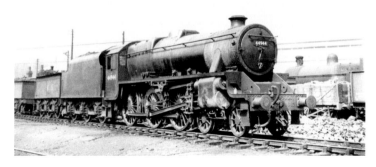

Also at Grimesthorpe in 1951 is ex-LMS 'Black Five' No. 44944 with several pre-nationalisation engines in view. (H. Casserley)

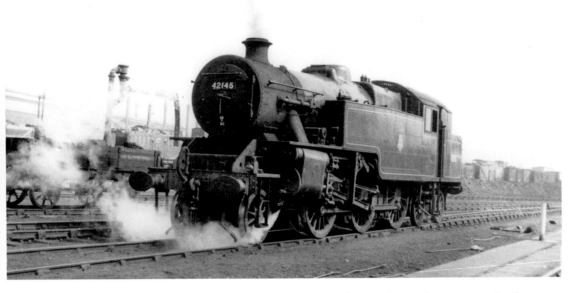

Ex-LMS Fairburn 2-6-4T No. 42145 awaits its turn of duty at Grimesthorpe on 20 April 1951. (H. Casserley)

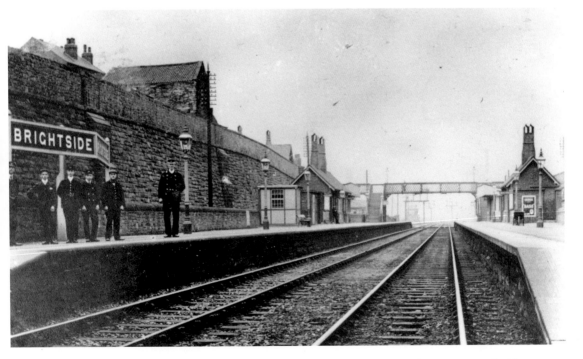

The station at Sheffield Brightside as it appeared in the early twentieth century. Brightside was the junction of the Lancashire, Derbyshire & East Coast Railway and the Sheffield & Rotherham Railway, which gave the MR access to Sheffield from its main line. (LOSA)

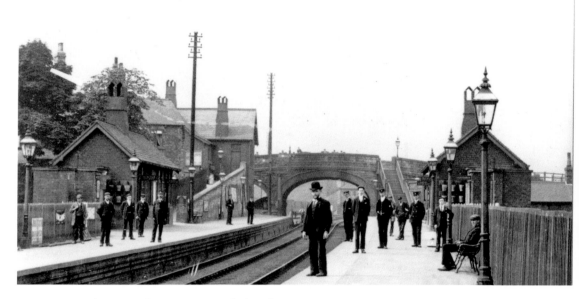

An early twentieth-century view of Chapeltown station on the MR branch from Brightside to the Leeds main line. (LOSA)

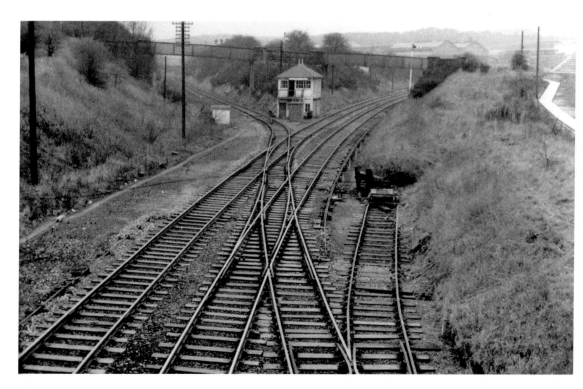

The ex-MR junction near Chapeltown in the late 1960s, facing Cudworth with the colliery branch on the left-hand side. (R. Carpenter)

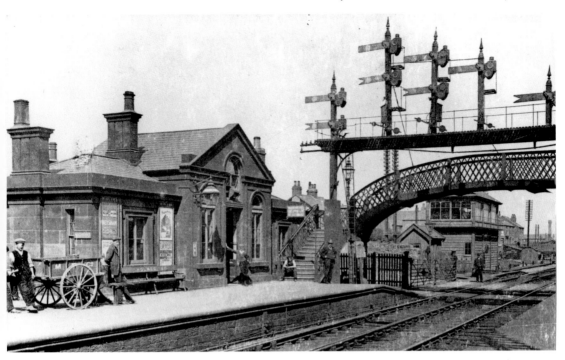

On the line from Brightside to Rotherham, trains pass Blackburn Forge before reaching Holmes station. Between Blackburn Forge and Holmes, a little branch took trains to the terminus station at Rotherham Westgate. Holmes station is seen here in MR days, complete with typical Midland station architecture, footbridge and signal box. A gantry of lower quadrant MR signals gives an indication of an approaching junction to Rotherham and the line from Chesterfield. (LOSA)

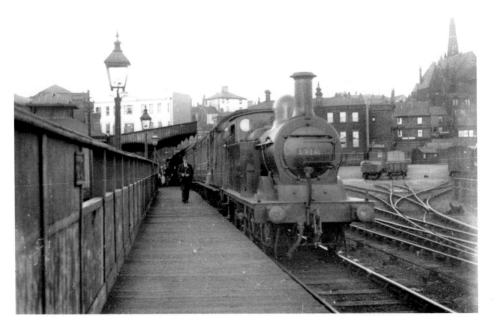

The terminus at Rotherham Westgate in August 1935 with 0-4-4T No. 1416 on the local branch train. (R. Carpenter)

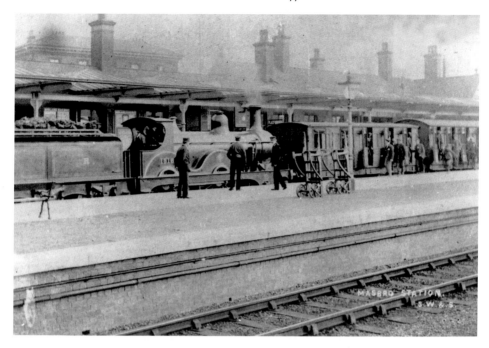

The station of Rotherham Masborough as it appeared in MR days with Johnson 2-4-0 No. 1518 at the head of a passenger train of ancient Midland four-wheel coaches. Summer rain in September 1931 caused flooding at Rotherham & Masborough station, causing disruption to passenger services. (LOSA)

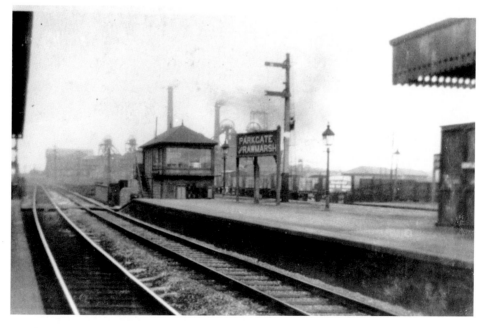

Heading to Barnsley from Rotherham is the station of Parkgate & Rawmarsh, which served a nearby colliery, the pithead being visible on the right. Between Rotherham and Barnsley the MR line ran parallel to that of the GCR, both having passenger stations in close proximity. The MR had originally opened this line for freight only, but decided to open passenger stations in competition with the GCR. (LOSA)

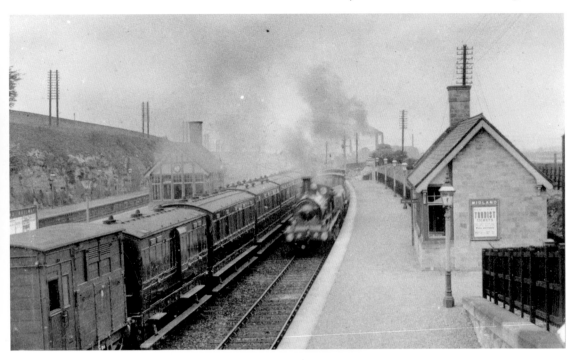

Another station, Kilnhurst, on the route to Barnsley with MR trains in view and an industrial scene in the background. Just to confuse matters, there was also a Kilnhurst station on the GCR, its line on an embankment to the left of this view. (LOSA)

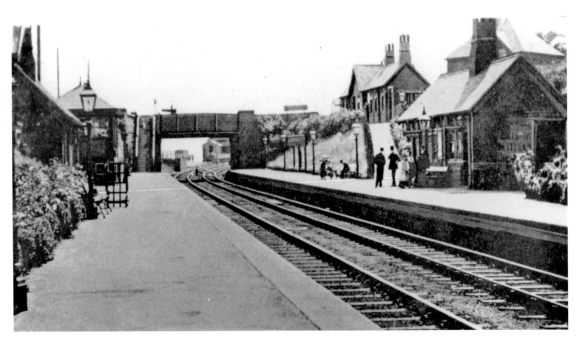

Between Kilnhurst and Barnsley, a branch went off to Leeds, again parallel with the GCR, with a station at Wombwell, seen here at the end of the nineteenth century. (LOSA)

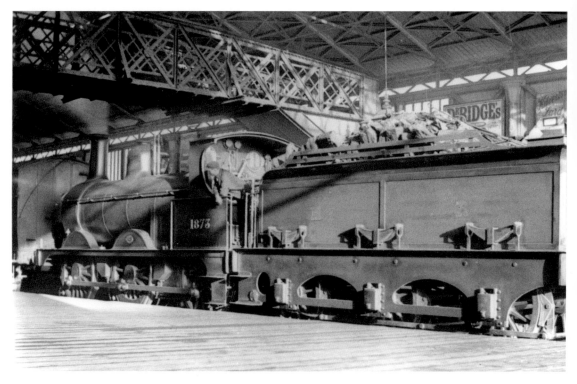

Barnsley Court House station in MR days with 'Johnson' class 2 0-6-0 No. 1873. A branch from the main line at Cudworth was built by the MR in 1869 to a new station at Barnsley, Court House being opened some three years later. An intermediate station was opened at Monk Bretton in 1876. The branch was 4½ miles long and its main feature was the 1,087-foot Oaks Viaduct, which crossed two railways, a main road, a river and two canals. A shuttle service connected Court House with the main line, reaching a peak of twenty-two trains each way on weekdays, with an extra two on Saturdays, and seven on Sundays, in 1912. Monk Bretton station closed in 1937 and the shuttle service ended in 1958. The Oaks Viaduct was demolished in 1969 and a half-mile spur to Monk Bretton glassworks was all that remained. On 11 March 1959, notice of closure for Court House station was issued, and it closed officially on 19 April 1960. (R. Carpenter)

A 1910 timetable for MR shuttle services between Barnsley Court House station and Cudworth for connections with the main MR Leeds–St Pancras line. (Author)

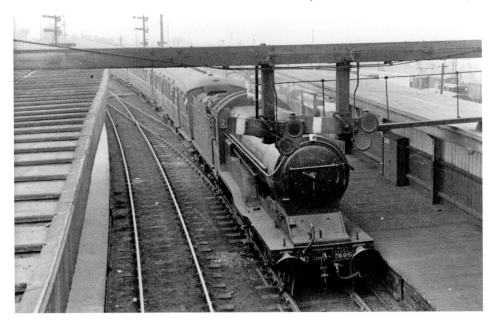

Arriving at Barnsley Court House station at the head of the 4.50 p.m. Penistone to Mexborough train is ex-GCR enlarged 'Director' class 4-4-0 No. 2665 *Mons* on 18 April 1847. (H. Casserley)

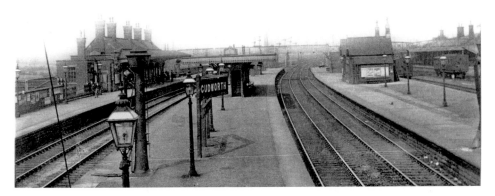

On the MR main line, and the other end of the shuttle from Barnsley Court House, was the station at Cudworth, seen here in MR days. The station here was shared with the Hull & Barnsley Railway, which paid rent to share facilities. In its time, there were only two accidents at Cudworth. The first was on 12 January 1843, which killed one person, while the other occurred on 19 January 1905 when two MR trains collided with a third in fog, which killed seven passengers. By 1967, the MR main line between Leeds and Normanton was suffering from subsidence, caused by coal mining in the area, and trains were often rerouted, first along the Swinton & Knottingley Railway and then at Cudworth, traffic ceasing here in 1972, although such passenger trains were brought back in 1996. However, Sheffield–Leeds services had ceased altogether in 1967 and all stations were closed. (LOSA)

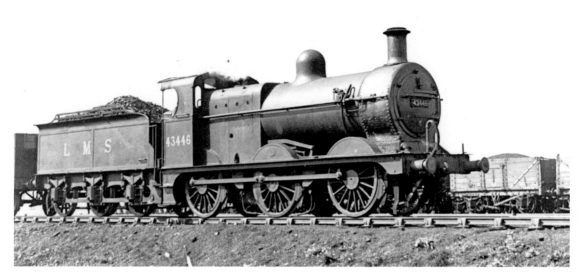

Back in happier times, a selection of views on the main line to Leeds. Here, LMS (ex-MR) 3F 0-6-0 No. 43446, still with LMS ownership on the tender, is seen at Royston on 29 April 1949. (H. Casserley)

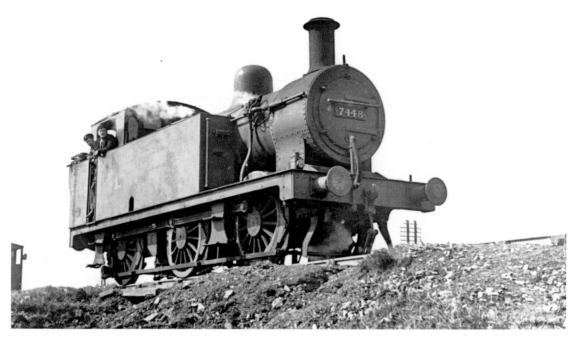

Also at Royston, on 29 April 1949, is 'Jinty' 3F 0-6-0T, still carrying LMS No. 7448, on shunting duties. (H. Casserley)

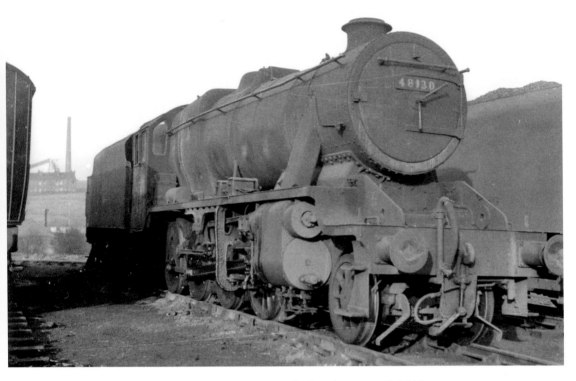

Ex-LMS 8F 2-8-0 No. 48130 rests at Royston shed in the 1950s. (LOSA)

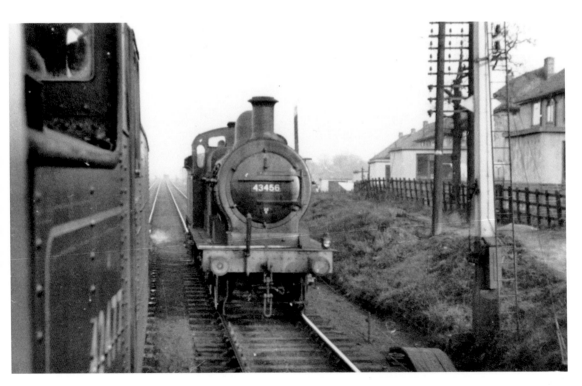

Approaching a passenger train at Methley is ex-MR 3F 0-6-0 No. 43456 running light engine. (H. Casserley)

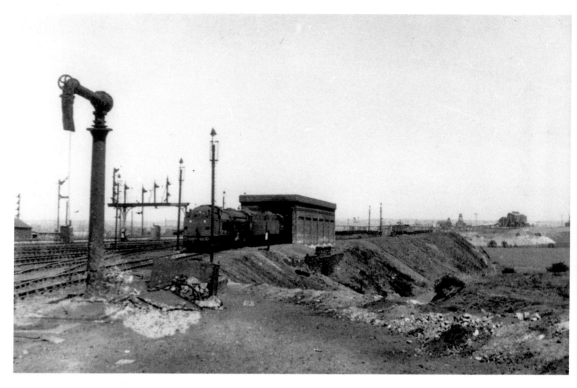

A line of steam locos await their fate at Normanton locoshed on 2 June 1963. (H. Casserley)

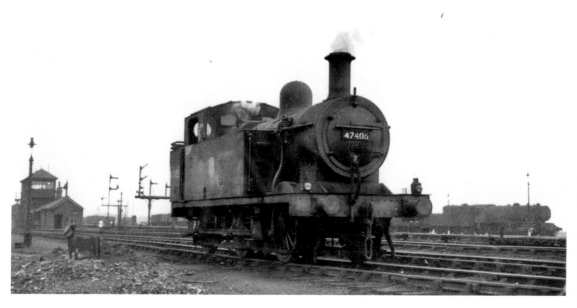

Also at Normanton shed on 28 May 1951 is 'Jinty' 0-6-0T No. 47405. An ex-WD 2-8-0 is in the background. (H. Casserley)

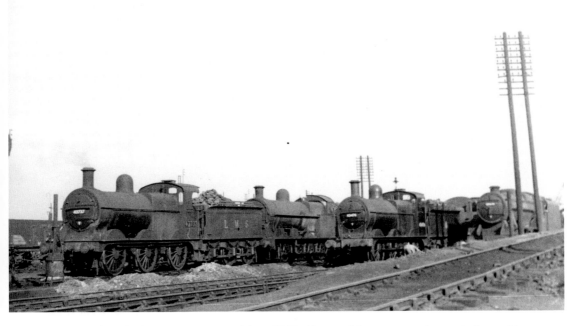

Stourton locoshed on 26 June 1950 with ex-LMS 3F 0-6-0s Nos 43737 and 43476, along with 8F No. 48641 and ex-LNWR 7F 0-8-0, still carrying its LMS No. 9112. (H. Casserley)

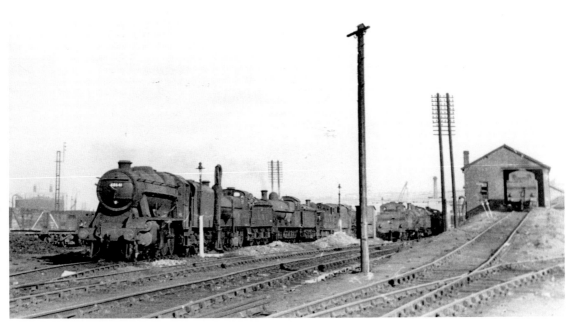

Also at Stourton shed on 26 June 1950 is a line of ex-LMS engines, some still with LMS ownership marked on their tenders, with an unidentified 8F 2-8-0 leading. (H. Casserley)

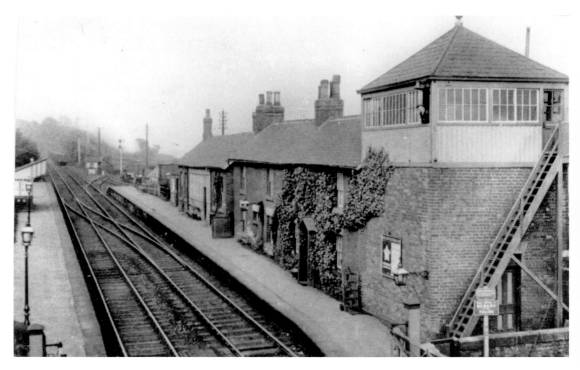

Shunting at Stourton on 5 September 1953 is ex-LMS 'Jinty' 0-6-0T No. 47538. (H. Casserley)

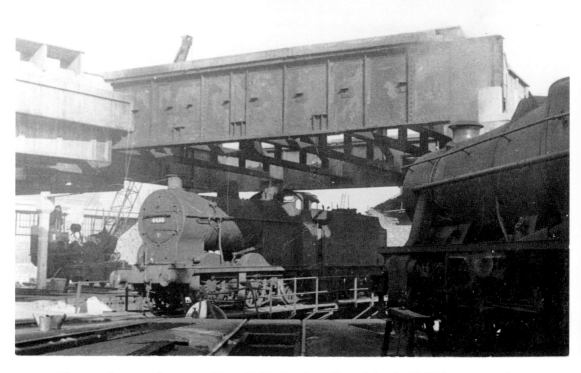

The roundhouse at Stourton with ex-LMS 4F 0-6-0, still retaining its LMS No. 4435, and an unidentified 8F 2-8-0 on shed on 26 June 1950. (H. Casserley)

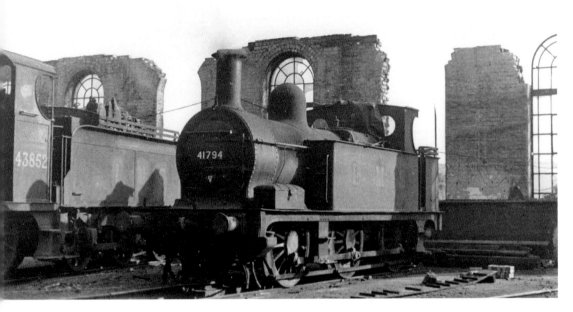

Ex-MR 1F 0-6-0, with open cab, No. 41794, is seen at a half-demolished Stourton locoshed in the company of 3F 0-6-0 No. 43852 on 26 June 1950. (H. Casserley)

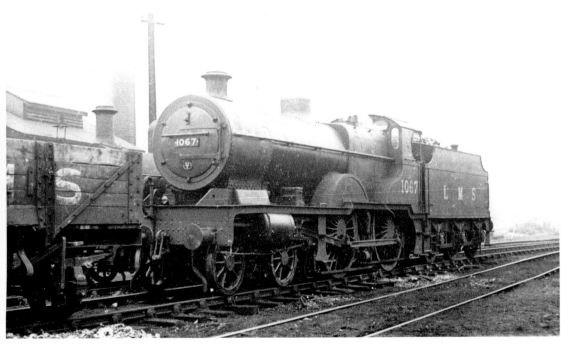

At Manningham shed on 2 October 1948 is LMS 'Compound' 4-4-0 No. 1067. (H. Casserley)

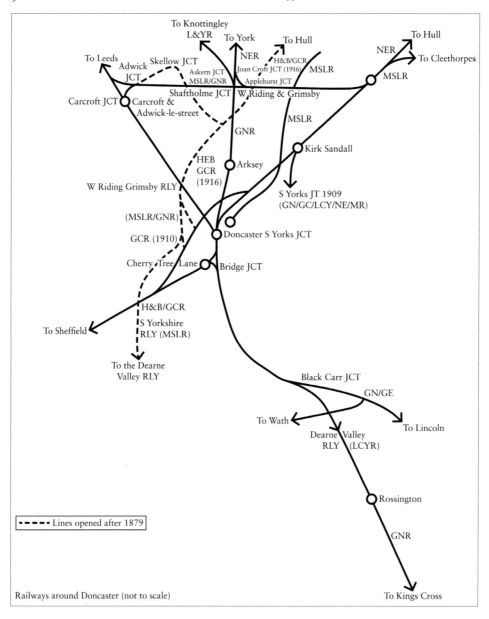

A map showing the railway network around Doncaster. The GNR has its main line running from King's Cross through Doncaster to Shaftholme Junction, where it makes a head-on connection with the North Eastern Railway, giving access to York, before heading on to Edinburgh (on the East Coast Main Line). At Black Carr Junction, the joint line with the Great Eastern from Lincoln joins the GNR to Doncaster. There is also a connection to the Dearne Valley Railway, giving access to coal traffic. Access to Leeds is via a joint line with the MS&LR (as the West Riding & Grimsby Railway). The South Yorkshire Joint Railway can be seen leaving the MS&LR at Kirk Sandall and access to Sheffield is via the MS&LR's South Yorkshire Railway. (Author)

THREE

DONCASTER AND THE GREAT NORTHERN RAILWAY

Doncaster was destined to become famous as the centre of locomotive construction for both the Great Northern Railway and the later London & North Eastern Railway, building many famous engines, such as A1 Pacific *Flying Scotsman* and streamlined A4 Pacific *Mallard* among very many others. Doncaster was the most northerly point reached by the independent GNR, the company only reaching further north over the tracks of other companies. The GNR gained access to York over metals of the North Eastern Railway and shared access to Leeds with the MS&LR. Indeed, it was the MS&LR that connected Doncaster with Sheffield. Thus, Doncaster was not seen as particularly important to the King's Cross company, as other railways, like the Midland and Lancashire & Yorkshire, were better connected to main centres of population, and the GNR was happy to concentrate its locomotive activities at Boston, Lincolnshire and Peterborough.

The GNR had originally set out to build a main line to York, which was to become part of the East Coast Main Line from King's Cross to Edinburgh, as well as to the eastern part of Lincolnshire. The original GNR route ran to Peterborough, then northeast to Boston (where the original repair shops had been opened since 1848) and on to Doncaster, via Lincoln, Gainsborough and Retford. A more direct line from Peterborough to Doncaster, via Grantham, Newark and Retford, did not open until 1852. In order to reach its planned destination at York, the GNR had to use NER metals from Shaftholme Junction to York, the NER then operating trains from York to Edinburgh via the North British Railway in Scotland. Initially, any plans that the GNR had of reaching York were resisted by the 'Railway King' George Hudson, whose York & North Midland Railway (Y&NMR) was centred on York; he fiercely resisted any attempt to break his monopoly in the city. However, his power had declined by the late 1840s due to his dubious business practices. By 1854, the NER had come into existence due to the merger of Hudson's Y&NMR, the York, Newcastle & Berwick Railway and the Leeds Northern Railway. Yet the new company did not make much effort to improve the NER line south of York and did not complete the line from York to Shaftholme Junction until 1871. Prior to these improvements, the GNR operated its services to York from Shaftholme Junction, via the roundabout Lancashire & Yorkshire Railway line through Knottingley, to join the mistrusted Y&NMR outside York. Once the GNR and NER were connected, the GNR ran its trains to York and the NER took them on to Scotland, using jointly owned coaches over what was to become something of a racetrack between the English and Scottish capitals. Indeed, it was on a section of the ECML, at Stoke Bank, that LNER A4 Pacific 4468 *Mallard* took the steam speed record of 126 mph on 3 July 1938.

By 1850, as the GNR was planning to expand its network, it became clear that the works at Boston were too small for the company's requirements. The then-locomotive engineer, Archibald Sturrock, gave thought to building a new, more extensive works. Sturrock and the majority of the GNR Board favoured a move to a more central location at Peterborough. However, chairman of the GNR Edmund Denison fought to have Doncaster become the centre for its locomotive engineering facilities, winning the argument in 1851. By 1853, all heavy locomotive work was transferred to Doncaster, although it would not be until 1867 that the first locomotive was built at what was to become known as 'The Plant'. In that year, Patrick Sterling, who had become locomotive superintendent in 1866 and was known for his famous single-wheelers, obtained approval to build three 0-4-2 engines at Doncaster. One of these, No. 18, was the first of many locomotives to be built at Doncaster for well over a century, the works providing express engines through to humble tank and shunting locos for the GNR, LNER and British Railways.

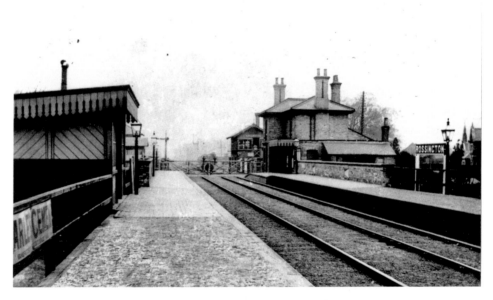

South of Doncaster and before the joint line from Lincoln joins the GNR at Black Carr Junction lay the station at Rossington, seen here in around 1905. (LOSA)

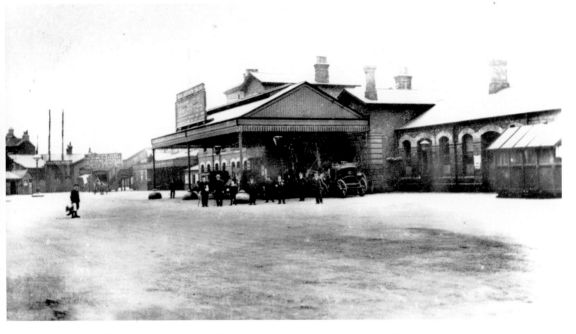

Exterior of Doncaster station, with staff, as it appeared in 1905. The station was built by the GNR in 1850 and was made up of two platforms with a central crossover in the middle. (LOSA)

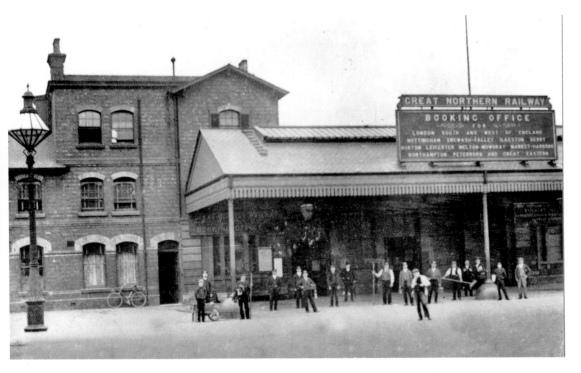

Entrance to Doncaster station in 1905, the board above it emphasising that the station is owned by the GNR and that the booking office will offer tickets to London, the South and West of England, Nottingham, Erewash Valley, Ilkeston, Derby, Burton, Leicester, Melton Mowbray, Market Harboro (*sic*), Northampton, Peterboro (*sic*) and Great Eastern. (LOSA)

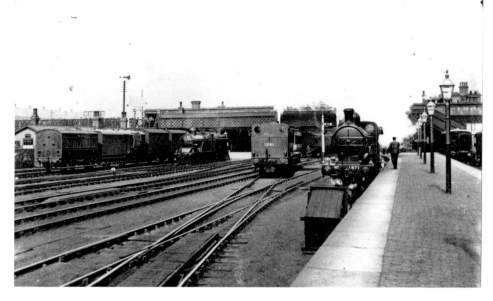

Interior of Doncaster station at its south end in GNR days. On the left of the picture is an Ivatt 4-2-2, built between 1898 and 1901. In the centre is 0-6-0 saddle tank No. 1241 on shunting duties while, on the right, is Ivatt 4-4-0 No. 1371 (LNER class D3/4) of 1900–02. The footbridge at the rear gave access to the locoworks, known as 'The Plant'. As can be seen, coaches were largely of the four-wheeled variety. (LOSA)

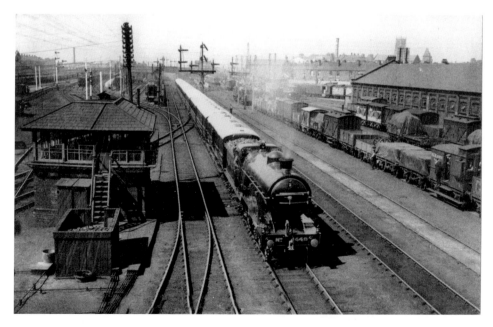

A GNR 'Atlantic' heads south through Doncaster with the royal train in 1908. Doncaster had long been a crossing point on the River Don, developing as a commercial and trading centre since medieval times. Horse racing became popular here from the early nineteenth century and the town had developed something of an aristocratic image, so much so that contemplation of a railway here was viewed with distaste. Therefore, after some difficulty, the GNR finally arrived here with a temporary station in 1849. (LOSA)

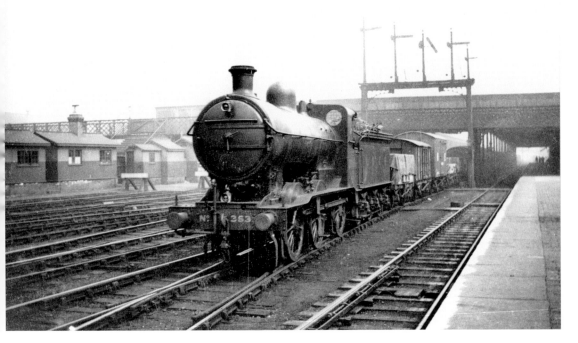

Doncaster station in the 1930s with ex-GNR 0-6-0, as LNER J6 class 3532, on an 'up' freight. (R. Carpenter)

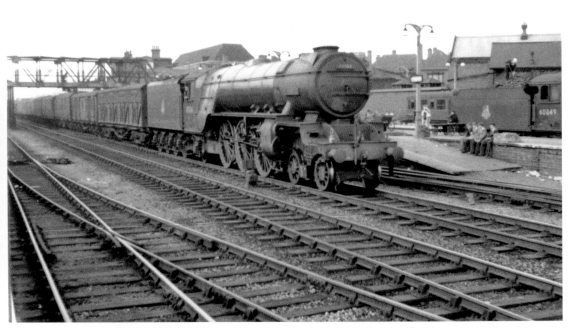

Ex-LNER A2/2 Pacific No. 60504 *Mons Meg* is seen passing through Doncaster station at the head of a parcels train in 1957. Members of this class were originally built in 1934–36 by Gresley as 2-8-2s for services between Edinburgh and Aberdeen. They were rebuilt by Thompson in 1943–44 as Pacifics. All had 6-foot 2-inch wheels and three cylinders. All were withdrawn between 1959 and 1961. (R. Carpenter)

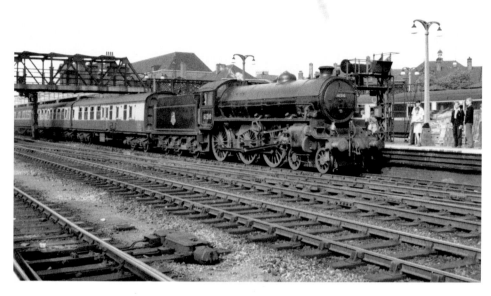

Ex-LNER B1 4-6-0 No. 61210 waits in 1957 at Doncaster station with an 'up' express. The engine was built at the North British Locomotive Company, with maker's plate No. 26111, and entered service on 3 July 1947. It started life based at New England shed, was then transferred to March on 27 April 1952, returning to New England on 8 June 1952. From there, the loco was transferred to King's Cross on 14 December 1952 and went back to New England on 8 March 1953. The loco stayed at New England for another decade before moving to Colwick on 22 September 1963 and finally arrived at Doncaster shed on 28 November 1965. She was condemned at Doncaster on 10 February 1966 and sold to A. Draper of Hull for scrap in March 1966. (R. Carpenter)

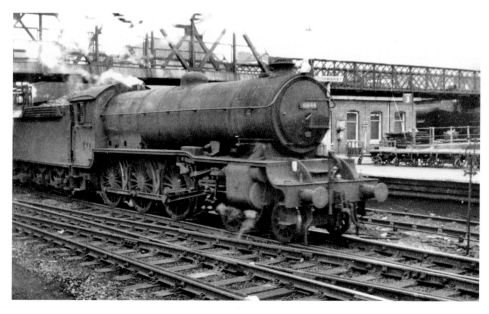

Waiting at Doncaster station in the early 1960s, and in rather dirty condition, is ex-LNER B16/3 4-6-0 No. 61444. These engines were originally ex-NER engines, built between 1919 and 1924. This engine is an example of those rebuilt with a Walschearts valve gear to their three cylinders and raised running plate, so treated in 1937. (LOSA)

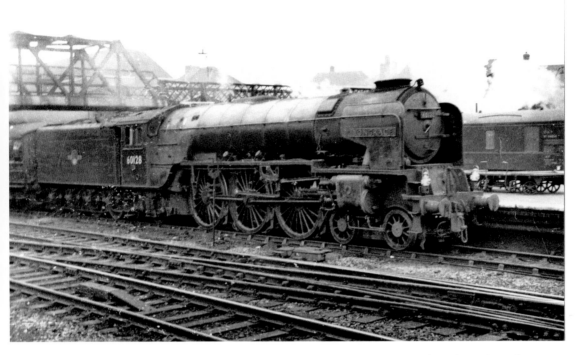

BR Peppercorn A1 Pacific No. 60128 *Bongrace* at Doncaster with a train of Gresley teak stock in the late 1950s. (LOSA)

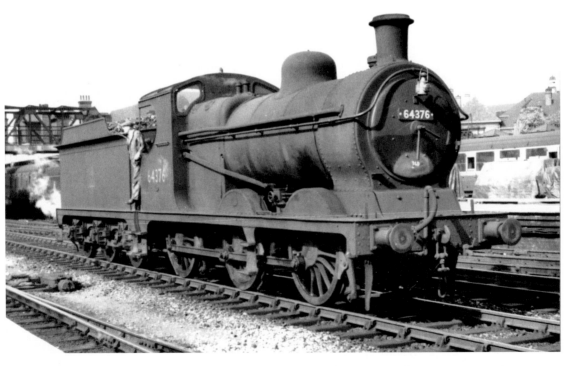

Ex-GCR/LNER J11 class 0-6-0 No. 64376 waits on the centre road at Doncaster station in 1957. These engines were built between 1901 and 1910, all surviving until 1954 when withdrawals began. All had gone by 1963.

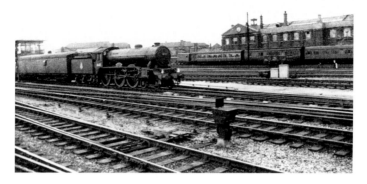

Ex-LNER Gresley B17 4-6-0 No. 61638 *Melton Hall* approaches Doncaster with a March–York train. The engine was built at the old NER works at Darlington in 1933 and numbered 2838. She entered traffic on 2 March 1933 and was allocated to Doncaster shed before transfer to Norwich on 15 March 1933. From here the loco went to Stratford on 14 January 1944 and then to Cambridge on 8 January 1945. She then went to March on 12 September 1951, having been renumbered 1638 on 18 August 1946. Two years later, on 11 August 1948, her BR number, 61638, was given to her. She was condemned on 17 March 1958 and, to complete the circle, she returned to her first allocated shed at Doncaster to be cut up. (J. Suter)

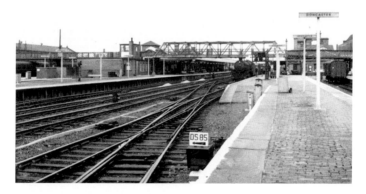

Standing at Doncaster station with an 'up' freight in 1961 is BR Thompson B1 4-6-0 No. 61329, another of the North British-built engines (No. 26230). The loco entered service on 18 June 1948 and, once again, was allocated to New England shed. From there she went to March from 12 June 1949, thence to Lincoln from 20 October 1949. She then found herself going south to Stratford on 21 October 1951. For a short while, from 19 March 1953, she went to the Southern Region before returning to Stratford on 23 May 1953. From there she went back to March from 16 September 1962. Only a month later, on 28 October, she was allocated to Doncaster where, like many others, she was condemned on 17 April 1966 and was sold for scrap a month later to Cohen's of Kettering. The station itself was considerably enlarged between 1873 and 1877 as traffic increased. The station was crossed by the Great North Road and protected by a level crossing, which must have caused considerable traffic problems given the amount of rail traffic – not least the constant numbers of coal trains, all having to use the line here. Things were not to improve until a bridge that took the road over the railway was built between 1909 and 1911. The two-track bottleneck here was only relieved when a new railway bridge that took Leeds trains was built at the same time (H. Priestley)

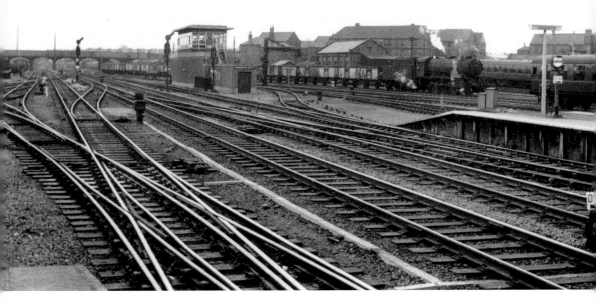

Ex-WD loco heads a north-bound mineral train through Doncaster in 1962. Major changes at Doncaster began in 1850, although the MS&LR line from Sheffield had arrived in 1849, from the north. First, the MS&LR arrived from the north-east, then the West Riding & Grimsby Railway came in from the north-west, all funnelling on to the two tracks that crossed the Great North Road, as previously mentioned. The station footbridge was replaced by a subway in 1939 when a new platform one was built, making an island platform. The line from Hull was separated from the rest of the main line by converting sidings into a main line. The Second World War intervened and it was not until 1949 that tracks were laid on the bridge over the River Don, giving Leeds its own lines. The station was modernised in the early 1970s, with BR investing £125,000. A further £4 million was spent in 2007 to further improve Doncaster station. (H. Priestley)

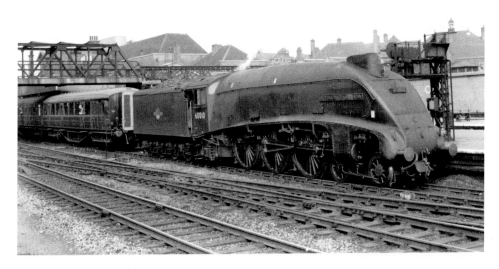

One of the famous ex-LNER Gresley A4 Pacifics, No. 60010 *Dominion of Canada*, is seen taking over a Leeds–King's Cross express at Doncaster station on 16 July 1961. These engines are so famous that no further explanations are needed here, except to say that they were all withdrawn by 1966 and several have found their way into preservation, including this one, which now resides in the country after which she was named. (D. Johnson)

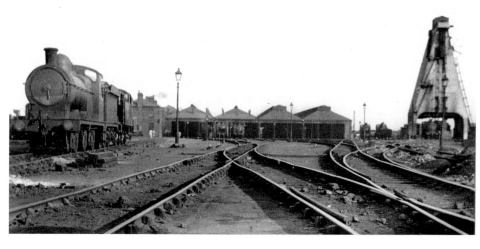

Doncaster shed in LNER days with an ex-GNR 0-6-0 in view with an unidentified tank loco behind. The shed itself can be seen in the background with the coaling stage, a recently installed concrete hopper type, and several locomotives in the background. (R. Carpenter)

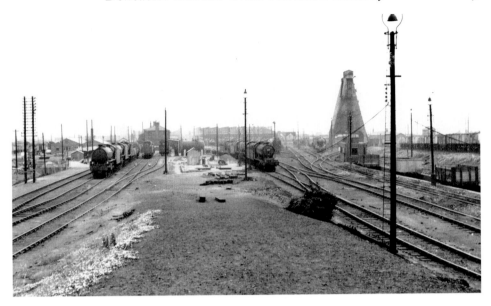

A general view of Doncaster locoshed on 9 July 1967, with several B1 4-6-0s in view. Doncaster was the principal shed of the GNR, opening with the line in 1850. It was a thirteen-road straight shed with a turning triangle. Coded 36A, it had an allocation of around 180 engines, as the allocation below shows:

Ex-LNER A3 4-6-2	60047 *Donovan* 60055 *Woolwinder* 60058 *Blair Athol* 60061 *Pretty Polly* 60064 *Tagalie* 60066 *Merry Hampton*
Ex-LNER V2 2-6-2	60849, 60852, 60857, 60861, 60867, 60870 60872 *King's Own Yorkshire Light Infantry* 60875, 60877, 60880, 60881, 60889, 60890, 60896, 60902, 60917, 60921, 60928, 60930, 60935, 60943, 60948, 60956
Ex-LNER B1 4-6-0	61026 *Ourebi* 61036 *Ralph Assheton* 61086, 61087, 61107, 61120, 61124, 61125, 61126, 61127, 61128, 61170, 61193, 61196 61246 *Lord Balfour of Burleigh* 61247 *Lord Burghley* 61248 *Geoffrey Gibbs* 61249 *Fitzherbert Wright* 61250 *A Harold Bibby* 61265
Ex-LNER K1/3 2-6-0	61861, 61907, 61918, 61978
Ex-GNR 2-8-0	63476, 63477, 63478, 63479, 63480, 63481, 63483, 63484, 63485, 63486, 63488, 63491, 63493
Ex-LNER 02 2-8-0	63925, 63926, 63928, 63941, 63942, 63943, 63945, 63946, 63947, 63951, 63952, 63953, 63954, 63955, 63956, 63957, 63958, 63959, 69361, 63962, 63964, 63967, 63961, 63962, 63964, 63967, 63968, 63973, 63974, 63986, 63987
Ex-GNR J3 0-6-0	64124

Ex-GNR J6 0-6-0	64179, 64183, 64185, 64193, 64195, 64209, 64218, 64219, 64232, 64236, 64243, 64255, 64258, 64259, 64261, 64262, 64263, 64264, 64270, 64279
Ex-GCR J11 0-6-0	64285, 64349, 64410
Ex-GNR J39 0-6-0	64713, 64721, 64737, 64758, 64835, 64885, 64893, 64902, 64909, 64910, 64951, 64952, 64976, 64977, 64984
Ex-NER J21 0-6-0	65095, 65117
Ex-LNER Y1 0-4-0T	68132s (operates at Rarnskill Wagon works)
Ex-LNER Y3 0-4-0T	68165
Ex GNR J55 0-6-0T	68319
Ex-GNR J52 0-6-0ST	68763, 68769, 68775, 68782, 68786, 68800, 68804, 68806, 68813, 68835, 68836, 68841, 68842, 68843, 68847, 68849, 68857, 68858, 68860, 68865, 68867, 68869, 68870, 68885, 68886
Ex-GNR 0-6-0T	68926, 68936, 68945, 68961, 68980, 68985, 68986, 68987, 68989, 68991
Ex-NER J72 0-6-0T	69014
	Total: 177

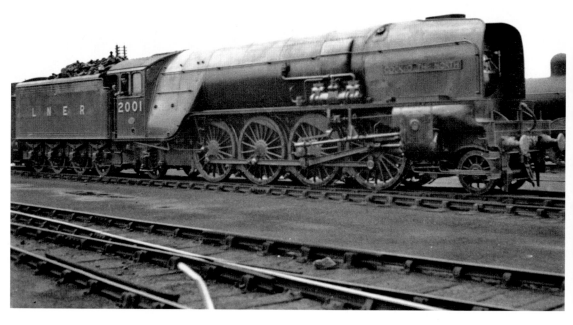

Awaiting servicing at Doncaster in 1935 is unique P2 2-8-2 No. 2001 *Cock o' the North*. The engine was built in 1934 and had a tractive effort of 43,462 lb and an axle load of 44,800 lb with a steam pressure of 220 psi. The engine had three cylinders and used poppet valves to actuate a rotating camshaft. The engine had a specially shaped front end to lift smoke clear to improve visibility and a double chimney was fitted to improve draughting with a minimum of back pressure. The engine was designed to work over difficult lines around Aberdeen, which could tax the Pacifics of the day. A second engine was built, No. 2002 *Earl Marischal*, with more normal Gresley motion. A further four members of the class were built, but these were more like the A4s. Despite the power of these engines, they did not eliminate double-heading over the Edinburgh–Aberdeen route and the heavy engines caused track wear on sharp curves. Also, they proved costly to maintain and were rebuilt in 1944 to a class A2/2 Pacific design by CME Edward Thompson. These engines remained non-standard and were not the most attractive, having an ungainly appearance. (LOSA)

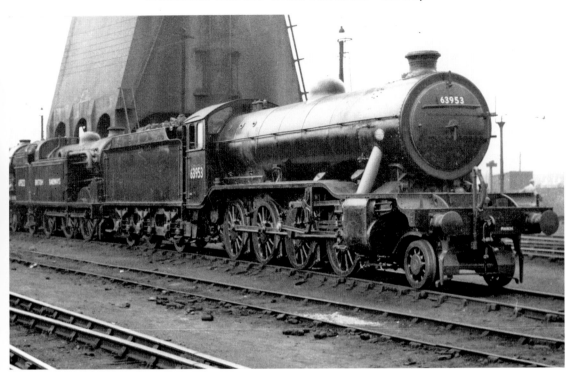

Newly outshopped and, as yet, without the new BR totem on the tender, ex-Gresley class 02/3 No. 63953 waits outside the coaling stage at Doncaster shed in 1948. (R. Carpenter)

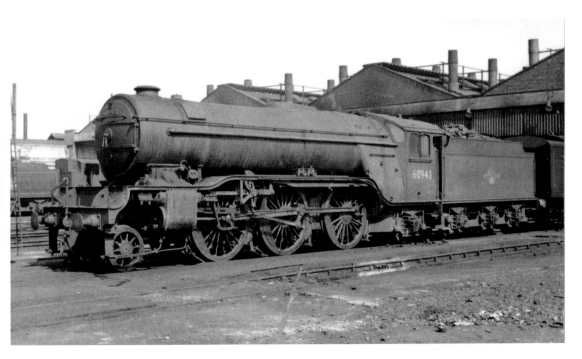

Ex-LNER Gresley V2 class 2-6-2 No. 60943 is seen sitting outside Doncaster shed in 1957. This class was built in 1936 for mixed traffic work and these locomotives mainly found themselves on express parcels service, including the newly inaugurated 'Green Arrow' fast parcels train, after which the doyen of the class, No. 4771, was named. (LOSA)

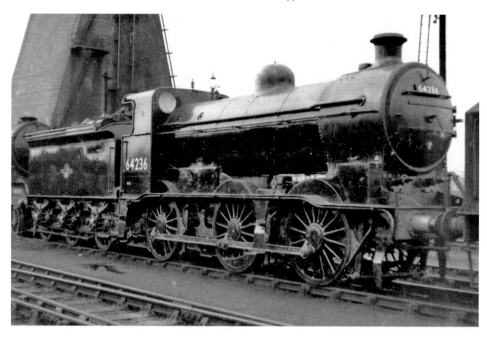

Ex-GNR/LNER class J6 0-6-0 No. 64236 is seen at the coal stage of Doncaster shed, its home base, in 1958. (R. Carpenter)

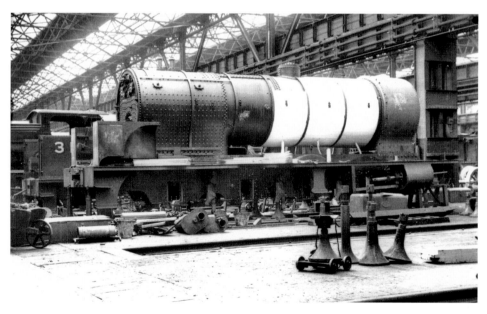

LNER ex-NER Q5 0-8-0 No. 658 is seen undergoing a major overhaul at Doncaster works in 1932. Along with the Pacifics, Doncaster works turned out many famous classes of locos, including the V2 2-6-2s and Peppercorn A1 Pacifics, along with many other more humble engines. Along with the old NER works at Darlington, the works turned out steam engines for both the LNER and BR. 'The Plant' is still going strong and is now in private ownership. Although early nineteenth-century residents were very much against a railway in Doncaster, they must surely have been proud of the contribution made to the national railway system by the town and would certainly have enjoyed holding a world speed record that is yet to be beaten. (R. Carpenter)

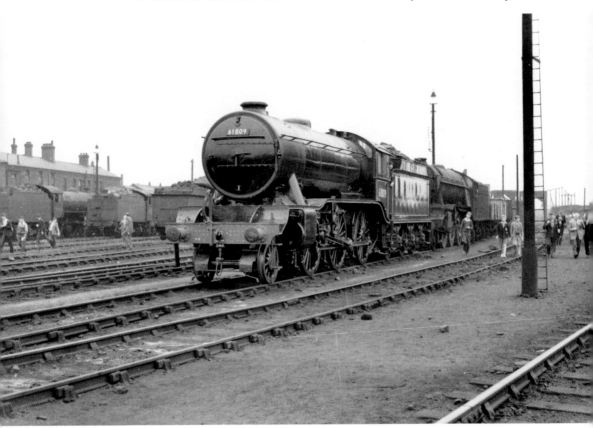

On 16 July 1961, Gresley K3/2 No. 61809, in clean condition, is at the head of a couple of locos on what appears to be an open day for railway enthusiasts. Several other of Doncaster shed's allocation can be seen in the background. By 1959, Doncaster's Carr shed, coded 36A, had reached a peak with an allocation of some 191 engines, including seven A3s, thirteen A1s, twenty-three V2s and twenty-seven B1s. There were thirty-one O2 2-8-0s and twelve ex-WD 2-8-0s and some BR 9F 2-10-0s were allocated at Doncaster. Withdrawn in that year, and allocated to Doncaster, was the solitary W1 4-6-4, the 1937 rebuild of Gresley's four-cylinder compound with water-tube boiler. Doncaster shed was closed in 1966, being the last steam shed operated by the Eastern Region. (R. Carpenter)

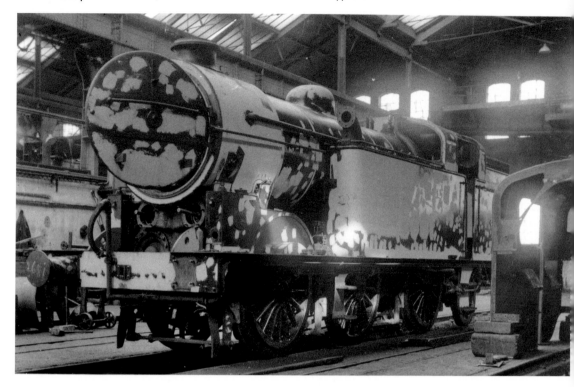

Ex-GNR N2 class 0-6-2T No. 2681 is being stripped down for repair at Doncaster locoworks in 1932. Known as 'The Plant', the works was established by the GNR in 1853 for the maintenance of locomotives and carriages. Locos entered the works from the south and carriages entered from the north. A new erecting shop was built in 1891, and in 1889 the wagon repair shop was moved near to the locoshed. In the early years, Archibald Sturrock was Chief Mechanical Engineer when the works was opened. Although he had favoured a base at Peterborough, he found himself at Doncaster. He was famous for his 2-2-2 and 2-4-0 express engines, although most of his designs were for goods traffic. He was followed by another Scot, Patrick Stirling, who joined the GNR in 1866, staying until his death in 1895. He was the famous designer of the 8-foot 4-2-2 'Single', which was involved in the 'Races to the North' with the London & North Western Railway. In April 1867, Stirling obtained approval to build three 0-4-2s at Doncaster, No. 18 being the first loco to be built at Doncaster and the first of 709 Stirling engines to be built at the works. The successor to Patrick Stirling was H. A. Ivatt, appointed after his predecessor's death. He had experience with the LNWR at Crewe and, following the introduction of heavier trains with dining cars (appearing in 1893), he found that there was inadequate motive power. He built some 4-4-0s with large boilers, but found them inadequate. He therefore designed the first 4-4-2 'Atlantic' locos to run in the UK. Unlike the L&YR types that followed, these engines had outside cylinders when introduced in 1899. The boiler size was increased from a 10-foot 1-inch diameter to a 13-foot diameter. Ivatt also built several goods engines which lasted well into BR days, including C12 'Atlantic' tanks and J523Ts. Perhaps the most famous CME at Doncaster was Sir Nigel Gresley, who arrived at Doncaster as carriage superintendent in 1905, becoming CME in 1911. His first design for the GNR was the H1 (LNER K1) 2-6-0 in 1912. In 1918, he designed the O1 2-8-0 for heavy freight work, which had his unique three-cylinders with conjugated valve-gear. The N2 seen here was one of those designed by Gresley and built at Doncaster between 1920 and 1921. As they were designed to work on the Metropolitan Railway, they were given short chimneys. A further fifty of the class were ordered and built by outside manufacturers, including the Yorkshire Engine Company of Sheffield. These 0-6-2Ts were the first with this wheel arrangement since construction of the N1s between 1907 and 1921. (R. Carpenter)

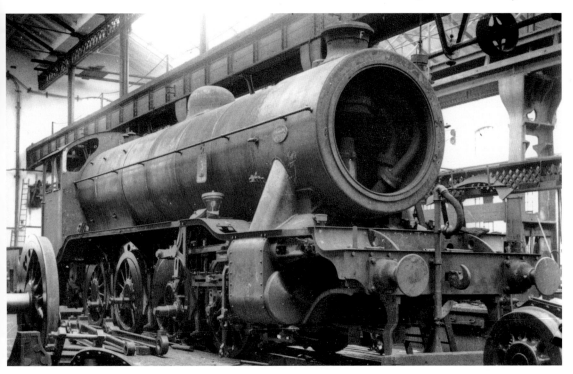

One of the Gresley O2 2-8-0s, No. 2956, under construction at Doncaster works in 1932. As early as 1915, Gresley had turned his thoughts to building a four-cylinder Pacific locomotive, no doubt inspired by Churchward's Pacific *The Great Bear*, built for the Great Western Railway in 1907. However, he had to wait until 1922 before his first Pacific appeared. This was the famous *Flying Scotsman*, although when turned out from Doncaster it was named *Great Northern* and numbered 1470, a second engine (No. 1471) following, both as GNR engines, before the 'grouping' of 1923 when they went into LNER ownership. It was the third engine, for the Wembley Exhibition of 1924, No. 1472, which was given the name of the *Flying Scotsman*, the title given, unofficially, to the 10 a.m. GNR departure from King's Cross to Edinburgh. Following the Wembley Exhibition, when the *Flying Scotsman* was displayed next to the smaller GWR 'Castle' class 4-6-0 No. 4073 *Caerphilly Castle*, which was advertised as Britain's most powerful express engine, the LNER directors arranged for the A1 Pacific to be tested against the GWR loco. In the event, the GWR engine won. Gresley went on to improve his Pacifics in the light of the competition by introducing long-lap piston valves and increasing boiler pressure from 180 to 220 psi, increasing superheating and slightly reducing cylinder diameter with such success that the rest is history. The A1s were transformed, leading to the streamlined A4s and the world steam speed record when 4468 *Mallard* reached 126 mph in 1938. That record still stands. (R. Carpenter)

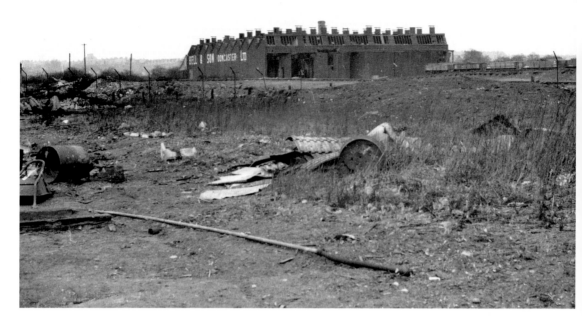

The LNWR had a small presence at Doncaster, its locoshed here closing with the 'grouping' of 1923, which provided engines for coal traffic emanating from the locality. The remains of the shed can be seen here as it appeared on 26 March 1961 after being abandoned by Bell & Son Ltd. (R. Carpenter)

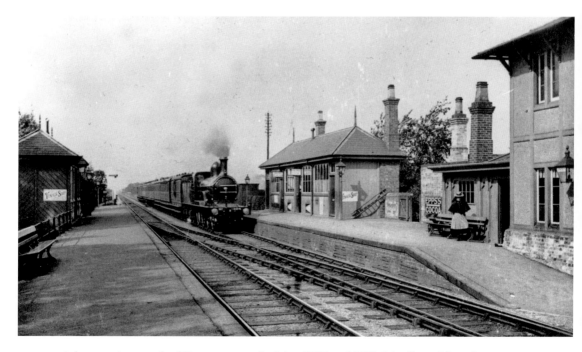

Arksey station, north of Doncaster, on the joint GNR and NER joint line with an Ivatt 4-4-0, No. 1304, at the head of a local train. The engine was one of the GNR Ivatt types built locally at Doncaster works. (LOSA)

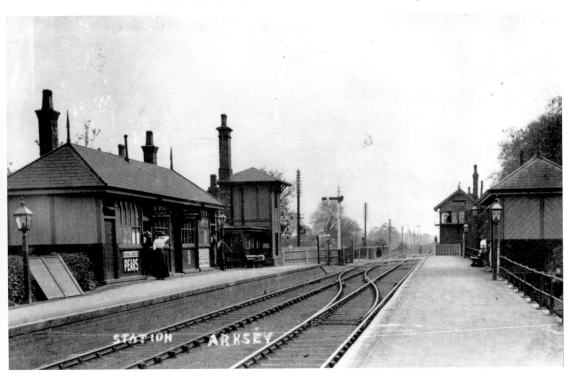

Another view of Arksey station in 1905, showing the waiting area and level crossing. The signal box is on the right, with a lower quadrant signal controlling the level crossing and railway. (LOSA)

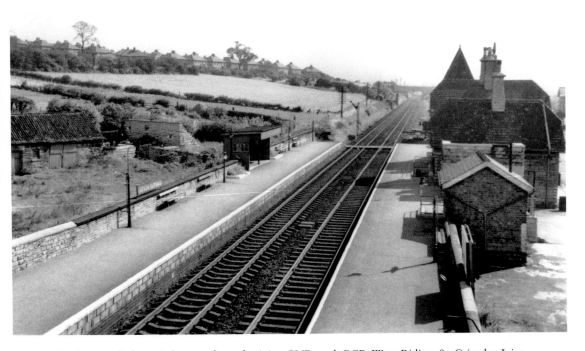

Further north from Arksey and on the joint GNR and GCR West Riding & Grimsby Joint Railway lay South Elmsall station, seen here looking north on 6 September 1966. (H. Priestley)

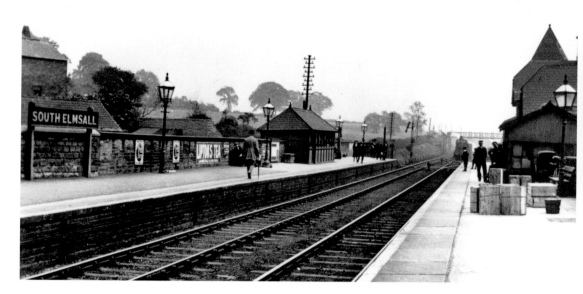

Another view of South Elmsall station as it appeared in the early twentieth century. (LOSA)

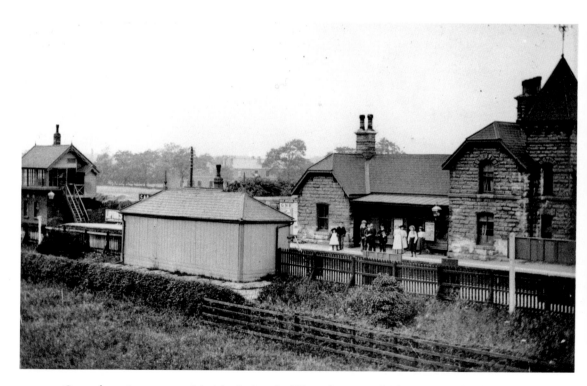

Carcroft station, seen as Adwick, during the Edwardian period. The junction for the line to Leeds was at this point. The station at this time was the joint property of the GCR and GNR, as was the line through to Leeds Central. (LOSA)

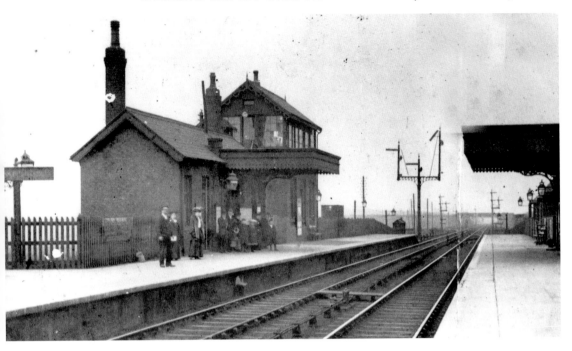

The station at Tingley on the line to Leeds in the early twentieth century. (LOSA)

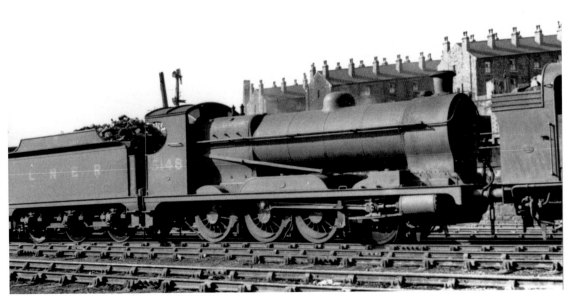

Between Tingley and Leeds lay the locoshed at Ardsley, seen here on 27 June 1937 with GCR Robinson Q4 0-8-0 No. 5148 in the shed yard. (H. Casserley)

LONDON, PETERBRO', NOTTINGHAM, MANCHESTER, LIVERPOOL, DONCASTER, WAKEFIELD, LEEDS, YORK, &c.—G.N.

Offices—King's Cross Sta., N. Gen. Man., Oliver R. H. Bury. Sec., E. H. Burrows. Chief Traff. Man., W. J. Grinling. Gen. Supt., J. Proud.

Week Days.

Miles	Down.	1	2	3	4	5	6	7	8	9	10	11	12	13	14	15	16	17	18	19	20	21	22	23	24	25	26	27	28	29	30
		mrn	mrn	mrn	mrn	mrn	mrn	mrn	mrn	mrn	mrn	mrn	mrn	mrn	mrn	mrn	mrn	mrn	mrn	mrn	mrn	mrn	mrn	aft	aft	Dd	aft	aft	mrn	aft	mrn
			Special Express to Leeds and York.								Mondays only.			Breakfast Car Express, London to Leeds.			Wednesdays only.		Saturdays only.			Luncheon and Dining Car Exp., London to York, Newcastle, Edinburgh, Dundee, and Aberdeen.	Luncheon Car Express, London to Leeds.			Luncheon & Dining Car Express.					
	KING'S CROSS (G.N.) ¶ dep.		3 15				5 5			5 20				7 15				7 45		8 45		10 0	1010			1035			1032		1145
—	Broad Street ¶ ″																	7 15		8 27						1011			1011		1127
2½	Finsbury Park ¶ ″						5 10			5 26								7 53		8 51						1041			1039		1151
17¾	Hatfield ¶ ″									5 50								8 23		9 15									1114		1217
32	Hitchin ¶ ″									6 12	8 10							8 45		9 35						1121			1145		1239
36	Three Counties									6 19	8 17							8 52											1153		
37	Arlesey and Shefford Road ‖									6 22	8 20							8 55											1158		
41	Biggleswade									6 31	8 29							9 4											12 7		
44	Sandy 441									6 37	8 35							9 14											1215		1255
47½	Tempsford									6 44	8 41							9 20											1221		
51¾	St. Neots									6 52	8 49							9 28											1230		
55¾	Offord and Buckden									6 59	8 56							9 35											1238		
58¾	Huntingdon 301, 599									7 5	9 3							9 42		10 6									1246		1 14
63½	Abbotts Ripton									7 14								9 51											1255		
69½	Holme 367									7 24								10 1											1 6		
72½	Yaxley and Farcet [383									7 31								10 8											1 13		
76¼	Peterbro' (Cowgate) 302, 304, a						6 32			7 37				8 41				1014		1028			1132			1212			1 19		1 37
160½	392 CROMER (Beach) arr.						1025							1257												3 26					
—	Peterbro' 388, 390, 443, dep.					5 30	6 36			7 45				8 44		9 15				1033	1037		1135			1216			Stop		1 42
84¾	Tallington ** [444, 593					5 44				7 59						9 31					1051										
88½	Essendine 367, 374					5 53	6 54			8 8						9 42					11 1					1234					2 2
92½	374 STAMFORD (Water Street) arr.					6 25	7 15			8 20						1010					1115					1246					2 15
	374 STAMFORD (Water Street) dep.					5 40	6 35			7 52						9 30					1045					1215					1 45
92¼	Little Bytham ‡‡					6 2				8 16						9 52					11 9										
97	Corby					6 13				8 25						10 3					1118										
102	Great Ponton					6 24				8 35						1016					1128										
105½	Grantham 368, 370, 384 arr.					6 30	7 19			8 41				9 23		1025				1111	1134	12 0	1211			1258					2 27
130	368 LINCOLN (High Street) arr.						8 14							1025		11½c				1211						1 48					
128½	370 NOTTINGHAM (Victoria) ″					7 54	8 6			9 28				1013						1218			1251			2 25					3 31
	373 NOTTINGHAM (Victoria) dep.					5 25				7 50				8 32			9 25			1010		11 0				1150					
—	Grantham dep.					6 32	7 21			8 43				9 25			1045			1114		12 5	1213		1235	1 2					2 31
109¾	Barkstone					6 39				8 50							1052								1244						
111½	Hougham					6 44				8 55							1057								1249						
115¼	Claypole					6 52				9 3							11 5								1258						
120	Newark §§ 368, 590, 600 arr.					7 0	7 38			9 11							1113			1132					1 9	1 20					2 50
—	373 NOTTINGHAM (Vic.) dep.						6 40			8 10							Stop			1024						1225					1 50
—	Newark dep.					7 2	7 39			9 13										1135						1 22				1 27	2 52
126¼	Carlton-on-Trent					7 12				9 23																				1 37	
127¾	Crow Park, for Sutton-on-Trent					7 16				9 27																				1 41	q
131¼	Dukeries Junction 660, 661									9 35																				1 49	
132	Tuxford †					7 26				9 38									1130											1 52	3 8
138½	Retford 584, 649, 654 arr.					7 37	8 2			9 48				10 3					1140	1158						1 46				2 2	3 18
146	654 WORKSOP arr.					8 6	8 35			Stop				1023						1 28						3 5				3 5	
161½	654 SHEFFIELD (Victoria) ″					8 31	9 0							1047						1 55						3 42				3 42	
237¾	655 STOCKPORT (Tiviot Dale) ″					9 46	1041k							1k26						3 25						5 22				5 22	
203	655 MANCHESTER (Lon. Rd) ″					9 53	1015							1213						3 23						5 10				5 10	
209	655 ″ (Central) ″					1024	11 9							1215						4 10						5 51				5 51	
202¾	655 LIVERPOOL (Central) ″					1035	1215a							1a15						4 30						6 37				6 37	
—	Retford dep.					Stop	8 4		8 8					10 5	1012					12 0						1 48				2 7	3 21
141¾	Sutton								8 14						1018															2 13	
144	Ranskill						8 13		8 19						1024															2 18	
145¾	Scrooby								8 23						1028															2 22	
147¾	Bawtry ††						8 19		8 28						1034					1213										2 27	3 34
151¼	Rossington [655, 721								8 36						1042															2 35	
156	Doncaster 382, 389, 648, arr.		6 4				8 30		8 44					1026	1050					1225			1 8			2 9				2 43	3 46
196¾	721 HULL (Paragon) arr.		8 15			mrn	1010		1010					1155	1228								2 29			3 41					4 58

Miles	Down.	1	2	3	4	5	6	7	8	9	10	11	12	13	14	15	16	17	18	19	20	21	22	23	24	25	26	27	28	29	30
				Wednesdays only.								Mondays only.												Through Train, Doncaster to Huddersfield and Blackburn.					Via Pontefract.		
—	Doncaster dep.	5 20	6 9	6 15		7 45	8 36						9 10	1030	1125								1 11	1 15		2 16		2 20			
160	Carcroft & Adwick-le-Street	5 26		6 30		7 52							9 18		1132									1 22				2 27			
162	Hampole					7 56							9 23		1136													2 32			
164½	South Elmsall			6 54		8 0							9 28		1140									1 30				2 38			
167¾	Hemsworth			7 11		8 7							9 35		1147													2 45			
170¼	Nostell					8 13							9 41		1153													2 51			
172	Hare Park and Crofton					8 18							9 45		1158													2 55			
174	Sandal [378, 669, 792					8 22							9 49		12 2													2 59			
175¾	Wakefield (Westgate) arr.		6 33	7 53		8 26	9 0						9 53	1055	12 6								1 35			2 41		3 3			
176½	″ (Kirkgate) 736 ″		6 44	7 50		9 8	9 8							1144	1244									1 45		2 51		3 23			
193¾	378 BRADFORD (Exchange) arr.						9 40							1128	1 6								2 10			3 23					
201¾	380 HALIFAX 736 ″		7j45	9j21			1013c								1j39									2j42		4 2		4j18			
190¾	736 HUDDERSFIELD j ″		7 37	8 45			1016L							12L8	1 45									2 28		4 7		4 7			
185¼	376 HOLBECK (H. Level) ″		6 52			8 51	9 18						1016	1111	1231								1 52			3 1		3 31			
202¾	708 HARROGATE arr.		7 50				1037						1144	1259	1 53								3 7					5 6			
214¼	708 RIPON ″		8 46				1157						1213		2 39								3 45					5 42			
185¾	376 LEEDS (Central) arr.		6 59			8 55	9 22						1019	1115	1234								1 56			3 5		3 35			
195¼	394 BRADFORD (v. Holbeck) ″		7 47			9 21							1053															4 11			
201	736 HALIFAX (v. Holbeck) ″					9 49	1013						1130	1231	1 32		noon						2 25						aft		
—	Doncaster dep.		6 13		6 55		8 33					1015			1153		12 0			1229			1 20			2 14			2 38	3 32	3 50
158	Arksey				7 0							1020					12 5														
163	Moss				7 10							1030					1215														
166	Balne				7 16							1036					1221														
168¼	Heck				7 20							1040					1225														
169¾	Temple Hirst				7 26			m		mrn		1046					1231														
174¼	Selby 696, 719, 724, 726				7 35		8 55	9 13		1025		1056					1239			1257			1 44			2 37	3 45			3 58	4 13
205½	726 HULL (Paragon) arr.				9 25		9 50					1232					2 4			2 4			2 34			3 59					5 50
178¼	Riccall				7 51			9 23		1034							1251										3 54				
181¼	Escrick				7 57			9 30		1040							1257			d							4 0				d
184	Naburn				8 3			9 36		1046							1 3										4 6				d
188	York 684, 714, 715, 720 arr.		6 55		8 15		9 18	9 49		1057					1235		1 14			1 25		1 42	2 10			3 0	4 17		3 54	4 25	4 40
208	708 HARROGATE 713, 714 arr.		8 20					11 8		1252					1 39							2 32	3 4			4 9					5 42
219½	708 RIPON ″		8 46		9 57			1157		1 46					2 39								3 45			4 47					6 25
230	715 SCARBOROUGH ″				1049		1114	1114							1 52								3 48			5 21					5 59
268½	684 NEWCASTLE (Central) ″		1012				11 7	1155							2 45							3 26	5 3			5 25					6 42
393	794 EDINBRO' (Waverley) ″						1 32	3 30														6 15				8 46					
440¼	808 GLASGOW ‡ ″						3 25	5 7														7 35				1028					
452¼	800 DUNDEE (Tay Bridge) ″						3 53	6 23														8 6				11 7					
523½	800 ABERDEEN § ″						6 10	8 50														10 5									
440¾	806 PERTH (v. Forth Bridge) ″						3 32	6 26														7 51				1036					
558¾	806 INVERNESS ″						8 0																			5A10					

For Notes, see pages 346 and 347; for Continuation of Trains, see pages 344 to 347.

A 1910 timetable for Great Northern Railway main line passenger services between King's Cross, Doncaster, Wakefield and Leeds showing connections to Sheffield Victoria. (Author)

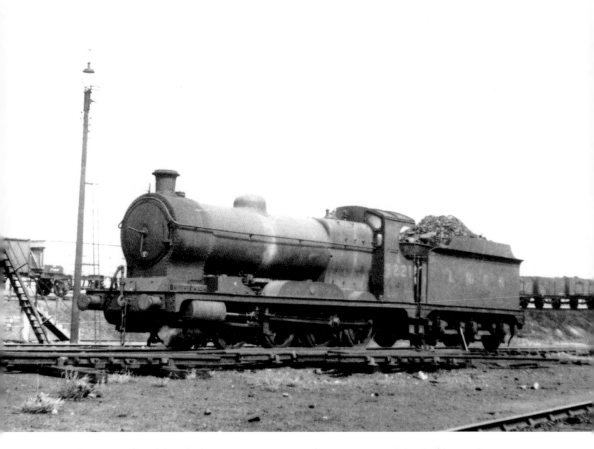

Another view of Ardsley shed on 26 June 1950 with ex-LNER ex-GCR Robinson Q4 0-8-0 No. 3221 on shed, still with its pre-nationalisation livery. Its condition suggests that it is due for a major overhaul, perhaps at Doncaster, when it will receive its new BR number of 63221 and cycling lion totem of the new British Railways. (H. Casserley).

FOUR

THE HULL & BARNSLEY RAILWAY

The Hull & Barnsley Railway had the distinction of being the last complete and independent Victorian railway, surviving in its own right for thirty-seven years before being absorbed into the North Eastern Railway in 1922, a few months before the 'grouping' of 1923.

It was at the NER Station Hotel in Hull that the Hull, Barnsley & West Riding Junction Railway & Dock Company was established in 1879 (the Hull & Barnsley Railway title did not come into existence until 1905). An Act was obtained in 1880 and the H&B was opened in 1885 at a cost of around £4 million, making it the most expensive railway ever built. The problem for the HB&WRJR&DC was that the NER's Hull–Selby line had taken the low ground at the Humber estuary, leaving the new company to find a route through the Yorkshire Wolds, further north. Many embankments and cuttings were required – the longest cutting being at Little Weighton, over three-quarters of a mile long – as well as three tunnels, two of which were short (the 1,226-yard Barnsdale Tunnel and the 685-yard Brierley Tunnel), but the third of which, Drewton, was 2,116 yards long. The line rose to a summit of 250 feet, which meant that heavy coal trains, the mainstay of freight traffic on the line, required double-heading. The line had two junctions with the Lancashire & Yorkshire Railway south of Carlton, connecting with that company's line to Leeds and Goole and, at Brierley Junction, for access to the coalfields at Wakefield and Grimethorpe.

Lack of finance was always a problem and a plan to bring a new station to Hull city centre had to be abandoned. Therefore, the H&B terminus was based on its carriage sheds at Cannon Street in a rather rough part of town. The station was reached by a spur from the freight line, which went around northern Hull to its Alexandra Dock, the largest in Hull, opened just before the railway. A special train was run from Hull to Stairfoot, near Barnsley, on 25 May 1885, but it was not until 27 July that regular passenger services began, with thirteen weekday trains each way and four on Sundays. Substantial stations were provided at Beverley Road (north Hull), Willerby and Kirkella, Little Weighton, South Cave, North Cave, Newport, Sandholme, Eastrington, Howden, Barmby, Drax and Carlton before the line entered South Yorkshire and passed stations at Balne Moor, Kirk Smeaton (with its junction for branches to Denaby and Wath), Upton and North Elmsall, and Hemsworth and South Kirkby (opened in 1881), arriving at Cudworth.

An agreement with the MR for access to Barnsley was rejected by the House of Lords, and the H&B had to make do with its terminus at Cudworth, which had been built by the MR, the H&B having to pay £20,000 for its own platform and footbridge to connect it with the rest of the station. The Hull company was offered refreshment facilities by the

MR, at a cost of £600, but this was rejected. By 1905, the H&B closed its own station at Cudworth and began using the MR platforms. In 1905, the H&B gained running powers to Sheffield and began operating four trains a day between the Steel City and Hull. The company built 4-4-0 tender locomotives for this service and even brought in 'comfortable' bogie coaches. Despite these efforts, the service only ran for twelve years, ceasing in 1917.

A working agreement was reached with the NER for freight traffic and, by 1900, there were exchange sidings at Carlton, increased connections with local collieries, and a 3-mile freight-only line to the GCR at Stairfoot. However, passenger services were a failure, only four-wheeled coaches being used for the first twenty years, claims often being made that three-coach trains would often arrive at Cannon Street without a single passenger. Indeed, there was a disparity of receipts between passenger and freight traffic, there being some twenty-eight goods trains operating each way in comparison to the small number of passenger services; by June 1900, only £14,058 was obtained in passenger receipts compared to £174,043 for freight. By 1922, only two of nine weekday trains went beyond Howden to Cudworth, the H&B being absorbed into the NER in April of that year, all becoming part of the new LNER eight months later. The LNER introduced name changes to some stations: Newport became Wallington, Eastrington and Howden added 'North' and 'South' respectively, Drax had 'Abbey' added, and Carlton had 'Towers' attached. In 1924, the LNER opened a link to Hull Paragon station, closing Beverley Road and Cannon Street to passengers. Sentinel steam railcars were introduced on passenger services in 1928, and the following year the eastern section of the old H&B became part of the Hull & District Interval Service, providing an hourly service to South Howden, with an additional unstaffed halt provided at Springhead. When opened in 1929, this new halt was regarded as possibly the smallest station in Great Britain and was situated close to the former H&B workshops. The line west to Cudworth was the first British main line to lose all of its passenger services when they ceased in 1932, evidence that the H&B never succeeded as a passenger line.

Although the H&B was not a great financial success, the company did have plans to reach Halifax and Huddersfield, but these came to nothing and the only extensions to the main line were two branches. The first of these was the 11-mile line from Wranbrook Junction, 3 miles south-west of Kirk Smeaton, to mines at Cadeby and Denaby. The local colliery company proposed and built the line, using the title of 'South Yorkshire Junction Railway', but it was always operated by the H&B. Although it was a freight line, passenger stations were situated at Pickburn and Brodsworth, Sprotborough, and Denaby and Conisbrough. Passenger services began from the opening in 1894, with two trains each weekday between Denaby and Carlton. Withdrawal of such services was proposed as early as 1895, but they lasted until 1903 and the line then concentrated on freight for the next sixty-four years, miners' trains operating as required. The line was finally closed in 1967. The Denaby end, however, continued in use into the 1970s, the old GCR link across the River Don being the last to close in 1981. Only Sprotborough station survives as evidence that the branch once existed.

Wrangbrook Junction was also the starting point for the eight-mile H&B branch to Wath, which began as the independent Hull & South Yorkshire Extension Railway in

1897 and was taken over by the H&B in 1898. Although mainly for freight, it also had a passenger service that was more numerous and lasted longer than that on the Denaby branch. When opened in 1902, there were five weekday trains between the H&B station at Wath and Kirk Smeaton (which was rebuilt with an extra bay platform for this service). There were also another six weekday trains from Wath to Hickleton and Thurnscoe, with one going through to Moorhouse and South Elmsall. By 1922, there were still seven weekday trains due to the proximity of the GCR station at Wath, which provided connections for Barnsley and Doncaster. Regular passenger services, however, ended in 1929, although seaside excursions continued until 1939. The branch closed in stages, but the whole line had gone by 1964. Only the station buildings at Wath still survive.

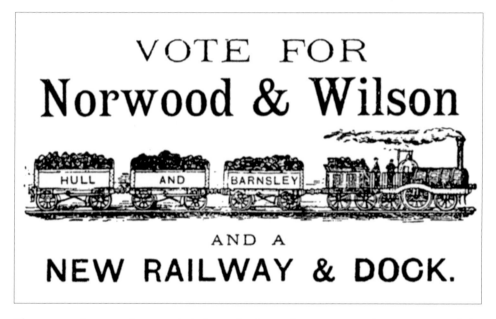

The proposed new railway and dock received popular support and some 7,000 of the population of Hull turned up to witness the cutting of the first sod on 15 January 1881 by the chairman of the HB&WRJR&DC. Prominent members of Hull Corporation gave support to the project, giving it a sense of respectability. A large fireworks display at the event increased the sense of celebration. Enthusiasm for the plan to build the new line and dock was not confined to Hull and inflammatory speeches were made to fire up enthusiasm, the chairman claiming, in a speech of 22 March 1880, that the new line would unite the working people of Hull with those of the West Riding of Yorkshire, as well as serve the interests of the traders and merchants of Hull. Such was the strong feeling towards the new railway that a deputation was sent to represent some 200,000 miners in South Yorkshire and North Derbyshire. Although it was not to be apparent at that time, it would be the labour of these miners that would become the very lifeblood of the Hull & Barnsley Railway. Such was the popular feeling of goodwill towards the proposed new project that three of the four candidates in the general election of 1880 declared their support for the new railway; the fourth, Charles Wilson, resigned from the board of the NER and was in favour of the scheme. The Conservative candidate, J. B. Pope, had interests in Denaby Main Colliery, which would be served by the new railway. Another candidate, a Mr Atkinson, had been a supporter of the Hull, South West & Junction Railway plan of 1874. It was, however, the Liberals, represented by Norwood and Wilson, who won the election. It is their poster shown here that demonstrates their support for the new line. It is interesting to note that the train shown is hauling coal. (Beverley Record Office)

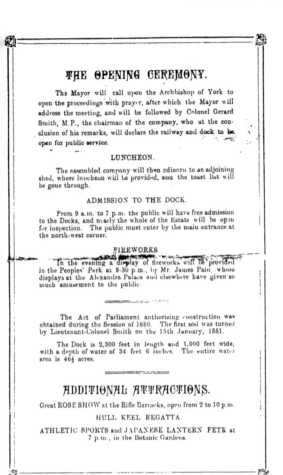

THE OPENING CEREMONY.

The Mayor will call upon the Archbishop of York to open the proceedings with prayer, after which the Mayor will address the meeting, and will be followed by Colonel Gerard Smith, M.P., the chairman of the company, who at the conclusion of his remarks, will declare the railway and dock to be open for public service.

LUNCHEON.

The assembled company will then adjourn to an adjoining shed, where luncheon will be provided, and the toast list will be gone through.

ADMISSION TO THE DOCK.

From 9 a.m. to 7 p.m. the public will have free admission to the Docks, and nearly the whole of the Estate will be open for inspection. The public must enter by the main entrance at the north-west corner.

FIREWORKS.

In the evening a display of fireworks will be provided in the Peoples' Park at 9-30 p.m., by Mr. James Pain, whose displays at the Alexandra Palace and elsewhere have given so much amusement to the public.

The Act of Parliament authorising construction was obtained during the Session of 1880. The first soil was turned by Lieutenant-Colonel Smith on the 15th January, 1881.

The Dock is 2,300 feet in length and 1,000 feet wide, with a depth of water of 34 feet 6 inches. The entire water area is 46¼ acres.

ADDITIONAL ATTRACTIONS.

Great ROSE SHOW at the Rifle Barracks, open from 2 to 10 p.m.

HULL KEEL REGATTA.

ATHLETIC SPORTS and JAPANESE LANTERN FETE at 7 p.m., in the Botanic Gardens.

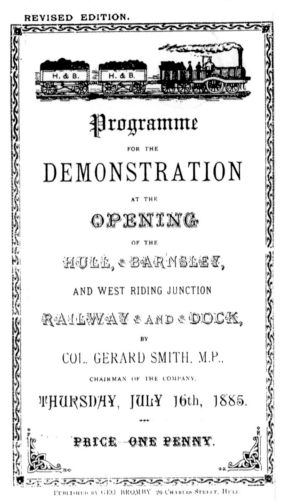

REVISED EDITION.

Programme

FOR THE

DEMONSTRATION

AT THE

OPENING

OF THE

HULL, BARNSLEY,

AND WEST RIDING JUNCTION

RAILWAY AND DOCK,

BY

COL. GERARD SMITH, M.P.,

CHAIRMAN OF THE COMPANY.

THURSDAY, JULY 16th, 1885.

***

PRICE ONE PENNY.

PUBLISHED BY GEO. BROMBY, 26 CHARLES STREET, HULL.

The programme of events for the opening day of the Hull & Barnsley Railway on 16 July 1885. Construction of the new line was always hampered by lack of funds, the route being an ambitious one involving deep cuttings and tunnels through the limestone Yorkshire Wolds. Indeed, when the Hull & Barnsley was originally registered, it only had capital of £500,000 in 25,000 shares at £20 each. A deposit of £2 2s per share was required on application. Following the engineers' report on the proposed route, capital was raised to £700,000. Proposed branches to join the Midland Railway and another to Market Weighton (which never materialised) and Driffield meant that a further £350,000 in capital was needed and shares were issued. Shares were mainly taken in small amounts of £100 to £1,000, although some bought between £3,000 and £7,500's worth. As the line became more expensive to construct, there were exchanges between shareholders in Hull and London investors. The latter had provided most of the capital but were not interested in Hull or the independence of the H&B. However, when the chairman, Gerard Smith, favoured takeover by a larger company in 1889 as a way of resolving the company's financial difficulties, Hull shareholders felt betrayed. In contrast to the early years of enthusiasm and rejoicing, there were bitter conflicts as the line was constructed. The H&B, however, did not fall into the hands of larger rivals and maintained its independence right up until 1922, when it was taken over by the North Eastern Railway, just prior to the 1923 'grouping' whereby the whole system in the Hull area became part of the new London & North Eastern Railway. (Beverley Record Office)

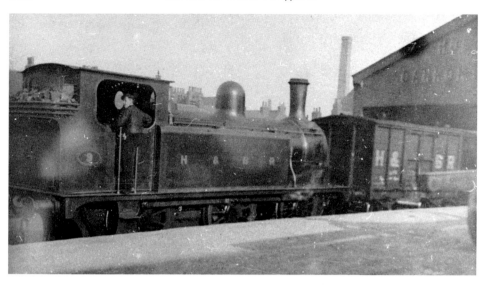

Cannon Street station of the H&B in 1905 with Beyer-Peacock-built 0-6-0 tank loco No. 9 on a freight train. The H&B at Hull was carried on an embankment which encircled the city and ran roughly parallel with the NER's Victoria Dock line. The eastern end started at Alexandra Dock and was linked to King George Dock, jointly owned with the NER. The western end of the dock line terminated at Neptune Street goods station. A spur was constructed from Sculcoates Junction which ran south to serve Beverley Road station at Fitzroy Street and the H&B terminus at Cannon Street. Both stations closed to passengers in 1924. Cannon Street, however, remained open to goods traffic until 1964. A power station was opened at Sculcoates in 1895 on a site bounded by the H&B, the railway company transporting the coal used from the mines of South Yorkshire. The goods yard at Neptune Street was leased from BR by Albert Draper & Sons to store redundant rolling stock between 1963 and 1969. Some 732 steam locos were scrapped on the site. The yard was closed in 1984. (R. Carpenter)

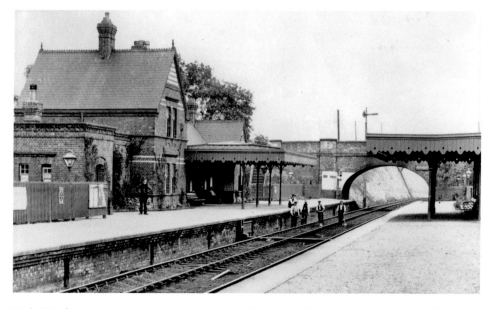

Little Weighton station as it appeared early in the twentieth century. Despite being little used, the buildings are quite substantial, a sign of hope that was never fulfilled. The canopies over the platforms were most unusual in design and were a feature of the stations along the route. (LOSA)

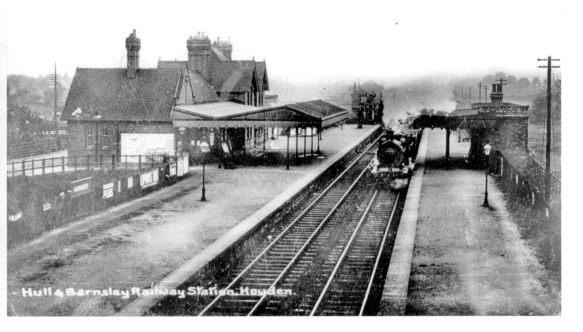

The substantial station at Howden with a coal train from South Yorkshire passing through. The area around the station had the highest population between Hull and the South Yorkshire coalfields served by the H&B, which guaranteed local train services long after such trains had ceased over the rest of the line. Indeed, the Hull–South Howden section had four to seven passenger trains a day. However, the last scheduled passenger train, the 8.30 p.m. from Hull to South Howden, ran on 30 July 1955. The line itself remained open all the way to Cudworth for freight, which state of affairs lasted over the whole route until 1958. (LOSA)

HULL, KNOTTINGLEY, CUDWORTH, and SHEFFIELD.—Hull and Barnsley.

Gen. Man., Edward Watkin; Sec., George Scaum; Supt. of the Line, R. Y. Vickers; Eng., R. Pawley; Loco. Eng., M. Stirling.

A 1910 timetable for H&B trains between Hull and Cudworth, when the line was still owned by the H&B and a reasonable passenger service was still operating. (Author)

SHEFFIELD, CUDWORTH, KNOTTINGLEY, and HULL.—Hull and Barnsley.

Miles from Cudworth	Down. Temple Meads Station,	aft	mrn	mrn	mrn	aft	mrn	aft	mrn	aft	aft	aft	aft	aft		aft	aft	mrn	aft	NOTES.
	539 BRISTOL ....dep.	1135		1 b 3				9 45		2 17	3 25		4 52			7 55		1125		
	578 BOURNEMOUTH WEST ‖ ″	6 45						8 37		9 40	1220		2 5			4 20		8 & 5		
	578 CARDIFF (G.W.) ...... ″	1039					7 54			1250	1 25		4 0			6 8		1021		
	578 CHELTENHAM ! ...... ″	9 32		2020			1045		1149	3 24	4 37		6 12			9 32		1232		b Except Mondays.
	539 BIRMINGHAM (NewSt.) ″	2 12		3055	6 5		1147		1250	4 28	5 45		7 18			1125		1 42		c Leaves at 7 aft. on
	538 LONDON (St. Pancras) ″	12 5		2045	5 0		1025		12 0	3 30	4 55		6 0			12 5		1130		Saturdays.
	538 LEICESTER (Lon. Rd.) ″	2 28		4043	7 10		1133		2 5	5 0	6 15		7 35			2 28		1 42		d Through Train,
	538 NOTTINGHAM ...... ″	12 5			7 25		1255		2 43	5 50	7 20		7 42			1245		2 5		Sheffield to Hull.
	539 DERBY .... ″	3 28		5035	7 52		1243		2 5	5 30	6 57		8 38			3 28		2 45		h Stop to set down
	566 LIVERPOOL (Central). ″				5 10		1030		1255	3 30	5 30		6 30					1115		from beyond Cud-
	566 MANCHESTER (Cen.).. ″				6 32		1120		1 50	4 50	6 35		7 25					12 0		worth and Knot-
	539 SHEFFIELD (Mid.)..... ″	4 38		7 30	9 8		2 43		3 55	6 58	8 28		9 50			4 38		3 34		tingley.
	619 BARNSLEY (Crt. Hse.) ″	mrn		7 50	9 0		2 5		4 8	6 c 3	8 44		11 3					3 40		k Bournemouth Cen-
—	Cudworth ....dep.	5 10		8 15	9 55		2 35		4 30		7 29	8 58		1115			5 10		4 30		tral.
4	Hemsworth & South Kirkby.			8 24	10 4		2 45		4 39		7 38	9 7		1124					4 39		
8	Upton and North Elmsall...				10 9						7 44								4 44		* Central Station.
12	Kirk Smeaton (below).......				1016		Sig.		Sig.		7 52								4 51		‡ Queen's Road,
—	730 BLACKPOOL (T.R.) ..dep.			7 40			9 55			3 0								1 37		Lansdown.
—	730 MANCHESTER (Vic.).. ″			7 5	9 5		1140			5 10								4 0		§ Nearly 1 mile to
—	M‖s Knottingley ......dep.			9 57	1237		2 20			7 45								7 35		North Eastern
—	6 Hensall			10 7	1247		2 30			7 54								7 45		(Paragon) Station.
—	10½ Carlton ....arr.			1015	1257		2 38			8 1								7 52		‖ Queen's Road Station.
22	Carlton			1029	1220		3 9			8 7								5 37 53		
23	Drax...........			1033	1224		3 13			8 11								5 7 7 57		
25	Barmby.....			1039	1230		3 19			8 17								5 13 8 3		
29	Howden 726	5 52	40	59	1046	1236		3 24		5 14	8 23	9 37				5 52		5 2 08 10		
32	Eastrington		7 49		1062	1242				5 20	8 29							5 26 8 16		
34	Sandholme		7 5		1057	1247		2 15		5 25	8 34							5 31 8 21		
35	Newport (Yorks)		3 2		11 1	1251		2 19		5 29	8 38							5 35 8 25		
38	North Cave.	6 c8	9 9	12 11	7	1257		2 25	3 58	4 45	5 35 6 30	8 44	h	10 0				2 0 5 41 8 31		
59	South Cave.		8 14	16	1111	1	1		2 30	3 42	4 49	5 39 6 34	8 48	h	10 4				2 4 5 45 8 35		
44	Little Weighton...		8 24	25	1120	1	10		2 39	h	4 58	5 43 6 57	h	1013				2 13 5 54 8 44		
47	Willerby and Kirk Ella....		8 31	32	1127	1	17		2 46	3 56	5 5 5 56 50 9	4 10 6	1020				2 20 6 1 8 51		
52	Hull 716 { Beverley Road arr.	6 26	8 41	9 41	1136	1	27		2 56	4 6 5 14 6 6 7	0 9 14 1016 1030					6 26		2 29 6 10 9 1		
53	724, 728 { Cannon Street § ″	6 30	8 45	9 45	1140	1	31		3 0 4 10 5 18 6 10 7	4 9 18 1020 1034					6 30		2 33 6 14 9 5		

The return H&B timetable of 1910, from Cudworth to Hull. (Author)

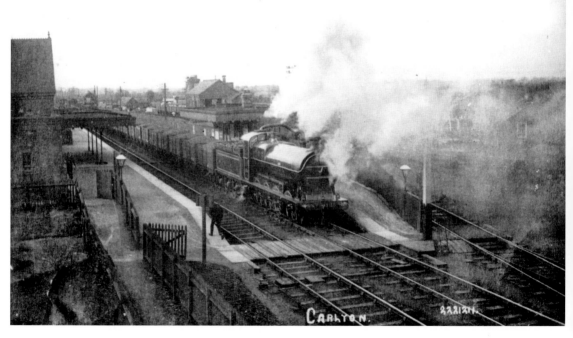

Carlton station in the early twentieth century, with a coal train waiting. Despite the general failure of passenger services along the line, the H&B made a good profit from its coal traffic after reaching agreement with the NER for such trains; the company had heavy freight locos for such work. Here, an 0-8-0 designed by CME Matthew Stirling can be seen at the head of this substantial coal train. A unique feature of these, and other locos built by Stirling for the H&B, was their domeless boiler. These particular engines were introduced in 1907, a total of fifteen were built, and they had 19x26-inch cylinders and Allan straight link motion. The large boilers had Belpaire fireboxes and a total heating surface of 1,859 square feet and a boiler pressure of 200 psi. These engines weighed about 61½ tons. As can be seen, these locos were fully lined out, showing their importance to the H&B. All of these engines were withdrawn under LNER auspices in 1931. (LOSA)

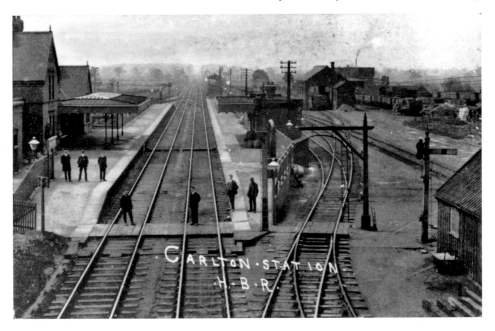

A general view of Carlton station showing the main building and goods yard. The last pick-up goods service from Neptune Street and along the H&B to Carlton was withdrawn in April 1959. Other pick-up goods services ended in stages; the last section to be served was between Hull Springhead and Little Weighton, which finished in 1964.

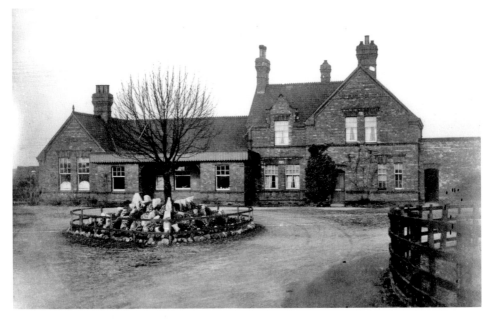

The exterior of Carlton station in the early twentieth century. The line was closed in 1964, the only surviving sections being the freight line through northern Hull; it became the favoured route to Hull's eastern docks, allowing the ex-NER Victoria Dock branch to close. Another small section of the line survives to serve the mighty Drax coal-fired power station with MGR trains. Station buildings have also been restored at South Cave, Drax and Carlton. (LOSA)

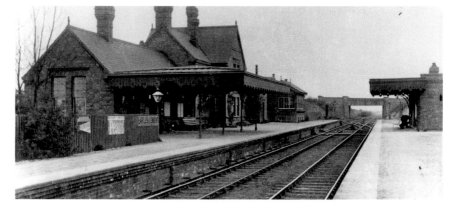

HULL, CUDWORTH, and SHEFFIELD. — North Eastern (Hull and Barnsley Section).

Offices — Hull.

NOTES.

a Stops at 11 34 mrn. when required.

b Except Mondays.

b Stops when required.

c Except Sunday nights.

d Morning time.

e Except Saturdays.

F Arrives Manchester at 9 2 aft. on Saturdays.

g Victoria Station, via Derby.

h Except Sunday mornings.

h Stops at 11 51 mrn. when required.

i Leaves Liverpool 2, (Thurs. only) and 1 30 aft., (Sats. only); Manchester 3, (Thurs. only) and 2 20 aft., (Sats. only).

* ¼ mile to South Eastrington Station.

† Nearly 1½ miles to Hemsworth Station, G.N. and G.C.

‡ Queen's Road, Lansdown.

§ Cannon Street Station; over ¼ mile to Wilmington Station and nearly 1 mile to Hull (Paragon) Station.

¶ 1 mile to North Howden Station.

☞ **For other Trains**

BETWEEN   PAGE

Hull and Howden 768

After takeover by the NER, and before absorption into the LNER, this timetable of 1922 shows the extent of passenger services along the H&B. (Author)

South of Carlton and on to Cudworth, the line passed through Baine Moor before arriving at the junction station of Kirk Smeaton, seen here in the early twentieth century. From here, trains served the branches to Wath and Denaby, the latter branch serving the coalfield there. From Kirk Smeaton, the H&B continued to Cudworth. (LOSA)

KIRK SMEATON and WATH.—North Eastern (Hull and Barnsley Section).

Miles	Up.	Week Days only.									
		mrn	mrn	mrn	aft	Except Sats. { aft	Sats. only { aft	aft	aft	aft	
	Kirk Smeaton ....dep.	7 10	8 50	1055	....	....	....	....	....	5 28	
6	Moorhouse & South Elmsall.	7 24	9 0	11 5	....	....	3 1	....	....	5 38	
9	Hickleton and Thurnscoe ..	7 36	9 6	1111	1 14	3 7	3 7	3 56	....	5 44	
12	Wath 702, 709 ....arr.	7 42	9 12	1117	1 20	3 13	3 13	4 2	....	5 50	

Miles	Down.	Week Days only.									
		mrn	mrn	mrn	aft	Except Sats. { aft	Sats. only { aft	aft	aft	aft	
	Wath.. ....dep.	8 15	9 40	1155	....	1 55	1 55	3 40	4 45	7 10	
3	Hickleton and Thurnscoe ..	8 23	9 47	12 1	....	2 1	2 2	3 46	4 53	7 17	
6	Moorhouse & South Elmsall.	8 30	9 54	12 1	....	2 8	....	....	5 0	7 24	
12	Kirk Smeaton *(above)* .. arr.	8 40	10 4	....	....	....	....	....	5 10	7 34	

A 1922 timetable for branch line trains from Kirk Smeaton to Wath. (Author)

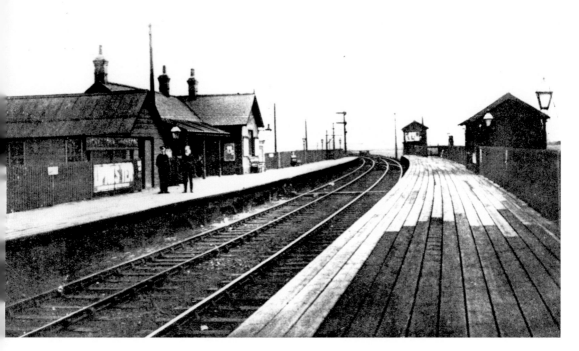

Hickleton and Thurnscoe station on the Wath branch, as seen at the end of the nineteenth century, where a connection could be made with the Manchester, Sheffield & Lincolnshire Railway (later to become the Great Central Railway) for Sheffield. (LOSA)

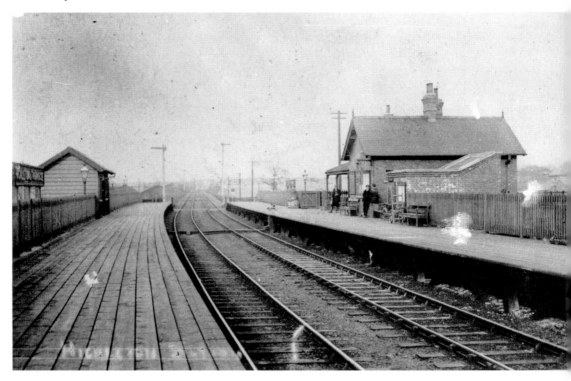

Another view of Hickleton and Thurnscoe station in the same period. (LOSA)

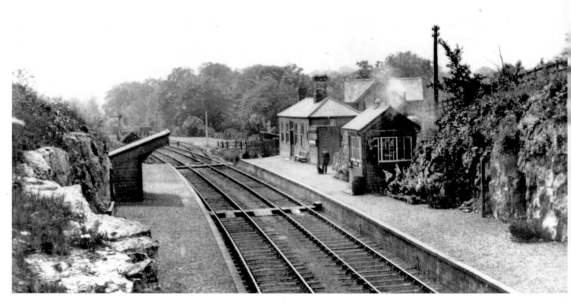

The attractive little station of Sprotborough, at the end of the nineteenth century, on the branch to Denaby from Kirk Smeaton. The only other station on the branch was Pickburn and Brodsworth, just north of here. Like the branch to Wath, this little line also connected with the M&SL at Denaby. (LOSA)

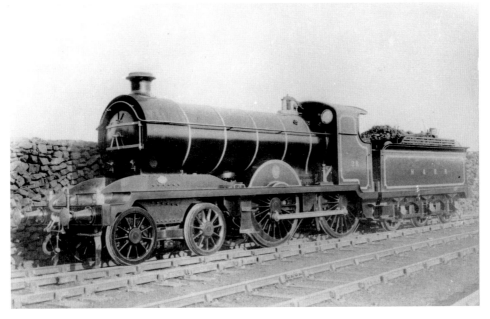

Stirling-built H&B 4-4-0 No. 38 stands outside Hull Springhead shed. These locos had the domeless boilers which were a feature of Stirling's locos and had two 18x26-inch cylinders. The driving wheels were 6 feet 6 inches in diameter and the engines had a boiler pressure of 170 psi. All H&B engines were painted in 'invisible green' which really appeared to be black (thus 'invisible' green). They were lined out in a very attractive bright blue, edged with red on both sides. Matthew Stirling was appointed Chief Mechanical Engineer to the H&B in 1885 at the young age of twenty-nine, after he had been trained under his father, Patrick Stirling, on the Great Northern Railway. During his long service as CME at Hull, he followed the practice of his father and uncle and never built a loco with a domed boiler. (LOSA)

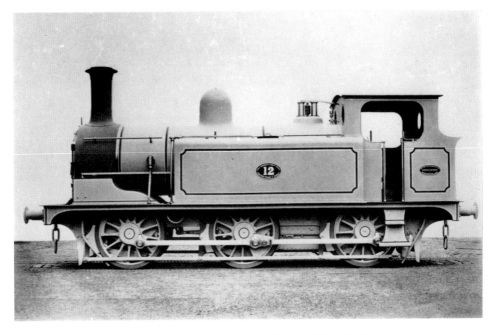

A grey photo of Beyer-Peacock 0-6-0 No. 12, built for the H&B. (LOSA)

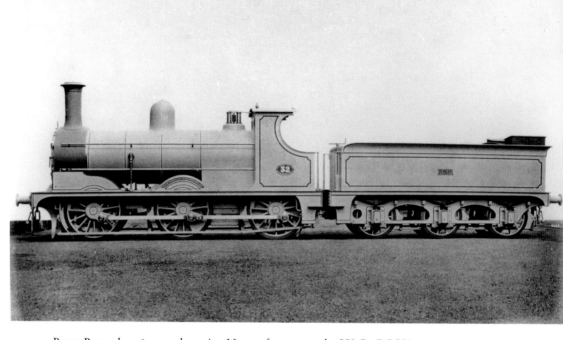

Beyer-Peacock 0-6-0 goods engine No. 32 for use on the H&B. (LOSA)

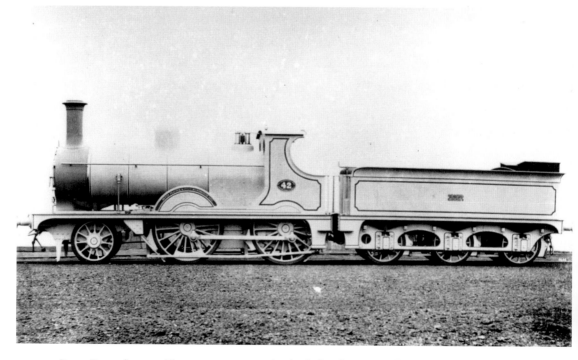

Beyer-Peacock 2-4-0 No. 42 passenger engine built for the H&B. These locos were produced, as with the types in the previous two illustrations, to be used on the H&B while engines of the H&B's own design were built to operate trains over the new route. (LOSA)

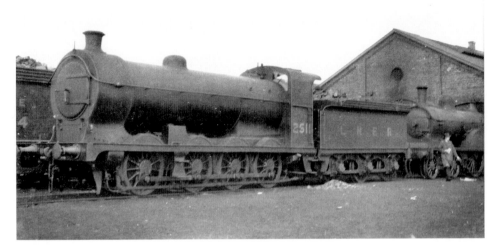

Ex-H&B 0-8-0, as LNER class Q10 No. 2511, on the shed yard at Hull Springhead. The original Stirling domeless boiler, as featured in the image of the 0-8-0 at Carlton station, has been replaced by an LNER domed one with the round-topped firebox replacing the Belpaire type of the original. All of these engines had been withdrawn by 1931. (LOSA)

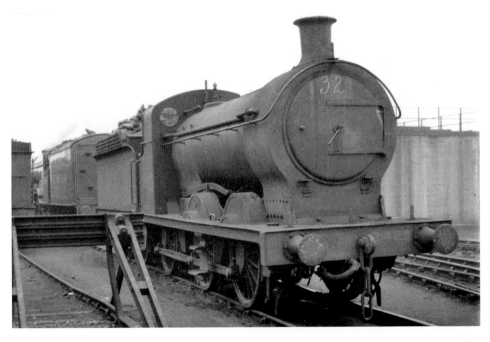

Ex-H&B 0-6-0, as LNER J23 No. 2423, is seen at Hull Springhead shed around 1930. The loco still retains its Stirling domeless boiler and was built at Kitson's of Leeds with a large boiler at the time of 4 feet 10¾ inches. The locos had 5-foot driving wheels, 18x26-inch cylinders and a boiler pressure of 170 psi. (LOSA)

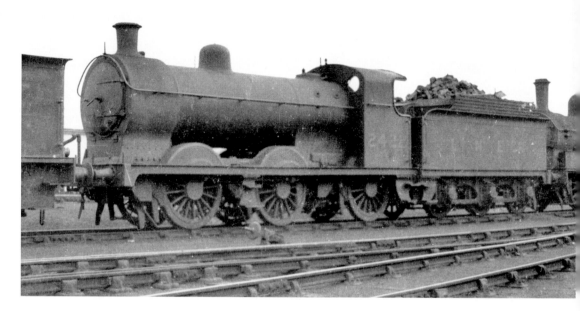

Ex-H&B LNER J28 0-6-0 No. 2422 on the shed yard at Hull Springhead around 1930. These locos did not survive into BR ownership. (LOSA)

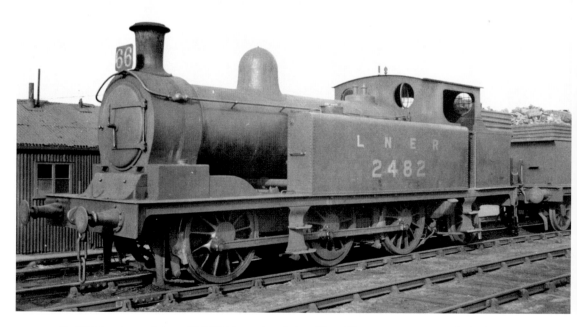

Ex-H&B 0-6-2 tank loco, LNER No. 2482 of class N11. These engines originally had Stirling domeless boilers, this one carrying an LNER domed type. These engines were often used on local passenger trains, and this example is seen at Hull Springhead shed. None of these engines survived into BR ownership. (LOSA)

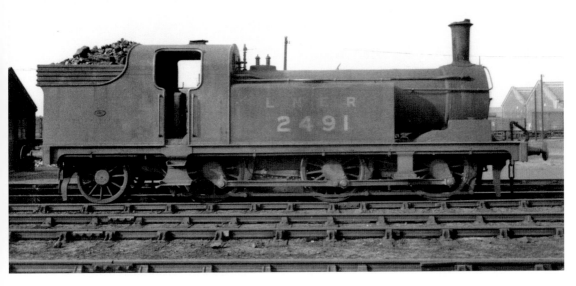

Ex-H&8 0-6-2 tank loco, as LNER class N12 No. 2491, with its original domeless boiler. The engines were built in 1901 and had 4-foot 6-inch driving wheels. None of this class survived into BR ownership. (LOSA)

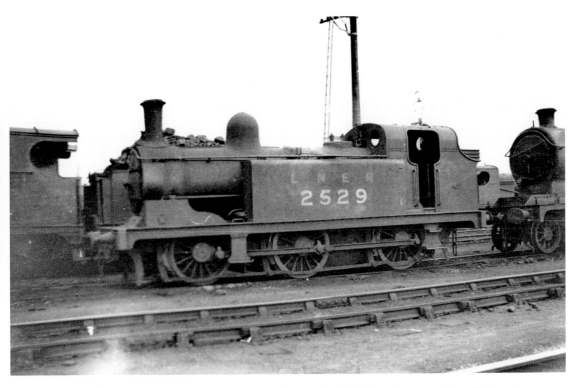

Ex-H&B LNER J75 0-6-0T No. 2529 at Hull Springhead shed in the 1930s. These little tank engines were used on local passenger trains, for the pick-up of goods and for shunting duties in the various freight depots on the H&B. None, however, survived into BR ownership. (LOSA)

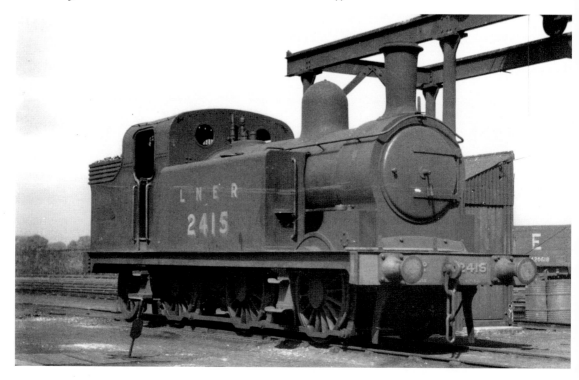

Ex-H&B 0-6-2T, as LNER N13 No. 2415, at Hull Springhead shed around 1934. This loco has an LNER domed boiler – all were originally built with domeless boilers. They were an enlarged version of the H&B N12 class. (LOSA)

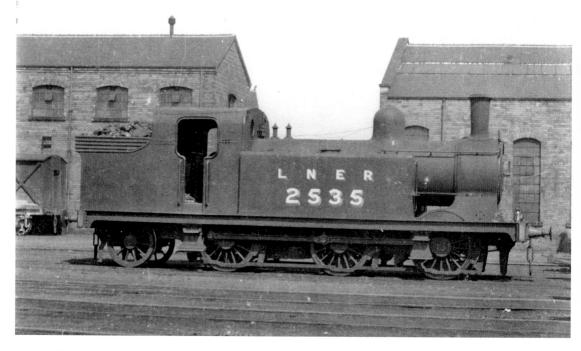

Ex-H&B 0-6-2T, as LNER N13 No. 2535, in Hull in 1934. These engines were built between 1913 and 1914, with 4-foot 6-inch driving wheels, and they survived into BR ownership. (LOSA)

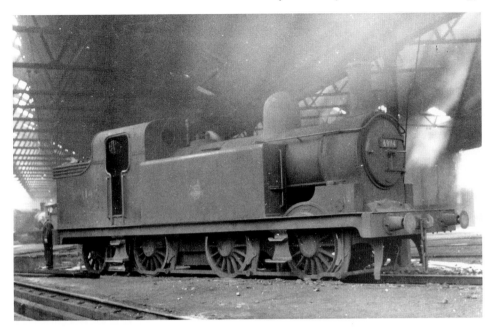

The last N13 0-6-2T to survive, as BR No. 69114, seen here in the shed at Hull around 1954. Only two years later, in 1956, the loco went for scrap, ending a link with the Hull & Barnsley Railway locos that had lasted since opening. (LOSA)

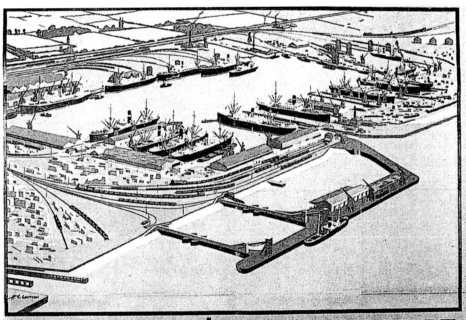

A 1928 poster showing a panoramic view of the Alexandra Dock, which was then in the hands of the LNER. It gives a good idea of the expanse of the dock and the network of railway needed to serve it. (Author)

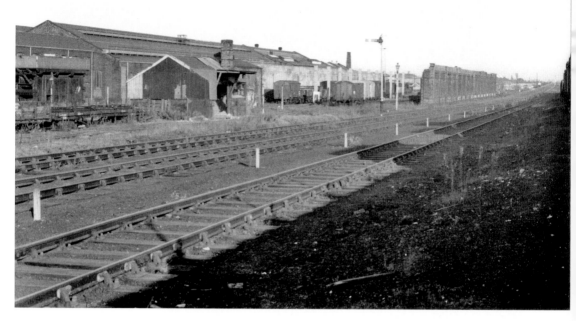

The remains of Hull Springhead shed as it appeared on 13 October 1963, having closed on 22 October 1956. The H&B had a shed here since opening and it was handed over to the NER on 1 April 1922. Before the LNER was formed, however, forty-three of the engines allocated to Springhead had to be condemned and the NER needed to bring in some of its own engines to keep the H&B route running. Thus, when the LNER was formed there were forty-nine former NER locos operating over the H&B, of which twenty-six were based at Springhead shed. Although the shed provided motive power for freight and shunting, there were two 4-4-0s and one 2-4-2 tank allocated for passenger duties. December 1923 saw Springhead with an allocation of 122 engines, 96 being ex-H&B types. As services along the H&B were modified as then LNER, ex-NER locos were gradually transferred away and the last of the Q6 0-8-0s left on 24 May 1927, the last three N9s on 31 May 1927, the last Q5 went on 4 June 1927, and the last J27 0-6-0 on 28 July 1928.

For a year, Springhead relied on ex-H&B locos. In September 1929, 04 2-8-0s Nos 6581 and 6613 arrived for trials on the H&B in an attempt to remove the necessity for double heading of mineral trains, as was the usual practice with native 0-6-0 locos. These new locos were so successful that, within a year, Springhead had an allocation of nineteen 04 locos. Ex-H&B class 8 (J23) 0-6-0s at Springhead were steadily decreasing due to withdrawals and transfers as use was found for them elsewhere after six had gone to York on 12 March 1927. Eventually, they were scattered all over the NE area. By 31 December 1932, the introduction of 04 locos meant that only eight J23 0-6-0s were at Springhead, compared with thirty-four in 1923. Also displaced at this time were H&B class A (Q10) 0-8-0s and, in October and November 1929, examples were sent to Dairycoates, Selby, Borough Gardens and Tyne Dock for trials.

Eventually, only two, Nos 2498 and 2502, were left at Springhead. Six Q6 0-8-0s were transferred from Selby to Dairycoates, allowing a further six 04 2-8-0s to move from Dairycoates to Springhead. By January 1939, only ten former H&B engines were left at Springhead, all being N12 0-6-2Ts, which, along with two J21 0-6-0s and fifteen 04s, completed the allocation of twenty-seven. Early in 1940, the 04s were transferred away to Darlington, Heaton, and West Hartlepool for working extra coal traffic to the south as part of the war effort; they were replaced at Springhead by Q6 0-8-0s from Dairycoates and West Hartlepool. Under a reallocation scheme in March 1943, Springhead lost its 0-8-0s, receiving ten ex-NER Atlantics, Nos 295, 649, 699, 702 703, 705, 742, 1753, 1776 and 1794, along with J24 0-6-0 1892, J25 0-6-0s 1723, 1976, 2056 and 1139, N8 0-6-2T Nos 267, 345, 445, 1104, and N11 0-6-2T Nos 2481 and 2482 from Cudworth shed.

In March 1944, WD Austerity engines returned to this country from Europe and became the mainstay of traffic until the shed closed. Other classes to appear in the post-war years were A7 4-6-2Ts, J73 0-6-0Ts and 350-hp diesel-electric shunters. The shed closed to steam on 15 December 1958, the remaining steam locos having been transferred away on 30 November 1958. They were: J73 0-6-0T 68360 and 68361, BR 3MT 2-6-0 77000 and 77010, WD Austerity 2-8-0 90011, 90233, 90352, 90378, 90427, 90482, 90503, 90511, 90586, 90623, 90677 and 90688. The shed continued in use for diesel locos and DMU maintenance until July 1961. During the Second World War, one GWR Dean Goods 0-6-0 was sold to the War Department and spent some time at Springhead. USA 2-8-0s and 0-6-2Ts were also serviced here. The last H&B loco at Springhead was N13 No. 69119, transferred to Leeds Neville Hill in September 1953; this loco, together with 69117, was withdrawn on 5 July 1955. Only one other surviving H&B loco, No. 69114, was withdrawn on 22 October 1956.

The allocation at Hull Springhead in June 1950 was as follows:

LNER Code SPHEAD
BR Code 53C, becoming 50B in January 1960

Ex-LNER J25 0-6-0	65667, 65705, 65728
Ex-LNER J73 0-6-0T	68360, 68361, 68363
Ex-LNER J77 0-6-0T	68402, 68413, 68429, 68435, 68440
Ex-LNER J72 0-6-0T	68670, 68673, 68676, 68686, 68724, 68743, 68746, 68747, 68751, 68752, 68753, 69001, 69002, 69003, 69009
Ex-LNER N13 0-6-2T	69111, 69112, 69113, 69116, 69119
Ex-LNER A7 4-6-2T	69774, 69776, 69785, 69789
Ex-WD 2-8-0	90007, 90010, 90011, 90047, 90052, 90094, 90116, 90160, 90217, 90233, 90378, 90429, 90470, 90478, 90497, 90571, 90586, 90661, 90677, 90688
Total: 55	

Along with its freight duties, the shed also had five passenger duties, which were as follows:

1. 6.10 a.m. South Howden and return. The loco was on pilot duties until 12.30 p.m. Then three return trips to South Howden and North Cave (four on Saturdays), commencing with the 1.05 p.m. Hull to South Howden.
2. 6.50 a.m. Hull–Cudworth and return.
3. Pilot from 6.30 a.m.; 8.30 a.m. to North Cave and return; pilot 9.45 a.m. to 1.45 p.m.
4. 2.55 p.m. Hull–Cudworth and return.
5. 7.15 p.m. Hull–South Howden and return; 9.25 p.m. Hull–North Cave and return (10.40 p.m. Hull–North Cave and return on Saturdays only).

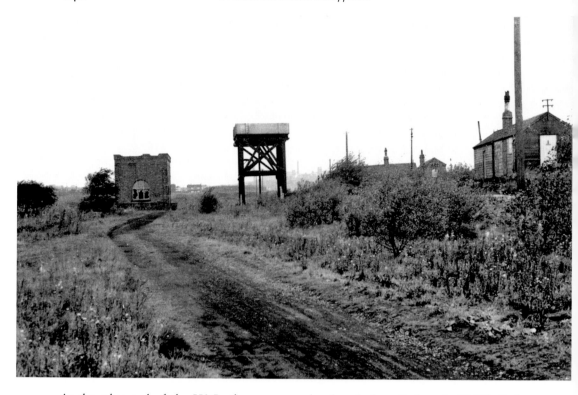

At the other end of the H&B, there was another locoshed at Cudworth (LNER Code: CUDTH, BR Code 53E). Shortly before the 'grouping', on 6 December 1923, Cudworth shed had an allocation of some thirty locos – in less than twenty years this would be reduced to six. All thirty were ex-H&B types, but in 1924 ex-NER class A (LNER F8) 2-4-2T was allocated to Cudworth to work passenger services on the Wath branch. This loco, No. 262, spent the summer back at York in 1925, but returned to Cudworth on 2 October. Between 20 April 1927 and 3 October 1927, 262 went to Malton. Passenger services to Wath were withdrawn on 6 April 1929 and 262 was transferred to Scarborough on 15 May 1929. Locos used on mineral trains from Cudworth were H&B class B 0-6-0s, withdrawals beginning in April 1925, which gradually reduced Cudworth's allocation. In addition, 0-6-0s were often double-headed on mineral trains, and to avoid the need for this GCR-designed 04 2-8-0s came to Cudworth, starting with No. 6576 on 5 October 1929, followed by 6549, 6577 and 6578. Cudworth's two 0-8-0s were sent to Hull on 23 October 1929 (No. 2500) and 18 November 1929 (No. 2508). By March 1932, the allocation at Cudworth shed was as follows:

LNER class J23 0-6-0	2438, 2439, 2445, 2451, 2452, 2456, 2461, 2462, 2464, 2465, 2466, 2467, 2468, 2477
LNER class N11 0-6-2T	2481
LNER class N12 0-6-2T	2483, 2484, 2487, 2489, 2490
LNER class N13 0-6-2T	2415
LNER class J75 0-6-0T	2525, 2526, 2527
LNER class J28 0-6-0	2414
LNER class 04 2-8-0	6549, 6576, 6577, 6578
Total: 29	

On 9 May 1934, ex-H&B 0-6-0s, very small in number at Cudworth, and two former NER classes were tried out, with two of each type sent (J21 875 and 1558 of West Hartlepool, J25 2038 of Shildon and 2136 of Darlington). On 29 June 1934, the two J21s were sent back and

replaced by two J25s (No. 25, ex-Wear Valley Junction, and No. 1990 from Darlington). The loan of the other two was made permanent on the same day. Only four weeks later, the four remaining H&B 0-6-0s at Cudworth were sent away; Nos 2445, 2456 and 2462 went to Hull and 2477 went to Whitby. In July 1933 and January 1934 0-6-0 2414, N13 2415, and J75 2525, 2526 and 2527 went to Hull, leaving only two classes of ex-H&B locos at Cudworth. Both were 0-6-2Ts: N12 Nos 2483, 2484, 2487, 2489, 2490; N11 No. 2481. On 27 July 1936, 2490 went to York in exchange for N12 2485 but on 19 October 1936 2490 returned to Cudworth, with 2483 being transferred away. N12 2490 went to Hull eleven days later in exchange for 2488. Locos 2484 and 2487 were transferred to the southern area in March 1936, and 2489 was withdrawn in February 1937, leaving 2488 as the only member of the class at Cudworth. This loco was exchanged for N11 2482 on 2 August 1937. Of the J25 0-6-0s, Nos 25 and 2038 were exchanged for J21 875 from Dairycoates on 26 July 1935 and the other went to Hull in 1936. No. 2072 arrived at Cudworth early in 1935, and J21 875 was replaced by J25 1970 in August 1937. Two J21s returned to Cudworth in June 1939 when 1970 and 2072 went to Darlington, being replaced by 613 and 1516. On 6 July 1940, A7 4-6-2T Nos 1114 and 1195 came to Cudworth from Dairycoates to release class 04 6549 for West Hartlepool, and 6611 for Heaton. Also arriving was Q6 0-8-0 2250 from Dairycoates on 25 March. The allocation now was as follows:

A7 4-6-2T	1114, 1195
J21 0-6-0	613, 1516
N11 0-6-2T	2481, 2482
04 2-8-0	6567, 6569, 6616
Q6 0-8-0	2250
Total: 10	

Duties for these locos were as follows:
- A7 – one on 8 a.m. Upton; one spare
- N11 – one double-shift pilot 5.30 a.m. – 9.45 p.m.; one spare
- J21 – one 10.45 a.m. Upton mineral; one away on loan
- 04 – one on 5.30 a.m. Hickleton mineral; one on 6.30 a.m. Wath mineral; one on 7 a.m. Brodsworth mineral
- Q6 – one on 9 a.m. Denaby mineral

In March 1943, Cudworth lost all of its locos except the two A7s. In place of Q6 2250, J21 613, N11 2481 and 2482, and 04 9576, 6579 and 6614, the shed received J25s 459, 1993 and 2080, along with C6 4-4-2 696 and 697, the last two proving unsuitable for mineral and heavy freight work. In March 1944 Q6s 2252, 2278 and 2287 arrived, but 2278 was exchanged for 2246 two months later. In October 1944, 696 and 697 went to Hull Dairycoates. The three Q6s left in September 1946 and were replaced by Q5 772 and 3311. The allocation for January 1947 was:

J25	5667, 5703, 5714
Q5	3311, 3332
A7	9771, 9789
Total: 7	

At the end of 1950, all had been sent away and replaced by 04 2-8-0s Nos 63620, 63667, 83751, 63754, 63845, 63849, 63857. Engines 63620 and 63667 were transferred away in the same year and replaced by 63772, and it was these six locos that were sent to Royston shed when Cudworth closed on NER 30 July 1951. Its remains can be seen here in 1963.

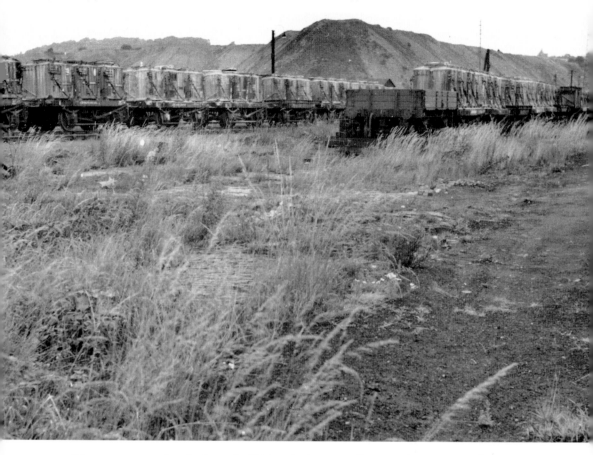

There were two other sheds on the H&B, which were still in use when the NER took control. The first was at Bullcroft, which had an allocation of one class B 0-6-0 and three class F2 0-6-2Ts on 6 December 1923. Early in 1925, the F2s were sent away and replaced by another class B and NER A7 4-6-2T. On 12 September 1928, 0-6-0 No. 2436 was withdrawn from the shed. On 29 October 1929, 04 2-8-0 No. 6611 came from York to replace A7 No. 1174, which went to York a few months later. On 9 July 1930, T1 4-8-0T No. 1657 brought from Stockton was replaced ten days later by No. 1658 from York. This loco was for Warmsworth pilot duty and on 8 December 1930 No. 1660 moved to Bullcroft for the same duty. This duty was taken over by Doncaster on 12 October 1931 and the two 4-8-0T7s went to Dairycoates, leaving only 0-6-0 No. 2469, 0-6-2T No. 2486 and 2-8-0 No. 6611 at Bullcroft, all transferring to Springhead when Bullcroft closed on 5 December 1931. The second shed was at Denaby, which was responsible for working passenger services along the branch until withdrawal in February 1903; from then on, the shed housed only one or two freight engines which, on 6 December 1923, comprised one J23 0-6-0 and one N12 0-6-2T. The N12, No. 2489, went to Dairycoates on 28 May 1927. Two days later, all the staff were moved away and the shed closed on 31 May 1927 when 0-6-0 No. 2461 went to Cudworth. The remains of Denaby shed can be seen here in 1961. (R. Carpenter)

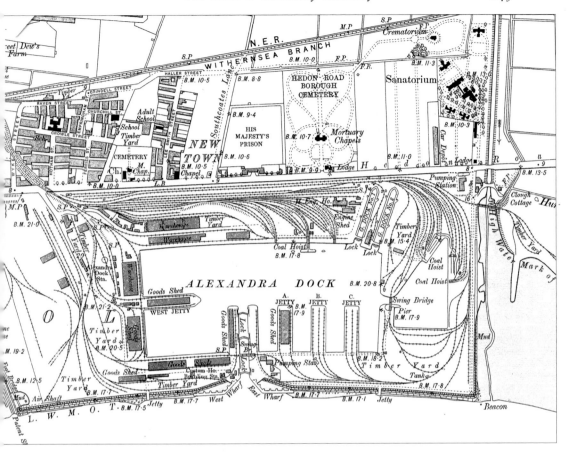

A map of Alexandra Dock in 1911, showing the complex rail network serving the port here. Schemes for lines from Hull to the West Riding had been proposed over the years. As early as 1845, a railway between Hull and Barnsley had been proposed yet suppressed. By 1870, however, Hull docks were struggling to cope with an upsurge in trade, so in an attempt to ease the situation the NER diverted traffic to Hartlepool, Goole and Grimsby, which angered locals; calls were duly made for a line that was independent of the NER. In 1880, plans were laid before Parliament for such a railway, although a new deep-water dock was considered more important. Hull Corporation agreed to sell to the fledgling railway company 126 acres of land on the site of what was to become the Alexandra Dock. Despite objections from the NER and the Hull Docks Company, the HB&WRJR Act was approved on 16 August 1880, the first sod being cut by Chairman Gerard Smith in January 1881 at the site of the new dock. Alexandra Dock opened on 16 July 1885, with freight traffic commencing four days later, and passenger services starting on 27 July. Initially, traffic levels did not live up to expectations and plans were made to amalgamate with the Midland Railway or the NER; but strenuous objections were made and such plans were abandoned. Fortunes gradually improved and a degree of prosperity was enjoyed as coal shipments grew. In 1880, the port handled some 600,000 tons, which grew by 1900 to some 2,200,000 tons, the bulk of which came through Alexandra Docks. To cope with such a huge increase in coal exports, the dock was extended in 1899. Pit props were carried on return workings from the docks. The H&B also carried wool from Australia and New Zealand for use in the mills of the West Riding to manufacture clothing. In 1906, jointly with the NER, the H&B built a new deep-water dock, most of the cost being borne by the NER. This new dock was completed in 1914, just in time to serve during the First World War, and was opened by His Majesty King George V, after whom the dock was named, on 26 June 1914. (Beverley Record Office)

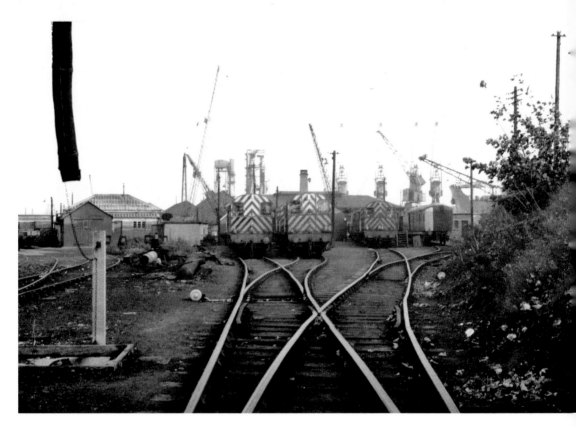

Another view of Alexandra Dock on 13 October 1963. At one time, the dock had its own locoshed providing motive power for the complex rail traffic on the site. The shed here was coded ALEX DOCK in LNER days, becoming 53C (a sub-shed of Springhead) in BR days. After takeover by the NER, the shed had to be supplied with NER locos and by 6 December 1923, out of twenty-nine locos allocated, only six were ex-H&B. The NER locos allocated comprised three types of 0-6-0Ts (J71, J74 and J76). Seven ex-NER Y7 0-4-0Ts were also allocated. The J74 and J76s disappeared by the end of 1931 and, until the introduction of diesel shunters in 1953, the bulk of work performed in the dock was carried out by J71 and J72 0-6-0Ts, sometimes helped out by the J73 and J77s. The last two Y7 0-4-0Ts were moved to Dairycoates on 11 June 1939 as part of a plan to only have J72, J73 and J77 tanks allocated to the dock shed. Various J71 locos were moved away at the same time. The allocation in September 1941 was as follows:

LNER J72 0-6-0T	462, 516, 524, 571, 574, 576, 1715, 1721, 1742, 1744, 2317
LNER J73 0-6-0T	549, 550
LNER J77 0-6-0T	145, 199, 614, 948, 1340, 1341, 1433, 1461
Total: 21	

Between May 1949 and November 1950, an ex-H&B N13 0-6-2T No. 69119 was allocated here, which seems a somewhat strange allocation. Perhaps it was surplus to requirements at that time. The first diesel-electric loco, No. 12114, arrived at the dock in October 1953 and all shunting in the dock was taken over by 204-hp and 350-hp diesel shunters. Locos at Alexandra Dock were transferred to Dairycoates on 27 October 1963, but the shed was retained as a signing-on point for crews, and locos continued to stand overnight in the dock area until closure. (R. Carpenter)

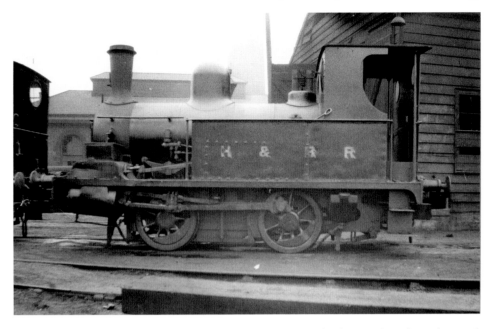

A little 0-4-0 dock tank loco of the H&B is standing outside the wooden Alexandra Dock locoshed in the years prior to takeover by the NER. It was probably these little tank locos which had to be withdrawn once the Darlington company had taken over and replaced them with NER 0-6-0 tanks. (LOSA)

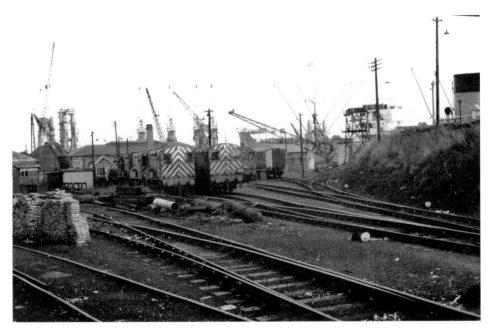

The Alexandra Dock at Hull on 13 October 1963 with a ship in port on the right and class 08 diesel shunters having replaced steam locos at the dock by this time. Within twenty years, Alexandra dock would be closed to traffic. The dock was finally closed to commercial shipping on 30 September 1982, with track removed and bridges dismantled in January 1988. (R. Carpenter)

The Hull & Barnsley Railway (not to scale)

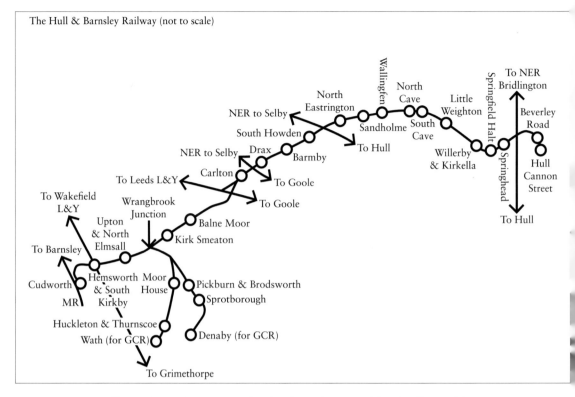

Dearne Valley Railway's junctions with other lines that served local collieries. The DVR was completed in sections as follows:

1. Shafton to Grimethorpe – 19 March 1902
2. Houghton to Thurnscoe – 13 March 1905
3. Thurnscoe to Hickleton – 26 February 1906
4. Hickleton to Denaby – 12 March 1906
5. Denaby to Cadeby – 6 August 1904
6. Section to Black Carr West – 7 October 1908

Passenger halts were at Ryhill (6 miles), Grimethorpe (8½ miles), Great Houghton (11¾ miles), Goldthorpe & Thurnscoe (13½ miles), Harlington (15¾ miles) and Edlington (20¼ miles). All were convenient for the villages that the DVR served, except Denaby, which was built after the line had been opened. The line was mainly to serve Melton Hall. (Author)

FIVE

OTHER RAILWAYS

With so many collieries in South Yorkshire, it was inevitable that a number of railway companies would take an interest in opening branches within the coalfield in order to maximise potential profits from the transport of the huge quantities of coal mined here. Thus, these lines were constructed primarily for freight traffic with passenger services being merely run as a secondary consideration.

One such line was the nominally independent Dearne Valley Railway, actually operated by the Lancashire & Yorkshire Railway, which commenced at Brierley Junction, on the Hull & Barnsley Railway, curved south-west to Shafton Junction and then ran via Grimethorpe, Great Houghton, Barnburgh, Denaby, Conisbrough and Edlington (south of Doncaster), where it made connections with the GCR, GER, MR, GNR and NER. The DVR also made a useful link with the South Yorkshire Joint Railway. A connection was made with the L&YR at Shafton, which gave access to Wakefield. The DVR opened in 1909, with passenger services starting in 1912. These services were usually worked by L&YR Hughes railmotors from the outset, replaced by push-pull fitted 2-4-2Ts when the railmotors were withdrawn. Passenger trains continued to operate until 1951 and much of the railway had disappeared by the end of 1966.

The previously mentioned South Yorkshire Joint Railway was owned by five railway companies, although it was the GCR which operated most of the early passenger trains. In 1902, all five railway companies were planning to build railways south of Doncaster to take advantage of potential profits from the haulage of coal traffic in the locality. The GCR and MR had taken over the Shireoaks, Laughton & Maltby project so that they could make an approach from the south while wishing to continue north through Maltby. At the same time, the NER and LY&R were planning a similar joint line, while the GNR planned a line west from Bawtry. As the plans of the five companies had similar intentions, they all agreed to combine and form the South Yorkshire Joint Committee, which was established in 1904. Between 1905 and 1909, a 17-mile line was built from the GCR/MR joint line at Dinnington to Kirk Sandall, just north-east of Doncaster.

As would be expected, the line concentrated on freight, mostly coal, which had reached over a million tons in 1913. Stations, however, had been built at Tickhill & Wadworth, Maltby & Dinnington and Laughton for goods traffic, but passenger services were soon under consideration. Excursions were tried to Doncaster and Cleethorpes in June and July 1910, with regular passenger trains operating soon after, with two GCR and two GNR trains each way between Doncaster and Shireoaks. Within a year, the service was reduced to three trains, all operated by the GCR, and, by 1912, a new passenger station was opened at Anston, on the GCR/MR joint line. A peak in passenger services of over 60,000 booked at its stations was reached in 1913, but the line still lost money.

In June 1917, passenger services were reduced to Saturdays only, as a wartime measure, and there was a reluctance to reinstate a full service when the war ended. By 1 April 1920, weekday services were recommenced with two trains a day, a 'market special' and an evening train (from October) on Saturdays. Passenger services ceased from 2 December 1929, although attempts were made to restore them in 1935 without success, but freight continued and coal trains were operated until the last remaining colliery at Maltby was closed.

Another line which captured coal traffic in South Yorkshire was the Swinton & Knottingley Joint Railway, its southern end connected with the Dearne Valley Railway near Frickley and Great Houghton Halt. The S&K also passed under the Hull & Barnsley Railway between Hemsworth and South Kirkby and Upton and North Elmsall.

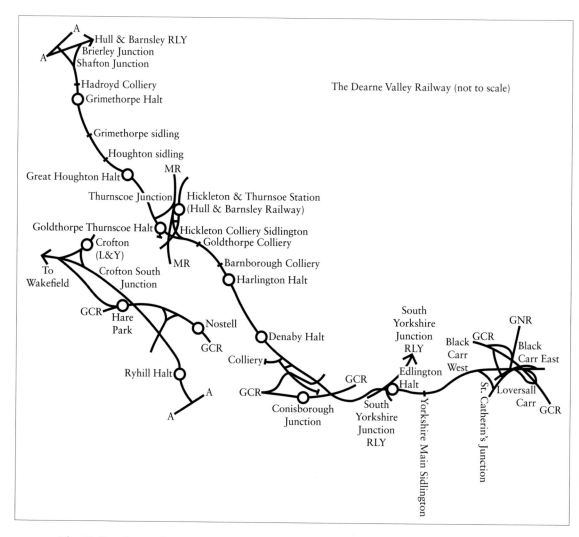

The Hull and Barnsley Railway showing the two branches and connections with the MR, GCR and NER.

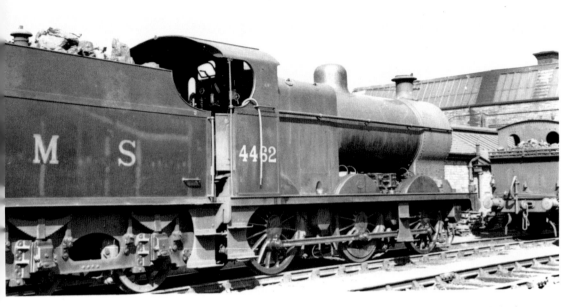

On 27 June 1937, LM class 4F 0-6-0 No. 4482 awaits its next turn of duty. Wakefield shed provided locos to work coal trains on the DVR. Its daily schedule was:

1. 5.45 a.m. to Grimethorpe, arriving at 6 a.m. Mondays only to work traffic to and from Black Carr as required.
2. 6 a.m. to Crofton Junction, then 6.10 a.m. Crofton Junction to Yorkshire Main colliery with empties, then trips as required.
3. From Crofton Junction at 7 a.m. to work up and down the line as required.
4. 6.55 a.m. to Crofton Junction, then 7.15 a.m. Crofton Junction to Hodroyd colliery, then as required.
5. 9.30 a.m. to Brierley Junction, then as required on the DVR.
6. 5.45 a.m. to Houghton coupled to 7. Call Crofton Hall for brake. Run Grimethorpe to Crofton Hall, arrive 8 a.m., then 9.50 am to Grimethorpe with brake in front of 5, then as required.
7. 5.45 a.m. (6 a.m. Mondays) coupled to 6, calling at Crofton Hall for brake. Run with brake to Houghton coupled to 6. Run trip Houghton to Crofton, then with brake to Grimethorpe, then Grimethorpe to Crofton Junction, then 11 a.m. Crofton Junction along DVR as required.
8. 9.05 a.m. to Crofton Junction coupled to 45 and Crofton 10, work 9.30 a.m. Crofton–Grimethorpe with Barnborough empties, then as required.
9. 9.05 a.m. to Grimethorpe coupled to 10, shunt along DVR and assist at Crofton Hall.
10. 9.05 a.m. to Crofton Hall coupled to 43 and 45. Leaves 9.25 a.m. for Grimethorpe, then as required.
11. 11.35 a.m. to Crofton Hall, depart 12.20 p.m. with Frickley empties.
12. 12.50 p.m. to Crofton Hall, then 1.35 p.m. to Grimethorpe with Exchange sidings empties.
13. 3.05 p.m. (Saturdays excepted), 1.45 p.m. (Saturdays only) to Crofton Hall, then 3.05 p.m. (Saturdays excepted), 1.45 p.m. (Saturdays only) with Frickley empties.

These schedules relate to days when Wakefield shed was in L&YR ownership and the numbers relate to locomotives. (H. Casserley)

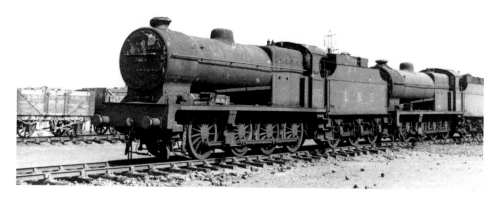

A pair of LMS Fowler 7F 0-8-0 locos, Nos 9533 and 9511, both fitted with oil-burning equipment at Wakefield shed on 30 April 1949. In 1948, oil burners were converted back to coal-firing after it was realised that the UK did not have the hard currency to purchase the oil in sufficient quantities. No. 9511 was the last to be converted, while No. 9533 and the other oil-burning Fowler 0-8-0s at Wakefield were scrapped. (H. Casserley)

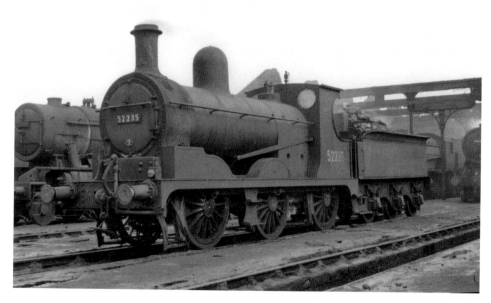

Ex-L&YR 3F 0-6-0 (L&YR class F19, No. 1240) BR No. 52235 at Wakefield shed in 1953 with an ex-WD 2-8-0 in the background. Back in L&YR days, a goods train left Crofton Hall at 6.35 a.m. for Cudworth on the H&B, reversing at Shafton Junction at 6.55 a.m. and again at Brierley Junction. The return working left Cudworth at 8.40 a.m. for Crofton Hall, passing Shafton Junction at 9.20. At the east end, there were two pilot trips from Black Carr East Junction, one at 3.30 p.m. down to Bessacarr Junction, arriving at 3.35; the other left at 4.10, arriving Loversall Carr at 4.15, returning at 4.30. From March 1902, the Grimethorpe and Houghton collieries were linked to the H&B. Contractors or colliery engines worked to Brierley Junction, where exchanges with the H&B took place. (L. Perkins)

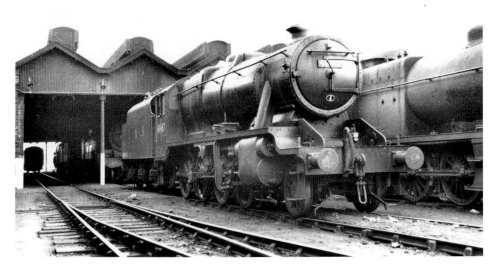

Ex-LMS 8F 2-8-0 No. 48457 at Wakefield shed in 1948, an example of motive power used on coal trains on the DVR from the 1930s until the end of steam. Back in the early years of the DVR, disputes arose between the DVR, H&B and NER. The latter were not happy that coal traffic was going to Hull over the H&B and that the NER had not been consulted. This led to the idea that coal traffic should be encouraged to go to the ports at Goole and Hull via Thurnscoe Junction and on to the Swinton & Knottingley Railway as convenient. Nothing was officially planned and traffic flowed as required. (N. Glover)

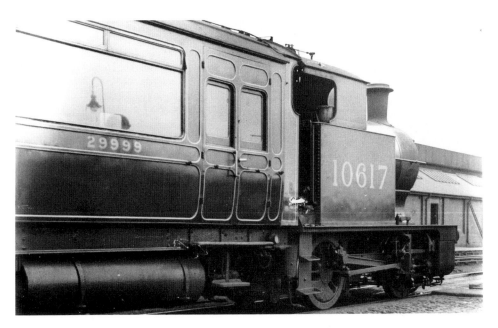

Hughes railmotor No. 10617 with coach No. 29999 at Wakefield on 29 June 1933 as it waits to operate its passenger service over the DVR. As well as the H&B, the S&K also had running powers to Houghton Main, its line running through to Pontefract. The GN also sent trains on to the DVR, taking loco coal from Yorkshire Main colliery to Doncaster. The GCR also had a branch to Houghton Main, running from Stairfoot Junction on the Barnsley–Mexborough line. (H. Casserley)

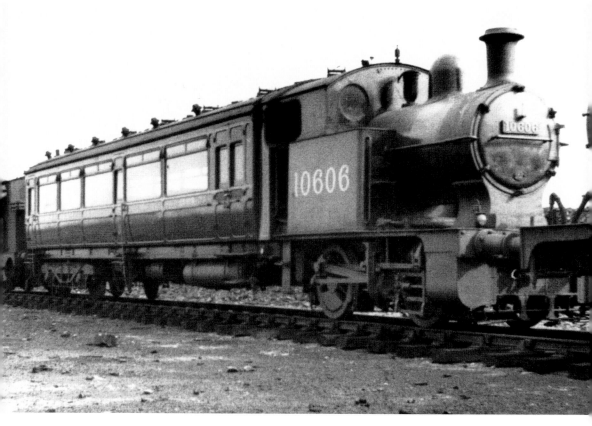

Ex-L&YR steam railmotor, as LMS No. 10606, at Wakefield shed. These little Hughes railmotors were used on DVR passenger services. The first suggestion for a new railway was proposed to the L&YR board, asking that a suitable railway be provided from Horbury Junction, west of Wakefield. However, no action was taken by the Horwich Company. Despite this, the Dearne Valley Railway Act was passed in 1897 to run from the H&B near Hemsworth to the GE and GN Joint line at Black Carr, south-east of Doncaster. Its directors were colliery owners within the area and the DVR was sponsored by the Hickleton, Houghton and Carlton Main collieries. The H&B was well placed to take coal for export and from 1898 a five-year agreement was signed which granted mutual running powers. This did not please promoters of the DVR Bill who had covert plans to link the DVR with the L&YR. With this in mind, contact was made with the L&YR in an effort to persuade them to run from Barnsley to Grimethorpe colliery over the GCR Houghton Main branch. Little was done and it transpired that the GNR and GER had adopted running powers, along with the H&B, when the line opened. Under the terms of its Act, the DVR had to be completed in five years, with a further two years for the dock, wharf and lay-by scheduled for construction near Denaby. An Act of 30 July 1900 allowed completion of the line by 6 August 1905 for the railway and 6 August 1908 for dock work on the River Don. The H&B obtained running powers to Grimethorpe and Houghton Main in exchange for DVR powers to Monckton Main and Carlton Main in H&B territory at Cudworth. (R. Carpenter)

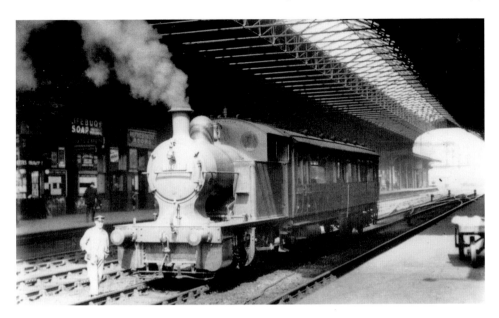

Ex-L&YR railmotor No. 10616 at Wakefield Kirkgate station, having just arrived from the DVR line, on 29 June 1933. Passenger services on the DVR were a natural development after the line opened, with halts at rail level. Ashes, lamps, a nameboard, fencing and an old coach body formed the stopping places. The coach bodies were decidedly battered and were painted yellow. The Hughes railmotors were fitted with retractable steps worked from the engine's vacuum system. The L&YR had built some eighteen of these units for use on its branches. The steam loco had 3-foot 7-inch wheels on an 8-foot wheelbase, driven by two 12x16-inch cylinders. The tanks carried 550 gallons of water and 15 hundredweight of coal was carried. The main loco used on the DVR was L&YR No. 12 (LMS No. 10610), built in March 1907 and rebuilt in 1912. The local press of the day thought that the new passenger service would be of great value to the local colliery communities. (H. Casserley)

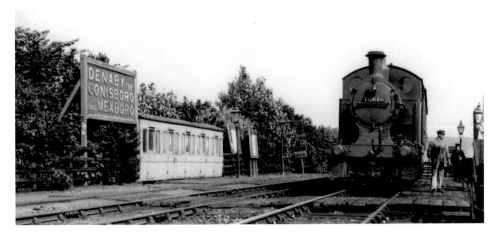

No. 10616 has arrived at Denaby, with its smart nameboard showing it as a junction for services to Conisborough and Mexborough. Also visible is the old coach body and the simple waiting area. The loco was operating the service on 29 June 1933. The original passenger service was four return trips a day from Wakefield to Edlington at 8.10 a.m., 10.25 a.m., 1.15 p.m. and 3.20 p.m. with a 9.30 p.m. Saturdays-only service. Trains from Edlington to Wakefield were at 9.13 a.m., 11.28 a.m., 2.15 p.m. and 4.20 p.m. with a 10.30 p.m. Saturdays-only service. (H. Casserley)

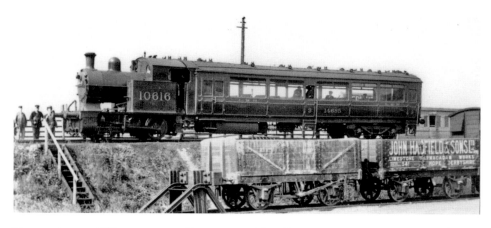

The terminus at Edlington on 29 June 1933 with railmotor No. 10616 waiting to depart. Wagons for John Hatfield & Son of Hope, Derbyshire, are in the foreground. After takeover by the LMS, the service improved slightly:

Wakefield depart	8.10 a.m., 10.25 a.m., 1.05 p.m., 3.28 p.m., 6.05 p.m.
Edlington depart	9.13 a.m., 11.28 a.m., 2.12 p.m., 4.25 p.m., 8.15 p.m.

On Saturdays there was a short working between Wakefield and Goldthorpe at 9.45 p.m., along with a 10.36 p.m. from Wakefield to Edlington. (H. Casserley)

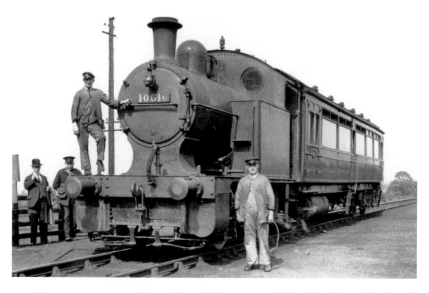

Also on 29 June 1933, crew, station staff and train are posed for this picture. By the winter of 1937, passenger services reached a peak as follows:

Wakefield depart	8.10 a.m., 10.25 a.m., 1.05 p.m., 3.50 p.m.*, 5.45 p.m., 8.15 p.m.*, 10.06 p.m.*
Edlington depart	9.13 a.m., 11.28 a.m., 2.13 p.m., 4.40 p.m., 6.50 p.m., 9.05 p.m.*, 10.57 p.m.*

* To or from Goldthorpe. A wait of between three and eight minutes was booked for return trips at Denaby. The last service to Wakefield was permitted to stop at Crofton South Junction when required to pick up locomen from sheds.

BARNSLEY and WAKEFIELD.—Lancashire and Yorkshire.

Miles	Down.						Week Days.																	Sundays.		
		mrn	mrn	mrn	**f**	mrn	**f**	aft	aft	**f**	aft	aft	**f**		aft	aft		mrn	aft				
	Barnsley ....dep.	6 15	8 13	9 40	9 57	11 55	12 0	2 43	4 17	4 38	5 56	5 78	0		9 3	11 0		10 15	6 20				
3¼	Darton	6 22	8 20	9 47	10 4	12 2	12 7	2 50	4 24	4 56	2 7	4 8	7		9 10	11 7		10 22	6 27				
4¼	Haigh.......................	6 27	8 25	9 52	10 9	12 7	12 12	2 55	4 29	4 50	6 7	7 9	8		9 15	11 12		10 27	6 32				
7	Crigglestone	6 31	8 29	9 56	10 13	12 12	12 16	2 59	4 33	4 54	6 11	7 13	5 16		9 19	11 16		10 31	6 36				
8¼	Horbury Junc. **736, 786**..	6 36	8 34	10 1	....	12 17	....	4 38	....	6 17	7 18	5 36		9 24			10 36	6 41				
11	Wakefield (Kirkgate)...arr.	6 41	8 38	10 5	10 40	12 21	2 34	3	6 4	4 25	2 16	2 17	22	9 17		9 28	11 23		10 40	6 45				

Miles	Up.						Week Days.																	Sundays.		
		mrn	mrn	**f**	mrn	aft	aft	**f**	aft	aft	aft	aft	aft	**f**				mrn	aft				
	Wakefield (Kirkgate)...dep.	7 25	8 27	8 59	11 15	10 2	0 2	18	3 38	5 20	6	5 8	20 10	0				11 30	3 55				
2¼	Horbury Junction........	7 30	8 32	....	11 20	16 2	5 2	23	....	5 25	6 10	8	25 10	5				11 35	9 0				
4	Crigglestone.............	7 35	8 37	9 31	11 25	21 2	10	....	3 46	5 30	6 15	8	30 10	10				11 40	9 5				
6¼	Haigh	7 40	8 42	9 36	11 31	1 26	2 18	....	3 51	5 36	6 20	8	35 10	15				11 45	9 10				
7¼	Darton	7 44	8 46	9 40	11 35	1 30	2 19	**n**	3 55	5 39	6 24	8	39 10	19				11 49	9 14				
11	Barnsley **548, 648** ....arr.	7 52	8 54	9 48	11 43	1 38	2 27	6 4	3 5	4 7	6 32	8	47 10	27	11 52				11 57	9 22				

| **n** Stops when required to take up. | **f** Via Horbury, changing there. | **o** Arrives at 8 40 aft. on Saturdays. | **s** Saturdays only. |

A timetable for L&YR services between Wakefield Kirkgate and Barnsley. The branch to Barnsley was started in 1847 and included a single-bore tunnel at Woolley that was due to an overrun on costs of construction. The tunnel would create a bottleneck as traffic built up. From 1 January 1850 passenger services started, with coal traffic commencing two weeks later. By 1853, coal traffic was so extensive that doubling of the line was authorised, with the exception of Woolley Tunnel, and opened throughout in the spring of 1855. In January 1858, the L&YR purchased the northern section outright, giving a complete line to Sheffield and Rotherham. In June of that year, the MS&LR opened its line from Penistone to Barnsley, and the L&YR enlarged its station at Barnsley, recovering the cost by charging tolls to other railway companies. The L&YR station at Barnsley was a single platform affair until Court House station closed in 1959 and all passenger services were diverted to a now-enlarged Barnsley Exchange station, which is still in use. Woolley Tunnel was finally doubled in 1902. Haigh and Crigglestone stations were closed in 1965, but a basic station remained at Darton. A wagon works was situated at the fork of Horbury Junction from 1876, having moved from Wakefield, where it had been established in 1856. (Author)

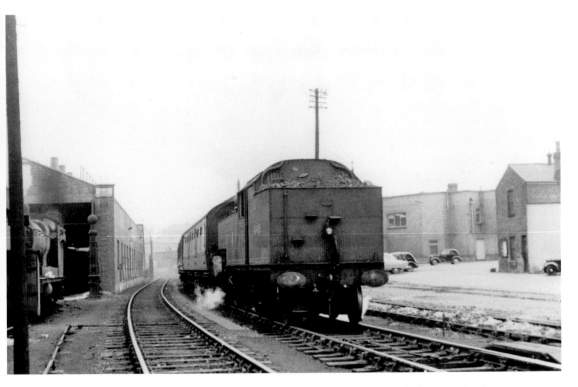

Leaving Barnsley Exchange station and passing the ex-GCR engine shed, on 13 April 1957, is ex-LMS Fowler 2-6-4T No. 42405 with the 1.55 p.m. local from Sheffield to Leeds. (H. Casserley)

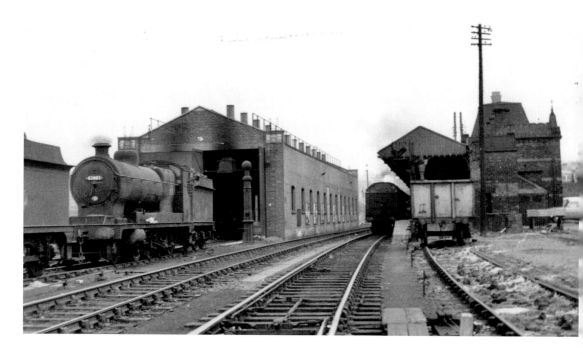

Having arrived at Barnsley Exchange, No. 42405 waits at the single platform with its train from Leeds. In the foreground is the ex-GCR shed with 2-8-0 No. 63883 at rest just outside. (H. Casserley)

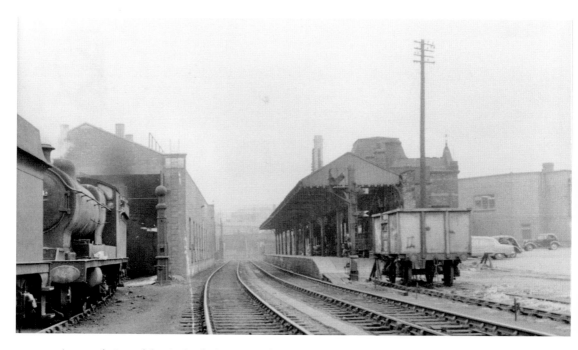

A general view of the single platform Barnsley Exchange station, looking towards Doncaster, on 13 June 1957. The single platform served both L&YR (LMS) and GCR (LNER) trains for many years. The station was only expanded to two platforms after closure of the GCR locoshed and Barnsley Court House station, despite the unpopularity of the exchange. (H. Casserley)

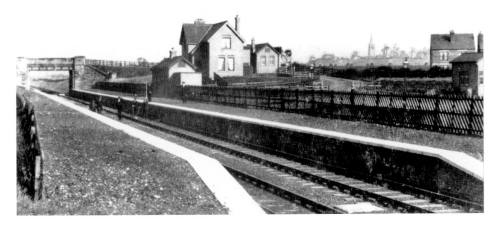

Dinnington and Laughton station on the South Yorkshire Joint Railway when it was new in about 1910. The station appears to have no traffic, a situation which occurred in 1921 when a coal strike caused complete closure of the line, after which discussions were undertaken to close all passenger services. However, Lord Scarborough, the local landowner, had a right to a passenger service to Maltby and, only reluctantly, the committee continued such a service. However, the Saturday evening service ceased in 1922. (LOSA)

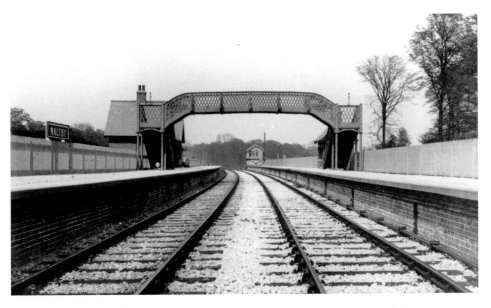

A view of Maltby station on the SYJR shortly after opening to passengers, looking very neat indeed. Further problems for passenger services arose with the General Strike of 1926, which caused complete closure of the line for fifteen months. When the line reopened, a Sentinel steam railcar was tried without success. After services had been reduced to a single Worksop–Maltby–Worksop train a day, Lord Scarborough agreed to withdrawal on 2 December 1929. An attempt was made to restore passenger services in 1935, but this failed. However, outward excursions continued until 1966, after which a few railtours were operated. (LOSA)

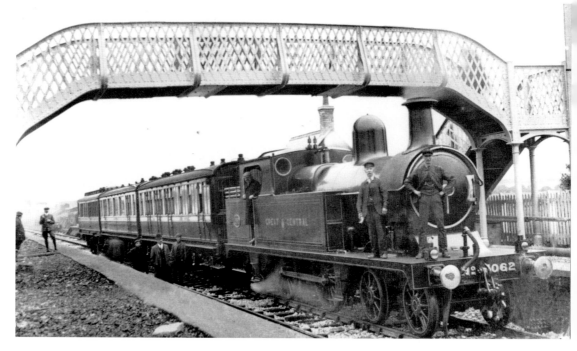

In happier times, GCR class 9K 4-4-2T No. 1062 is seen on a trial passenger service in September 1908 at Tickhill station with train crew and staff in view. A full passenger service commenced in 1910. (LOSA)

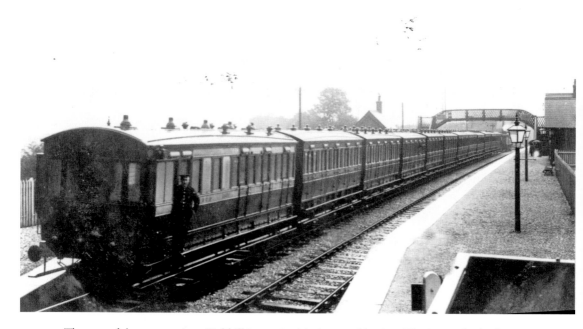

The rear of the same train at Tickhill in 1908 with the guard in view. The SYJR also had access to Rossington colliery on the DVR and trains of up to forty wagons would run directly from St Catherine's Junction to Black Carr West, reversing up the DVR to the colliery, where the engine would run round for shunting. Drivers of such trains would whistle at Tickhill station for advice on how they should be handled at Black Carr. (LOSA)

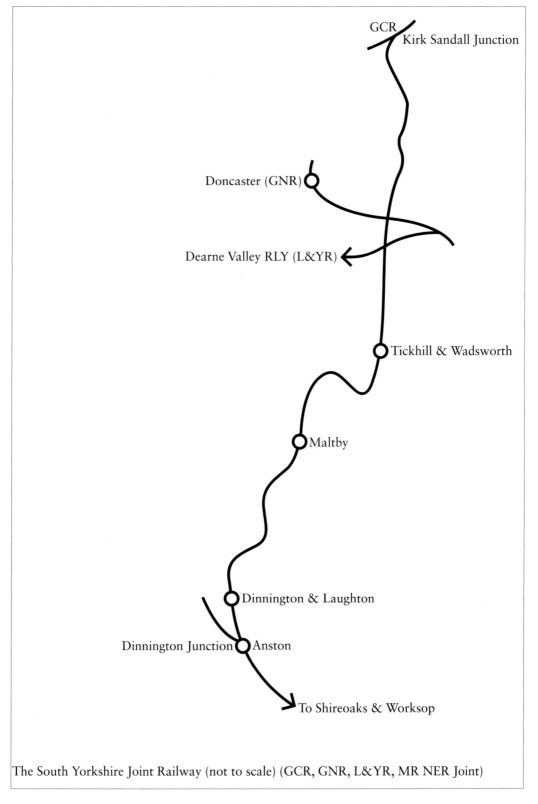

GCR
Kirk Sandall Junction

Doncaster (GNR)

Dearne Valley RLY (L&YR)

Tickhill & Wadsworth

Maltby

Dinnington & Laughton

Dinnington Junction   Anston

To Shireoaks & Worksop

The South Yorkshire Joint Railway (not to scale) (GCR, GNR, L&YR, MR NER Joint)

A map of the South Yorkshire Joint Railway showing junctions with the DVR and GNR just north of Tickhill station. (Author)

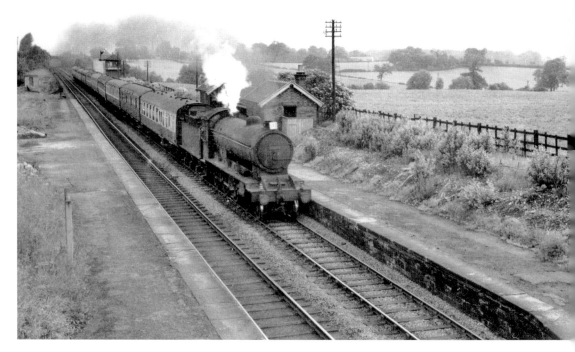

The southern end of the Swinton & Knottingley Railway, which was jointly owned by the MR and NER, with ex-LNER B16 4-6-0 No. 61459 passing through Frickley at the head of a southbound express from York on 29 June 1957. (H. Priestley)

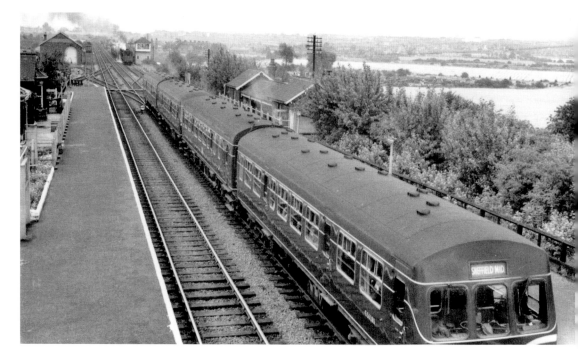

Three years later, a Sheffield-bound DMU waits at Bolton-on-Dearne on 4 August 1960. Loco No. 61424, another B16 4-6-0, can be seen in the distance. (H. Priestley)

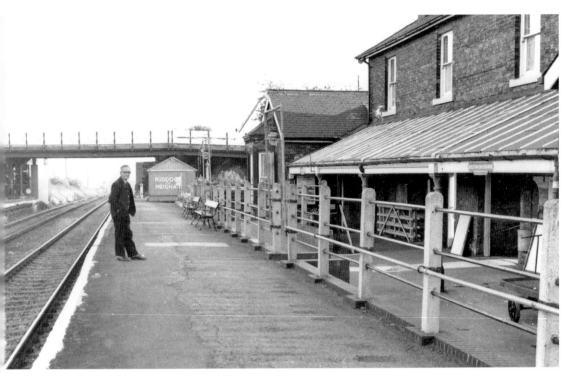

Bolton-on-Dearne station with a member of the station staff in the 1960s. Bolton-on-Dearne was another of the stations at the south end of the S&K. (LOSA)

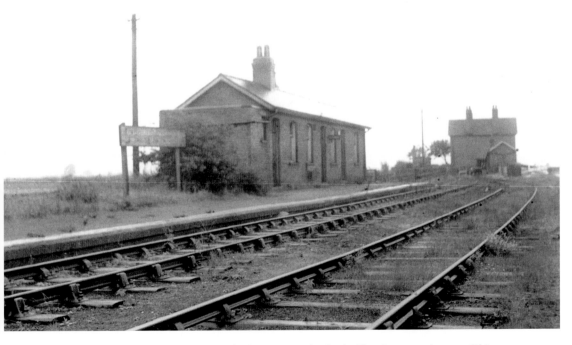

A view of Haxey Junction station, looking towards the buffers in around 1950. This was on the Axholme Joint Railway, owned by the NER and L&YR. The little branch lay east of Doncaster and south of Reedness Junction. (R. Carpenter)

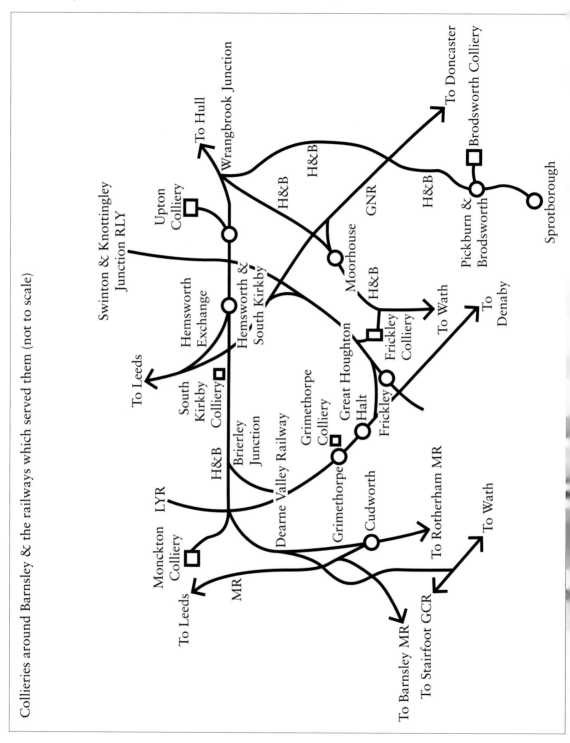

A map showing the collieries in the Barnsley area and the railways that served them, including the H&B, DVR, GNR, GCR, MR and S&K. The South Yorkshire coalfield stretched from the Barnsley area to the River Trent. Some famous collieries were situated here. Carlton Main (on the H&B) was one of the older mines, dating from 1876. Grimethorpe came in 1896 and was sunk on the estate of Mr F. J. S. Foljambe. The first coal left Manvers Main in 1870, Houghton in 1878 and Hickleton Main in 1894. (Author)

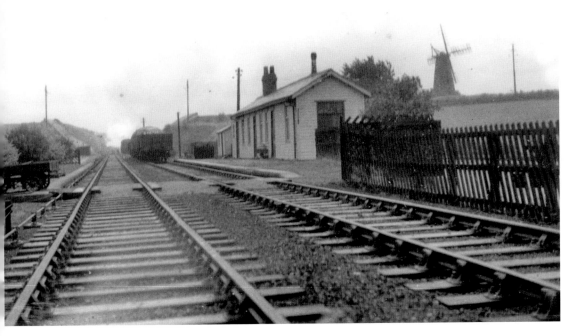

A very rural setting, complete with windmill on the right and tidy wooden station building, at Epworth on the Axholme Joint Railway in 1950. (R. Carpenter)

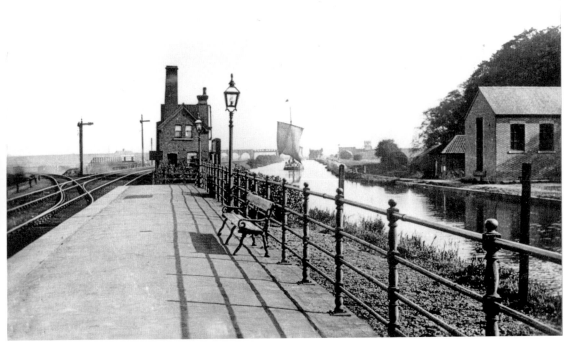

The GCR station at Crowle, facing Doncaster. A sailing barge is in view, approaching the station in this tranquil scene. (R. Carpenter)

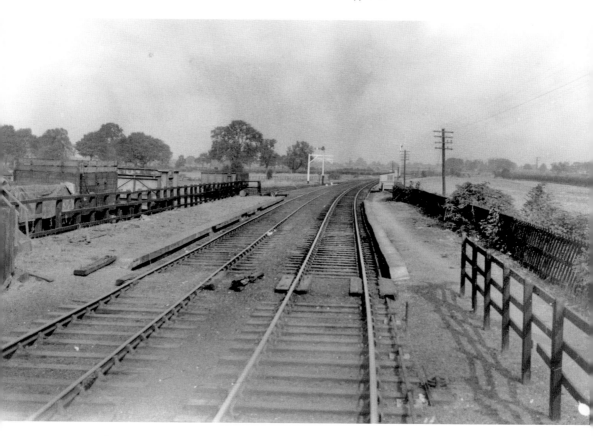

Crowle station on the Axholme joint Railway as it appeared on 17 July 1933 at closure to passengers. (R. Carpenter)

SIX

INDUSTRIAL LINES

With such large quantities of coal and steel products to be transferred from the collieries of South Yorkshire and the steelworks of Sheffield, the many companies built large and small industrial railways to transfer their products from mines, foundries and factories to the main railway network for onward shipment to all parts of Great Britain and beyond. So many of these railways were constructed that there would be sufficient material to produce a whole book on this subject alone. Therefore, only a small selection of these railways is included here.

These railways purchased locomotives, usually tank engines, from the many private locomotive manufacturers that existed throughout the United Kingdom in the late nineteenth and early twentieth century, including the Yorkshire Engine Company of Meadowhall, Sheffield, now near the site of the Meadowhall shopping complex. With such a large number of locomotive builders, there was almost as large a variety of motive power as on the main lines, bringing just as much interest to enthusiasts as the national system.

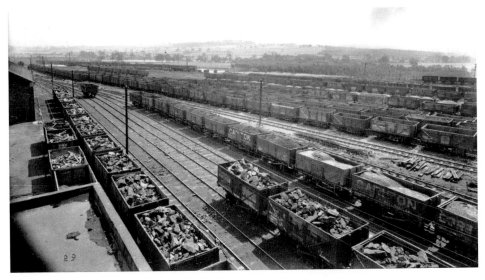

The sidings at Grimethorpe colliery, which belonged to the Carlton Main Colliery Company, as they appeared in 1946. Grimethorpe colliery was opened in the 1890s and was served by the Dearne Valley Railway when it opened completely in 1905. The line from Shafton to Grimethorpe was opened in 1902, with traffic from the colliery being connected to the main network via the Hull & Barnsley Railway at Brierley Junction. Prior to the opening of the DVR, the colliery's produce was transported to the H&B using their own engines, or those of the builders of the DVR. (R. Carpenter)

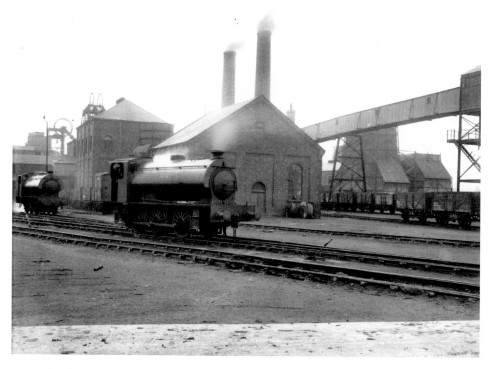

The pithead at Grimethorpe colliery with two of the colliery locos in view. These engines were purchased by the colliery company in April 1946 from the War Department. Numbered 4 and 5, these locos were built by Vulcan Foundry in 1945 (works Nos 5295 and 5296), sold to the War Department and given numbers 75305 and 75306. (R. Carpenter)

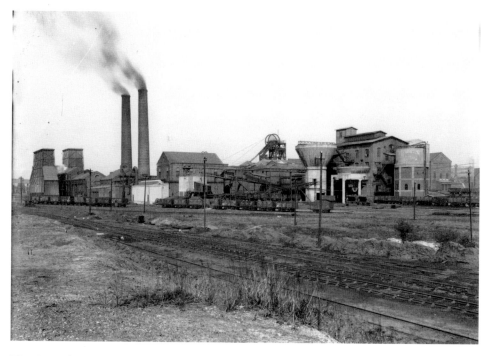

The Grimethorpe colliery and coking plant, with pithead in view, in 1946. (R. Carpenter)

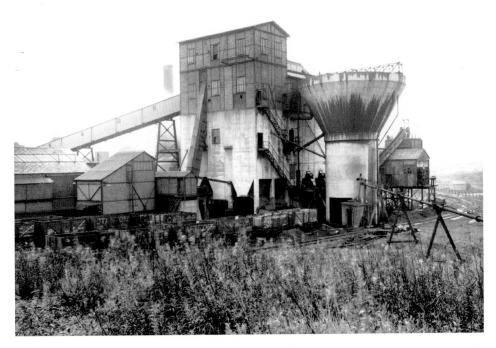

Another view of the coking plant at Grimethorpe colliery as it appeared in 1946. In the immediate post-war years, Grimethorpe, along with most other pits, was extremely busy turning out coal for export and for the domestic market, this being the fuel which powered Britain in those days. It is worth remembering that coal produced domestic gas, electricity, power for the railways and was the fuel most used for domestic heating. The fuel was to become even more important during the extremely cold winter of 1947. So important was coal to the economy that the new Labour government nationalised the industry, along with the railways, in 1948. (R. Carpenter)

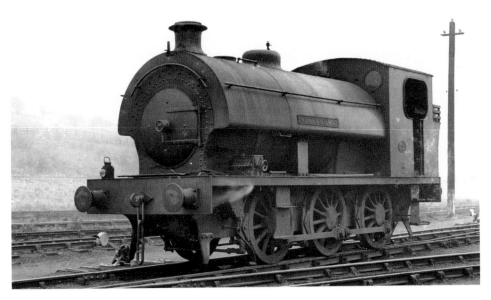

Cadeby Main Colliery, near Conisborough, with Hunslet loco No. 43 *Aberconway* in the sidings on 23 October 1949, a year after nationalisation. (N. Glover)

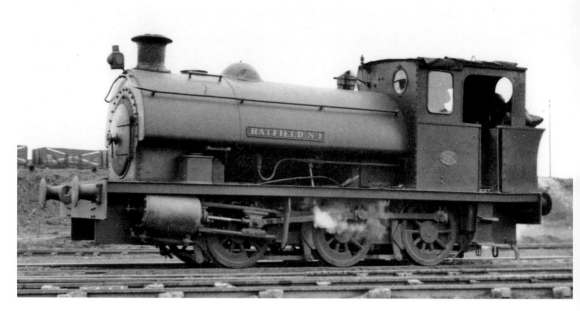

Standing in the sidings at Hatfield Colliery near Doncaster is outside cylinder loco *Hatfield No. 1* 0-6-0 saddle tank on 22 April 1954. (H. Casserley)

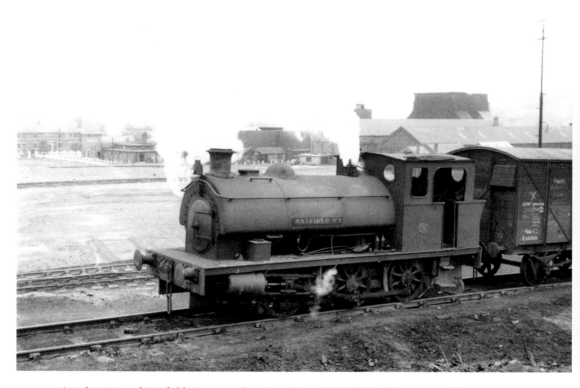

Another view of *Hatfield No. 1* on shunting duties at Hatfield colliery on 20 May 1952. (H. Casserley)

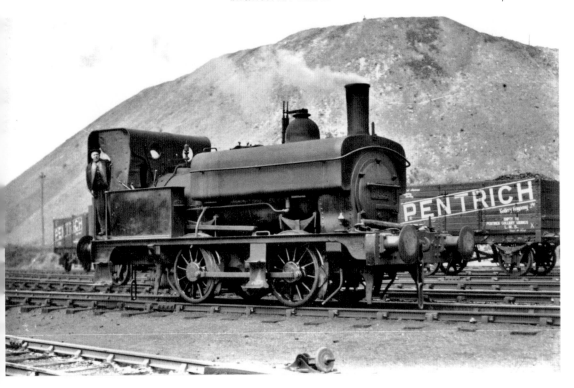

Pentrich colliery, Derbyshire, served by the Midland Railway, later the LMS (as the wagons are labelled), with an unusual 0-4-0 saddle tank in view. The engine gives the appearance of having been built by Kitson of Leeds, or is a withdrawn ex-Midland Railway engine rebuilt for colliery needs. (H. Casserley)

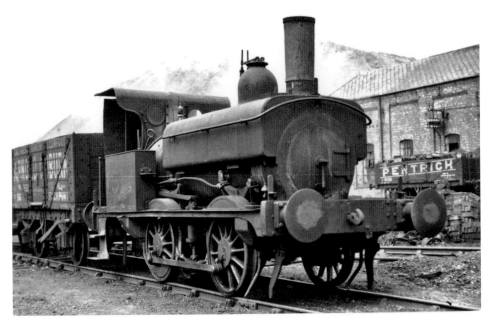

Also at Pentrich colliery on 30 May 1935 is another 0-4-0 saddle tank, with what appears to be MR No. 151, suggesting that it was originally built by the Derby company, or that the MR/LMS was providing motive power for the colliery. (H. Casserley)

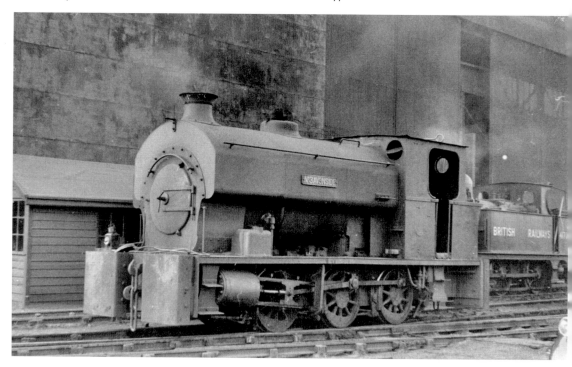

Seen at Staveley Ironworks on 3 June 1950 is No. 3 *Avonside*, an 0-6-0 saddle tank of 1924 (works No. 1919). At that time, the ironworks had two other Avonside locos, 0-6-0STs *Hartington* and *Devonshire*. The works was known to have as many as nine 0-6-0Ts at one time or another. In the background is ex-MR/LMS 1F 0-6-0T No. 41708 in early British Railways livery. (H. Casserley)

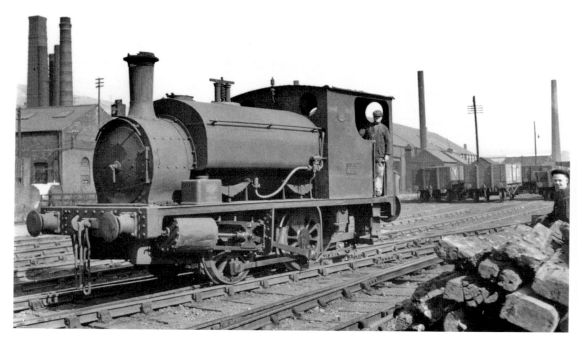

An 0-4-0ST is seen at Stocksbridge in the 1930s. No. 4 was an example of the locos built by the Yorkshire Engine Company. (R. Carpenter)

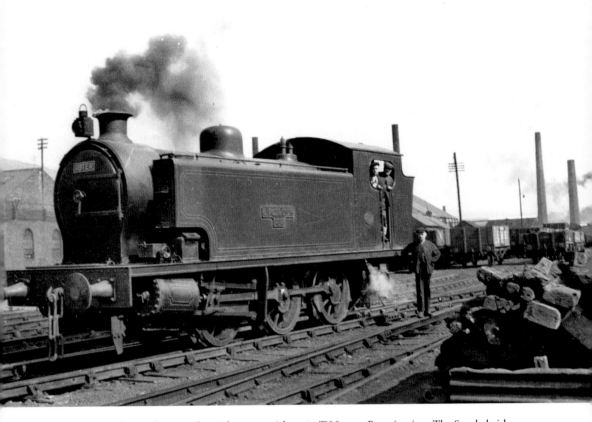

The Stocksbridge Railway in the mid-1930s with 0-6-0T No. 15 *Peter* in view. The Stocksbridge Railway was opened for traffic in April 1977, serving the major steelworks of Samuel Fox, which had been established in 1842, having taken over a disused corn mill near the centre of Stocksbridge and adapted it to make wire for textile pins. By 1848, Fox's began to make wire for umbrella frames. In the mid-1860s, the works had its own furnaces and rolling mills, which allowed production of railway track and springs. After the First World War, Samuel Fox & Co. merged with Steel, Peech & Tozer at Templeborough to form the United Steel Company. From that point, Fox's specialised in special steel products, concentrating on spring steels and, of course, stainless steel. From there, the company developed steel for the aviation industry and made springs for Rolls Royce cars. In 1967, the steel industry was nationalised, S. Fox & Co. becoming part of the new British Steel Corporation. Corus took over the works in 1999 and closed it in 2005, yet another industry to go abroad. (R. Carpenter)

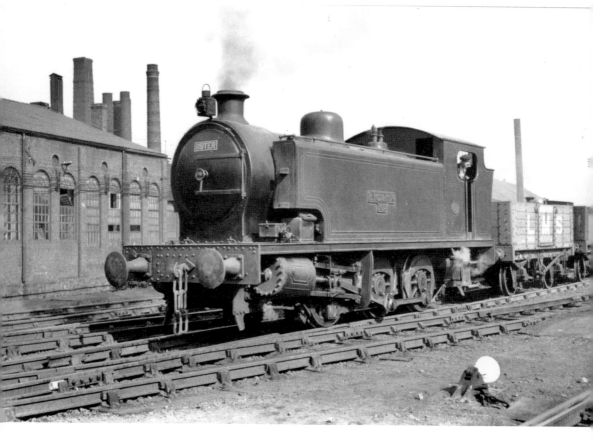

Another view of *Peter* on the Stocksbridge Railway. This 0-6-0T was built by the Yorkshire Engine Company of Meadowhall, Sheffield. The company began building locos in 1866, mainly industrial types for the British market or for export. The company did, however, build tank engines for the main line railways, notably GWR class 57xx 0-6-0 pannier tanks and the later 94xx 0-6-0PT. The Yorkshire Engine Company also turned out engines for the LNER. In pre-grouping days the company had turned out engines for the Lancashire & Yorkshire Railway, the Great Northern Railway, the Great Eastern Railway, the Hull & Barnsley Railway and the North British Railway. For a short time, from 1907, the company built motor cars and undertook other engineering work. After the Second World War, the company produced its first diesel locomotive in 1950, going into full production from 1953. In 1948, the company had been absorbed by the United Steel Companies, of which S. Fox & Co. was a member, and new diesels found their way onto the Stocksbridge works. The Yorkshire Engine Company ceased production of locomotives in 1965. (R. Carpenter)

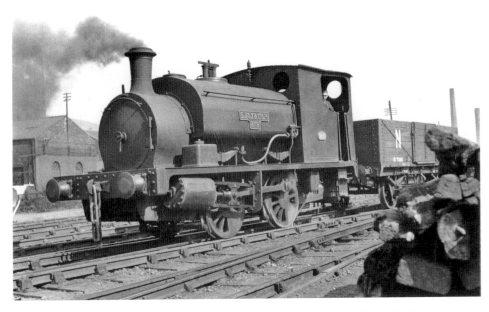

Shunting on the Stocksbridge Railway in the 1930s is 0-4-0 saddle tank No. 8, another Yorkshire Engine Company product. The Stocksbridge Railway route began just north of Deepcar station and then turned in a westerly direction into exchange sidings and over a viaduct across the River Don. From there, it continued down a slight incline past the Lowood works, on the south, then crossed a bridge over the Wortley Road. Passing the Ellen Cliff weighbridge and loop, it then passed Gregory's brickworks sidings just before crossing the Little Don. The line continued into the low yard of Fox's and passed the station yard. To Top Yard, the line went into Smithy Hill tunnel and into the Dam Bank sidings. (R. Carpenter)

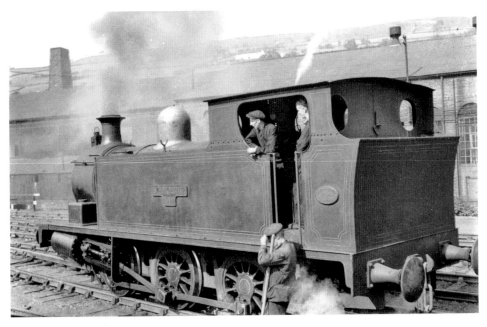

Yorkshire Engine Company 0-6-0T No. 14 at Stocksbridge in the 1930s. (R.Carpenter)

ACKNOWLEDGEMENTS

Without the assistance of the individuals and organisations mentioned below, this project would have been very difficult to complete. I should especially like to thank Gordon Sharpe, who provided much of the background on Sheffield, the local railway system and the Stocksbridge Railway. He spent many hours discussing his home city and the railways which served it. John Thurston supplied much material on the Dearne Valley Railway, and photographs came from Mr Richard Casserley, along with other pictures of the railways around Sheffield. Photographs of Sheffield, Rotherham, Barnsley, along with several areas in between, were supplied by Roger Carpenter, LOSA, and Jeremy Suter. To them, I offer my grateful thanks.

May I also thank Bernard Unsworth for spending some time working on the locoshed allocations in the Sheffield, Barnsley and Rotherham areas; he certainly saved me a considerable amount of time.

Organisations that helped with this project were the *Sheffield Star* and Filey Library. I hope my questions were not too much trouble for them to deal with.

Finally, thanks to my wife Hilary, whose job was to supply me with endless cups of tea as I worked on this book. I just hope that the finished product will be as enjoyable to read as it was to write.